Chappaquiddick Decision is more than the story of a fatal car accident.

It is also the story of the pressures put upon elected leaders.

It's the story of political infighting where all is fair as long as you don't get caught, where they play rough and for keeps, and where reputations are destroyed for political gain.

It's the story of the public's gullibility and penchant for gossip and how it is used to win votes.

It's the story of how democracy works . . . and does not work.

CHAPPAQUIDDICK DECISION

By
Larryann Willis

Library of Congress Catalog Card Number 80-67663
Copyright ©1980 by Larryann Willis

Cover design by Arvid Orbeck
              Petzold and Associates,
              Portland, Oregon

Printed in the United States of America
Times Litho
Forest Grove, Oregon

Better Books Publisher
Rt. 2, Box 69
Vale, OR 97918

CHAPTER page

PROLOGUE

At the inquest into the death of Mary Jo Kopechne, Joseph Gargan, Ted Kennedy's cousin, testified:

> I said to him, "What happened, Ted? Were you driving the car or was Mary Jo driving the car? Who was driving the car?" And then I said, "Well, what happened? WHAT THE HELL HAPPENED!"

The whole nation has been asking Ted Kennedy, "WHAT THE HELL HAPPENED!" Few have been satisfied with his answers.

Real life situations are often stranger than fiction. The closer one looks at Ted Kennedy's Chappaquiddick story the stranger it becomes. Kennedy himself often appears as frustrated as his questioners, and on November 3, 1979 he admitted to Roger Mudd, "I found the conduct and behavior almost — sort of — beyond belief myself. But I think that that's the way it was ... I find questions in my own soul as well."

To the consternation of his interrogators, Kennedy has held steadfastly to his inquest testimony, rarely deviating so much as a word from his original statements. On *Meet the Press,* Kennedy was asked, "Is there any new information you could offer between now and the election?"

The Senator replied, "... I wish there was new information that would serve to substantiate my sworn testimony, but I'm equally convinced that there's not going to be any new information ..."

Senator Kennedy is correct. There will be no new information ... unless he chooses to provide it. He is the only living witness to what happened on lonely Dyke Road the night of July 18-19, 1969. He has been the sole witness against himself and supplied the state with the evidence necessary to convict and sentence him for leaving the scene of the accident. Not even Joe Gargan or Paul Markham, both of whom claim to have aided Kennedy in his rescue attempts, were present when the accident occurred.

There are over 1000 pages of sworn testimony and volumes of information about Chappaquiddick. However, it is a time-consuming and tedious task to study the material and sift ignorant gossip from facts — an effort reporters have been unwilling to make. If the previous "investigators" had been more thorough in their research, the mystery of Chappaquiddick could have been solved years ago; all of the facts necessary to reveal what probably happened have been provided and are waiting to be pointed out.

Things are not always as we perceive them. Sometimes we think we have been very clever in seeing through something we were not supposed to, when all along there have been others more clever than we, lying in wait on the other side of the original deception to send us down a different path which also leads in the wrong direction. This is what has happened to the American people in regard to the Chappaquiddick accident.

The voter is the prize in this game of political chess. At times our democracy seems to degenerate into a struggle between various political groups for the coveted vote of the people. Politicians attempt to influence public opinion by manipulating the press, and the press in turn attempts to expose politicians who resort to such tactics. As a result, politicians play the game of helping the press expose their opponents while attempting to keep their own noses clean. It's a vicious game, and Ted Kennedy is an astute player, so are his opponents. With the stakes so high, one slip can be fatal in the rough and tumble political arena.

On July 19, 1969, Ted Kennedy awoke to find himself in a desperate situation which could have been the end of his political career. His performance during and after the Chappaquiddick accident has become the topic of heated debate. Unfortunately, the arguments, by and large, have been based on faulty information supplied by biased "investigators" more interested in political gain than the truth.

As a response to this "tradition" of rather questionable reporting, the author has made a sincere effort to report the facts completely and without bias. She has put Chappaquiddick in the social and political setting of its time.

The Kennedys leave Dukes County Courthouse after Senator Edward M. Kennedy pleaded guilty to leaving the scene of an accident. Kennedy received a two month suspended jail sentence and one year's probation. (July 25, 1969 Black Star)

CHAPTER I
THE CONFESSION

Judge James A. Boyle had reluctantly rescheduled the hearing from Monday July 28, 1969 to Friday the 25th. He had wanted it held as scheduled, but the attorneys presented compelling arguments for the surprise date change.

At first Judge Boyle had considered an assassination in his peaceful island court house absurd, but hate mail poured in at an alarming rate, public emotions pitched higher and higher, and pre-trial publicity gave every would-be assassin a front-row seat. The judge soon realized defendant Ted Kennedy could be killed in his court room.

The red brick Dukes County Court House was jammed with reporters from all over the world. Edgartown, a village on the island of Martha's Vineyard, Massachusetts, had never experienced such an invasion.

Court convened at 9:00 a.m. Ted Kennedy, looking pale and worried, arrived with his three lawyers. Local attorney, Richard J. McCarron, was handling the case. He was backed up by former District Judge Robert G. Clark Jr. and his son, Robert Clark III, who were considered the best accident lawyers in Massachusetts. County prosecutor, Walter Steele, and Police Chief Dominick "Jim" Arena were there to present the county's case against the Senator.

The reporters were tense and ready to flash the results of the proceedings to the anxiously awaiting world. The newsmen thought they knew what had happened, but no one was sure what Ted Kennedy would do. Would he plead not guilty to the charge confronting him? Would he try to explain away his involvement? So far, all that Kennedy had told the public was contained in a short statement he had given the police and the press:

"On July 18, 1969, at approximately 11:15 p.m., on Chappaquiddick Island, Martha's Vineyard, I was driving my car on Main Street on my way to get the ferry back to Edgartown. I was unfamiliar with the road and turned onto Dyke Road instead of bearing left on Main Street. After proceeding for approximately a half mile on Dyke Road I descended a hill and came upon a narrow bridge. The car went off the side of the bridge. There was one passenger in the car with me, Miss *_____, a former secretary of my brother Robert Kennedy. The car turned over and sank into the water and landed with the roof resting on the bottom. I attempted to open the door and window of the car but have no recollection of how I got out of the car. I came to the surface and then repeatedly dove down to the car in an attempt to see if the passenger was still in the car. I was unsuccessful in the attempt.

"I was exhausted and in a state of shock. I recall walking back to where my friends were eating. There was a car parked in front of the cottage and I climbed into the back seat. I then asked for someone to bring me back to Edgartown. I remember walking around for a period of time and then going back to my hotel room. When I fully realized what happened this morning, I immediately contacted the police."

No one knew what the Senator's whole story would be. How was he going to explain walking off and leaving that girl to drown without telling anyone she was in his car at the bottom of Poucha Pond until the police discovered it themselves nine hours later! He should have a convincing tale developed by now; after all he had been closeted all week at Hyannisport with a score of the best minds in the nation.

There were several legal grounds he could use for pleading not guilty. He had a battery of high priced lawyers working for him — there was no doubt that he would get off. The question was which loophole would be used to accomplish it.

---

* Because of the uncertainty of the spelling of Kopechne the space was left blank.

The reporters eagerly leaned forward to catch every word as the clerk read:

"Commonwealth versus Edward M. Kennedy of Boston, Massachusetts, on the 19th day of July, 1969, at Edgartown, did operate a certain motor vehicle upon a public way in said Edgartown and did go away after knowingly causing injury to Mary Jo Kopechne without stopping and making known his name, residence and the number of his motor vehicle. How do you plead, guilty or not guilty?"

All eyes swung to the famous Senator as he stood and quietly replied, "Guilty." He apparently realized that not all had heard. Taking a deep breath he repeated loudly, "Guilty."

GUILTY? The reporters looked wide-eyed at each other. There had been talk that he might do it, but no one had believed he would. Even an everyday reporter could see several legal technicalities he could use to claim innocence — a concussion, for instance. The Senator had just pleaded guilty to a charge that carried a maximum sentence of two years in the state penitentiary. He now had no recourse but to take whatever sentence the judge handed down. There could be no appeal. If Boyle wanted to, he could put Kennedy in prison and none of his high priced lawyers could save him. As far as anyone knew, there had been no pre-trial plea bargaining involving Judge Boyle. The atmosphere was tense as the audience waited in suspense for the sentencing while the judge listened to a summary of the evidence. Would Kennedy be treated like any other first time offender and receive a suspended sentence, or would the judge choose to treat him more harshly to avoid public criticism? They stared at Judge Boyle and tried to guess what he was thinking behind his stern-faced exterior. The judge was a staunch Republican and a Nixon supporter. Would he use the power he now held over the President's leading political opponent to completely destroy him? Kennedy was obviously worried. It appeared that he didn't know what Boyle would do either. Joan Kennedy, looking frightened, never took her eyes off her husband as she sat in the crowd with her brother-in-law, Stephen Smith.

Police Chief Arena completed his summary of the evidence; then Judge Boyle surprised everyone by asking a very pointed question, "I would be most interested in determining from the defendant or the Commonwealth if there was a deliberate effort to conceal the identity of the defendant."

Arena answered, "Identity of the defendant — not to my knowledge, your honor."

The judge then recognized Kennedy's lawyer, Richard McCarron, who said, "Your honor, the attorneys representing Edward M. Kennedy have advised him that there are legal defenses that could be presented in this case. However . . ."

The suggestion angered Boyle, who pointed an admonishing finger at the lawyer, "Mr. McCarron, just a moment. I don't think that is a proper statement to make. Do you now desire to say you want to plead not guilty?"

Kennedy had straightened up and was glaring at his lawyer. McCarron nervously glanced at his disgruntled client and quickly backed down, "No, your honor."

The judge wasn't finished with McCarron. He faced the lawyer and declared, "I'm concerned now with the question of disposition, mitigating circumstances, aggravated circumstances."

Kennedy was silently staring at his attorney. McCarron realized he had better do as he'd been told. "The defendant is adamant in this matter, your honor, that he wishes to plead guilty to the offense of operating a motor vehicle and going away after causing personal injury. It is his direction that this plea enter and leave the disposition to this court.

"I believe your honor has had experience in disposition on motor vehicle accidents of this nature. It is the contention of the defendant, your honor, and the defendant's attorneys that confinement to the house of correction of the defendant would not be the proper course. I believe his character is well known to the world. We would therefore ask that any sen-

4

tence that the court may impose be suspended."

The county prosecutor, Walter Steele, concurred, "May it please your honor, the commonwealth suggests for your honor's consideration that this defendant be incarcerated in the house of correction for a period of two months and that execution of this sentence be suspended.

"It would seem that having in mind the character of the defendant, his age, his reputation, prior to this occurrence, that the ends of justice would best be served were he given a suspended sentence."

Judge Boyle turned to the probation officer, "There is no record, Mrs. Tyra?"

The probation officer replied, "None, your honor."

The judge considered the notable defendant. The time had arrived. What would he do? Someone whispered that Kennedy looked sick. Joan's knuckles were turning white as she clenched her fists, her eyes still fixed on Ted. Judge Boyle cleared his throat and stated, "Considering the unblemished record of the defendant and the commonwealth represents this is not a case where he was really trying to conceal his identity . . ."

Steele anxiously interrupted in confirmation, "No, Sir."

The judge continued, "Where it is my understanding he has already been and will continue to be punished far beyond anything this court can impose. The ends of justice would be satisfied by the imposition of the minimum jail sentence and the suspension of that sentence, assuming the defendant accepts the suspension."

Kennedy slumped back in his chair, obviously relieved. McCarron quickly stated, "The defendant will accept the suspension, your honor."

The court clerk called, "Edward M. Kennedy". The Senator rose and the clerk continued, "On the complaint, the court has found you guilty and has sentenced you to serve two months in the house of correction at Barnstable: sentence is suspended."

The reporters exploded from their chairs in a mad rush to the nearest phones. The court filled with noise as the bailiff shouted for order. The next defendant was called to stand trial for driving without a license, while Kennedy was ushered out a back door and down a flight of stairs. Once on the first floor, the Senator went directly to the main entrance where a huge crowd of spectators, cameramen and reporters were waiting for him. The people were noisy and many were shouting to him. Kennedy tried to quiet them so he could talk, but the attempt was useless. He finally managed to get close enough to a group of reporters to be heard and announced, "I have asked the television network for time this evening to make my statement to the people of Massachusetts and the nation."

With that, Kennedy collected Joan and followed a wedge of state troopers who opened the way to a waiting car — and sped away, leaving the excited crowd eagerly anticipating that evening's telecast ... they were finally going to find out what had happened last Friday. All looked forward to Kennedy's logical explanation of the tragic accident which was mystifying the nation.

At 7:30 p.m. Eastern Standard Time, Senator Ted Kennedy went on the air with a carefully prepared statement.

My fellow citizens:

I have requested this opportunity to talk to the people of Massachusetts about the tragedy which happened last Friday evening.

This morning I entered a plea of guilty to the charge of leaving the scene of an accident. Prior to my appearance in court it would have been improper for me to comment on these matters.

But tonight I am free to tell you what happened and to say what it means to me.

On the weekend of July 18, I was on Martha's Vineyard Island participating with my nephew, Joe Kennedy, as for 30 years my family has participated in the annual Edgartown Sailing Regatta. Only reasons of health prevented my wife from accompanying me. On Chappaquiddick Island, off Martha's Vineyard, I attended on Fri-

Kennedy addresses constituents on T.V. after pleading
guilty to leaving the scene of a fatal accident. (July 25, 1969,
U.P.I. Photo)

day evening, July 18, a cookout I had encouraged and helped sponsor for a devoted
group of Kennedy-campaign secretaries.

When I left the party around 11:15 p.m., I
was accompanied by one of these girls, Miss
Mary Jo Kopechne. Mary Jo was one of the
most devoted members of the staff of Senator
Robert Kennedy. She worked for him for four
years and was broken up over his death. For
this reason and because she was such a gentle,
kind and idealistic person, all of us tried to help
her feel that she still had a home with the Kennedy family.

There is no truth whatever, to the widely circulated suspicions of immoral conduct that
have been leveled at my behavior and hers regarding that evening. There has never been a
private relationship between us of any kind. I
know of nothing in Mary Jo's conduct, on that
or any other occasion — and the same is true

7

of the other girls at that party — that would lend any substance to such ugly speculation about their character. Nor was I driving under the influence of liquor.

Little over one mile away, the car that I was driving on an unlit road went off a narrow bridge, which had no guard rails and was built on a left angle to the road.

The car overturned in a deep pond and immediately filled with water. I remember thinking as the cold water rushed in around my head that I was, for certain, drowning. But somehow I struggled to the surface alive. I made immediate and repeated efforts to save Mary Jo by diving into the strong and murky current, but succeeded only in increasing my state of utter exhaustion and alarm.

My conduct and conversations during the next several hours, to the extent that I can remember them, make no sense to me at all.

Although my doctors inform me that I suffered a cerebral concussion as well as shock, I do not seek to escape responsibility for my actions by placing the blame either on the physical and emotional trauma brought on by the accident or on anyone else.

I regard as indefensible the fact that I did not report the accident to the police immediately.

Instead of looking directly for a telephone after lying exhausted in the grass for an undetermined time, I walked back to the cottage where the party was being held and requested the help of two friends — my cousin, Joseph Gargan, and Paul Markham — and directed them to return immediately to the scene with me — this was sometime after midnight — in order to undertake a new effort to dive down and locate Miss Kopechne.

Their strenuous efforts, undertaken at some risk to their own lives, also proved futile.

All kinds of scrambled thoughts, all of them

confused, some of them irrational, many of them which I cannot recall, and some of which I would not have seriously entertained under normal circumstances, went through my mind during this period. They were reflected in the various inexplicable, inconsistent and inconclusive things I said and did — including such questions as whether the girl might still be alive somewhere out of that immediate area, whether some awful curse did actually hang over all the Kennedys, whether there was some justifiable reason for me to doubt what had happened and to delay my report, whether somehow the awful weight of this incredible incident might, in some way, pass from my shoulders.

I was overcome, I'm frank to say, by a jumble of emotions: grief, fear, doubt, exhaustion, panic, confusion and shock.

Instructing Gargan and Markham not to alarm Mary Jo's friends that night, I had them take me to the ferry crossing. The ferry having shut down for the night, I suddenly jumped into the water and impulsively swam across, nearly drowning once again in the effort, and returned to my hotel about 2 a.m. and collapsed in my room.

I remember going out at one point and saying something to the room clerk.

In the morning, with my mind somewhat more lucid, I made an effort to call a family legal adviser, Burke Marshall, from a public telephone on the Chappaquiddick side of the ferry, and then belatedly reported the accident to the Martha's Vineyard police.

Today, as I mentioned, I felt morally obligated to plead guilty to the charge of leaving the scene of an accident. No words on my part can possibly express the terrible pain and suffering I feel over this tragic incident.

This last week has been an agonizing one for me and for the members of my family. And the grief we feel over the loss of a wonderful friend will remain with us for the rest of our lives.

These events, the publicity, innuendo and whispers which have surrounded them, and my admission of guilt this morning, raise the question in my mind of whether my standing among the people of my State has been so impaired that I should resign my seat in the United States Senate.

If at any time the citizens of Massachusetts should lack confidence in their Senator's character or his ability, with or without justification, he could not, in my opinion, adequately perform his duties, and should not continue in office.

The people of this state — the state which sent John Quincy Adams and Daniel Webster and Charles Sumner and Henry Cabot Lodge and John Kennedy to the United States Senate — are entitled to representation in that body by men who inspire their utmost confidence.

For this reason I would understand full well why some might think it right for me to resign. For me, this will be a difficult decision to make.

It has been seven years since my first election to the Senate. You and I share many memories; some of them have been glorious, some have been very sad.

The opportunity to work with you and serve Massachusetts has made my life worthwhile.

And so I ask you tonight — the people of Massachusetts — to think this through with me. In facing this decision, I seek your advice and opinion. In making it, I seek your prayers.

For this is a decision that I will have finally to make on my own.

It has been written a man does what he must, in spite of personal consequences, in spite of obstacles and dangers and pressures.

And that is the basis of all human morality. Whatever may be the sacrifices he faces if he follows his conscience — the loss of his friends, his fortune, his contentment, even the esteem of his fellow men — each man must decide for himself the course he will follow.

The stories of past courage cannot supply courage itself. For this each man must look into his own soul.

I pray that I can have the courage to make the right decision. Whatever is decided, whatever the future holds for me, I hope that I shall be able to put this most recent tragedy behind me and make some further contribution to our State and mankind, whether it be in public or private life.

Thank you, and goodnight.

Like millions of other people across the nation, President Nixon sat glued to his television. He couldn't believe his good fortune. His sole threat in 1972 had just self-distructed. The President was fascinated by the Chappaquiddick incident. Within six hours of Kennedy's appearance at the Edgartown Police Station on Saturday, July 19th, Nixon's men were on the scene gathering information which was channeled directly to the Oval Office. The turn of events had amazed Nixon as much as it had stunned the rest of the nation. The most popular Democrat in the United States had actually walked into a police station and announced that he had been the cause of a young woman's death. What was even more astounding was that he waited nine hours to report the accident — the type of accident in which victims sometimes survive if rescued quickly enough.

Kennedy must have had a terrible attack of "the dumbs". There had been no witnesses to the accident. Why in the world would anyone, least of all a politician, accuse himself of the dastardly deed? He was the sole witness against himself. Yet, there he was, freely telling the nation what an evil thing he did. He was so bad, in fact, that he wasn't even sure he should stay in the Senate. He had to be crazy.

Kennedy must not have been kidding in 1968 when he said he wasn't interested in running for President. One thing was certain now, if he didn't want the job, he no longer had to worry about being pressured to try for it. But what a way to get out of it! There wasn't any reason Kennedy should be doing this. First of all, since there were no witnesses, all he would have had to say was that he didn't know anything about it. He could even have said that he was too drunk to drive, Mary Jo was taking him home and the next thing he knew he woke up in the drink. People would have been happy to believe that. He didn't have to put himself in the driver's seat. And not reporting the accident for nine hours! Why didn't he report it? Why didn't Gargan or Markham report it? After all, the Kennedy's weren't idiots; there had to be a good reason behind this madness. What could be so terrible that Kennedy would go to these lengths to cover it up? Richard Nixon intended to find out.

Ted was smart enough to try to bail himself out with a Checkers type speech such as had worked for Nixon in 1952 when he was in hot water for accepting an $18,235.00 slush fund from wealthy supporters to "run his office". At the time, Nixon had been nominated as Eisenhower's vice-presidental running mate and had asked people to write or wire the Republican National Committee whether or not he should stay on the ticket ... "Because, folks, remember, a man that's to be President of the United States or Vice President of the United States must have the confidence of the people. And that's why I'm doing what I'm doing." Within four days the GOP headquarters had received over two million responses running 350 to 1 in Nixon's favor. The public seemed to be quick to forgive a man who admits a mistake. It would certainly be ironic if Teddy managed to save himself with the President's personal salvation technique.

At first, Kennedy's speech appeared to have been successful. There was a tremendous inpouring of mail, over 100,000 letters and cards running 100 to 1 in his favor. A sympathetic public did not want to lose its last Kennedy, no matter what he said he had done. Of course, the Senator responded positively. After an appropriate waiting period he announced to his grateful constituents that because of their heartwarming letters he had reached the difficult decision of remaining in the Senate.

12

However, not everyone was pleased with Kennedy's performance. Soon the press began asking questions and widespread dissatisfaction began to grow. People asked, "How gullible does he think we are? He's got to come up with something better than that! If he couldn't save her, why didn't he go to the nearest house to call for emergency help?" On his way to church the following Sunday, Kennedy was confronted by a crowd of youths carrying signs which read, "Tell the truth, Teddy."

Letters to the editor of various news magazines were very critical. *Time* reported on September 5, 1969 that of the 1,817 letters received to date, 1,230 generally criticized the Senator while 587 expressed forgiveness or confidence in him.

Some of the more interesting letters read:
• "Senator Edward Kennedy today has made a slight revision in the magic 1961 inaugural pronouncement of his brother John F. Kennedy: 'Ask not what I have withheld from the people of Massachusetts, but what they can overlook for me.'"
• "Why did Senator Kennedy take a chance on drowning by swimming to Edgartown? It would have been much wiser for him to just walk across the water and certainly not beyond his capabilities."
• "Assume that your friend and cousin, having had a tragic accident, comes to your door late in the evening. He is completely exhausted, in shock, and has water in his lungs and a slight concussion. Do you call a doctor? Don't be ridiculous. The proper thing is to take your friend to the nearest ferry and when the ferry is shut down for the night just calmly stand there and watch him swim across the channel, preferably fully clothed. Now he'll be able to recuperate all by himself in a nice comfortable motel room.
• "Brothers Grimm, move over, You have been topped."

"If Kennedy did what he did, and was not drunk, and was not doing something immoral, then he is much too dumb to be a Senator."
• "It appears to me that Ted Kennedy has graduated from being the youngest Senator in the nation to

the oldest juvenile delinquent in the nation."

Not all letters were of this tone. A few showed more insight, such as one *Time* received:

● "Never have I witnessed such unity of opinion among the informed and uninformed — people who have acted as prosecutor, judge, witness, and jury. The verdict, guilty as charged, and a bit more so. Nearly all of these people say, 'If he had been a poor man, etc.' This little remark perhaps unconsciously reveals the real crime Kennedy is believed to be guilty of."

The public wasn't alone in its dissatisfaction with the Senator. The press was more than willing, in many instances, to add fuel to the fire.

The *New York Times* said, "His emotion-charged address leaves us less than satisfied with his partial explanation for a gross failure of responsibility, and more than ever convinced that the concerned town, country, and state officials of Massachusetts have also failed in their duty thoroughly to investigate the case because of the political personality involved."

Time magazine said, "The appearance did in fact answer a few questions, but left the most serious one unanswered, and raised a few that had not been asked before."

Newsweek, too, questioned, ". . . the hard fact was that Teddy's TV account of the tragedy of Chappaquiddick Island — and in particular of his indefensible ten-hour delay in reporting to the police — has not been enough to remove the suspicions, the doubts, the contradictions, and the unanswered questions that hang about the case."

Even *Life* attacked the Senator: "There was also some decidedly awkward talk of morality and courage, including an eloquent passage from his brother's book, which Teddy recited as though oblivious to the way the meaning rebuked him. He was simply hustling heartstrings, using words, cashing in on the family credibility . . .

"It was like a parody of the Cuban missile crisis, all surviving New Frontiersmen scheming to extricate their man from the scandal of accident."

Kennedy's popularity took a sharp drop. Before the accident the people of Massachusetts had given him a favorable rating 85% of the time. A poll taken on August 3, 1969 showed a favorable rating of 74%, an 11% drop in two weeks. He was still popular but the slip was alarming and was to continue downward as more questions were asked, much to the distress of Kennedy and his supporters.

As much as Kennedy may have wished it, the case was not closed with his guilty plea and subsequent conviction. Instead, the public demanded more information and the District Attorney decided to try for a manslaughter charge. The legal battles raged for months. To have or not to have the body exhumed for an autopsy? Should the inquest be open to the public? Should there be a Grand Jury investigation? Eventually, all of the participants were questioned, and every legal angle followed up. Kennedy testified for three hours, and all of the people connected with the tragic affair were called before Judge Boyle to give their stories under oath. Their testimonies filled 763 pages of transcript. Still the matter would not die. Especially when Judge Boyle indicated that he did not believe some parts of Kennedy's testimony.

Many people, both for and against Kennedy, delved into the accident in detail, examining official and unofficial investigation reports, the hearing and inquest transcripts and even the scene of the accident in an effort to discern the "truth". Instead of becoming clearer, the facts became more and more muddled. The investigators were confused. Kennedy's story just didn't add up with other evidence. His actions were illogical, and times didn't coincide, but try as they might, no one could figure out a better explanation of the accident or what Kennedy might be trying to hide.

The man who spent the most money and who had the most investigators on the case was none other than Richard Nixon. The President invested $100,-000.00 of his Campaign to Re-elect the President funds in the effort. This fact was proven in Congressional hearings and verified by the testimony of

Anthony Ulasewicz, Nixon's private detective, who did most of the work and received much of the money. In his *Memoirs,* published after he was finished politically, Nixon acknowledges his interest:

"It was clear that the full story of what happened that night on Chappaquiddick had not come out, and I suspected that the press would not try very hard to uncover it. Therefore I told Ehrlichman to have someone investigate the case for us and get the real facts out, 'Don't let up on this for a minute,' I said, 'Just put yourself in their place if something like this had happened to us.' In fact, our private investigator was unable to turn up anything besides rumors."

Nixon concurred with the Chappaquiddick Theorem as explained by James Doyle and demonstrated by Ted Kennedy. What it amounts to is that the best way to handle extremely bad news is to tell all immediately. If one follows the advice of friends and relatives and waits until things cool off to tell the story, the press will bring it out in bits and pieces which will make it look even worse than it would have been otherwise. Nixon may have figured out the theorem, but he wasn't bold enough to apply it to Watergate three years later.

It is now more than ten years after the tragic accident, and the public still is not satisfied with the case. Every time Kennedy is mentioned as a Presidential possibility, the word "Chappaquiddick" follows in the next breath. The problem is — if you aren't willing to believe Kennedy's explanation, what can you believe? The theories brought forth to date are even more flawed than Kennedy's imperfect story, and the public is frustrated. The theories range from the preposterous Zad Rust idea that Kennedy murdered the girl because he had gotten her pregnant and drove off the bridge to cover the crime, jumping out of the moving car onto the bridge in the nick of time to save himself, to the more widely believed idea that he was drunk, which also fails to hold up under scrutiny.

At this point, all rational people are in agreement that, as tragic as the incident was, IT WAS AN ACCIDENT. Things like that happen every day. It was very sad, but Kennedy can be forgiven for having caused it. Few doubt that he is sincere when he says that he cannot express the sorrow he has felt over the incident. Whether he is sorrowing over the loss of a friend or his subsequent public relations problems might be argued by his critics. However, no one can doubt that he wishes the accident had never happened.

That he says he drove the car off Dike Bridge and a young lady drowned because of it does not bother most people. But other things about the case do. Many questions linger.

Ted Kennedy listens to the charges being read against him. (July 25, 1969 Black Star)

Mary Jo Kopechne pictured at her desk in Robert Kennedy's office, 1968.

Island cottage where former RFK staff members attended cook-out the evening before the accident. (Willis, February 1980)

18

CHAPTER II
WHAT KIND
OF A PARTY WAS IT?

There is little doubt that the party itself was exactly what Kennedy described — a get-together for people who had worked on Robert Kennedy's campaign. It was unfortunate for the Senator that his wife or Mrs. Markham or Mrs. Gargan did not attend but their absence was probably coincidental. It was not at all unusual for Joan Kennedy to stay home. She and her husband have always led independent lives. In addition, she was pregnant and had a history of miscarriages, and her doctor had advised her not to exert herself.

In July of 1970 the Ladies Home Journal printed an interview Joan Kennedy gave to Betty Hoffman, which dealt with the Chappaquiddick party:

"Joan, how about Chappaquiddick?"

She was quiet for a long moment, obviously weighing her words.

"In following you around, I offered, "I've met most of the men who were at the party on Chappaquiddick. They hardly seem like the type that would ..."

"Yes," she said, in a rush of words, "you've seen what kind of men they are. For example, Jack Crimmins is a bachelor in his sixties — he's practically a member of the family, we've known him so long. As for the girls they invited to that party on Chappaquiddick, I know them all. When I wasn't on the road campaigning for Bobby, I'd often stop by his headquarters on L Street in Washington to say hello and to tell them how much their efforts were appreciated. Many nights they worked until midnight.

"They were all smart, hard-working, dedicated girls, all crazy about Bobby. They shared his ideals. When you're all working on a campaign together you become very close," she continued.

"After Bobby died, we kept in touch with his office staff, even after they found other jobs. Ted and I invited the girls, along with some other friends and staff people, to at least two cook-outs at Hyannisport; another time, we took them sailing on Ted's boat. It was a way to say thank you."

Yes, she said, she had known Mary Jo Kopechne, the girl who drowned in the car Ted was driving. Joan considered her "an exceptionally nice girl, very idealistic."

Joan explained why she had not gone to the party on Chappaquiddick. 'For the past six or seven years, Ted has sailed in the Edgartown Regatta. It's a fun regatta with lots of boats in the same class as his. He always wants to do well in the race. I crew for Ted every weekend in the club races at Hyannisport, but they're only about two hours long. The Edgartown Regatta takes six or seven hours. It's a man's race. I went once and it was pretty rugged. Also, I was two month's pregnant last July and taking it easy. I knew about the party they planned to have afterwards — it's traditional after sailing races — and that Joe Gargan had rented a small cottage because, on Martha's Vineyard, Ted's always recognized wherever he goes.

'Ted phoned me that Friday, after the race was finished, and told me, 'We came in fourth.' I knew how disappointed he must have felt. He's come close to winning so many times and never quite made it, and Ted always wants to win.'

Betty Gargan had intended to spend the entire week on Chappaquiddick Island with her husband and another couple. However, her mother became ill and was hospitalized. Naturally, Mrs. Gargan cancelled her vacation so she could stay near her mother. Joe Gargan cut his vacation down to the weekend. He did not cancel the barbecue altogether, because it had been planned for weeks, and the others had arranged time off from their jobs in order to attend. It should also be noted that the same group had gotten together on numerous other occasions, the last of which was at Ethel Kennedy's home where several of the wives had attended.

Many of Kennedy's enemies would like the public to believe that the girls involved were merely pick ups. Such was definitely not the case. They were all friends of the family, including the wives of the men who attended, and had every right to be there. As Esther Newberg was quoted, "It was a steak cook out, not a Roman orgy."

On August 28, 1969, *Time* magazine stated, "Kennedy wonders why people think he'd be so stupid as to get involved in a sex orgy in his own state accompanied by a middle aged chauffeur and girls from his own brother's staff." In retrospect, the idea does seem highly unlikely.

1968 photo of Robert Kennedy and Mary Jo Kopechne outside the Senator's office.

The five women who, along with Mary Jo Kopechne, attended the Chappaquiddick reunion for RFK staff workers. Left to right with 1970 place of employment: Rosemary Keough (Joseph P. Kennedy, Jr. Foundation for Retarded Children), Maryellen Lyons (Massachusetts State Senator Beryl Cohen), Nance Lyons (Senator Edward M. Kennedy), Susan Tannenbaum (Representative Allard Lowenstein), Esther Newberg (Urban Institute, Washington D.C.). (UPI January 8, 1970)

CHAPTER III

WHY WAS KENNEDY ALONE WITH MARY JO IN THE CAR?

Kennedy claims that he was merely giving Mary Jo a ride back to her motel. Perhaps he was. However, Mary Jo did not take her purse or motel key with her when they departed; also, she told no one that she was leaving — although she was overheard asking Kennedy for a ride. When he picked up his car keys from his chauffeur, Jack Crimmins, Kennedy told him that he was returning to his motel and was giving Mary Jo a ride because she was tired and not feeling well. Crimmins did not drive them because he was spending the night at the cottage, and chauffeuring the short trip would have been a pointless inconvenience. Since Kennedy and Mary Jo were not returning, the eight others who were also planning to later depart for Edgartown were left with only one car to transport all of them to the ferry.

Many people point to the Senator's reputation for appreciating a pretty face and say that he was obviously planning some hanky-panky. On the surface this seems a valid assumption. However, from what the investigators have been able to learn about Mary Jo, such conduct would be out of character for her. She had a good reputation and was a devout Catholic. She was so involved in the Catholic Church that upon graduation from New Jersey's Caldwell College in 1962, with a B.S. Degree in Business, she gave a year to the Lay Apostolate, and the church sent her to Montgomery, Alabama where she taught typing and shorthand to black youths. This experience led to her eventual involvement with the Kennedys. Mary Jo was definitely not a Washington party girl. She was a dedicated worker, hoping to make what she considered positive changes in government and society. This is not to say that she couldn't have had a moral lapse, but it would have been out of character. If Kennedy was looking for a little fun, he made a poor choice of girls.

The Senator himself presented a most convincing argument against such behavior when he told a friend that he was insulted that people would think he'd be interested in playing around in the back seat of a car. He had more class than that; he would have gone to the motel. How can that be argued? Kennedy had four different motel rooms at his disposal, and he knew no one would be back for a while. The mosquitos were terrible on the island, which would have made a roll in the bushes or on the beach unpleasant. He also had a bad back that was bothering him. It is difficult to imagine him considering such an encounter in the back seat of a car. In addition, it is apparent that Mary Jo did not have intercourse that evening because State Police Chemist, John McHugh, carefully tested her clothing for traces of seminal fluid and found none.

Be that as it may, the fact that Kennedy was alone with the girl in the middle of the night on a lonely island road, obviously not going to the ferry, naturally leads to a foregone conclusion about his moral character. Although Kennedy swore, "There is no truth whatever, to the widely circulated suspicions of immoral conduct ..." he was generally not believed. Joan Kennedy probably knows her husband better than anyone in this regard, and her views on the matter came through quite clearly in an interview by Lester David.

I asked her if she had felt betrayed or thought about ending the marriage because of the Chappaquiddick incident. "I never said that or felt that way," she replied. "It's absolutely untrue. Absolutely."

She grew angry as she discussed the stories that she had doubted her husband. "I believe anybody who did doubt has never really looked at the situation, hasn't talked to the eleven or twelve people who were involved. They made such a mountain out of a molehill, except that it ended in a terrible tragedy. I felt very badly for the girl's parents and her friends. It was a very, very, very tragic thing. But I see it just as that, an accident."

"It takes me a long time to have things jell in my mind," she told me. "Things occur to me almost like after the fact and I start thinking about them. As time went on, I got fiercely loyal to Ted. And if people would say anything derogatory or insinuate anything, that was the only time I'd show any kind of — well, maybe anger isn't the word but I'd get kind of mad at people for making little comments like 'Oh, poor Joan,' or 'You poor thing.' You know people love to think that you love sympathy. 'Oh, you poor thing' (mimicking) 'You must have gone through hell.' And I'd say to them, 'You know, I don't need, I don't want your sympathy. Don't feel sorry for me. Don't feel sorry for either of us.'

"When I said that, people would be startled. They kept giving me all this, 'You poor thing' and 'How can you live through all this' and a lot of other things I won't say. They kept insinuating that my life must have been pretty miserable because . . . and then they would give me all the rumors that were going around.

"And I'd find that absolutely repulsive. And some of these people were some of my good friends. I told them where to go. I said, 'Don't tell me that!' It was kind of like I got up on my high horse for the first time in my life. Not that I was being defensive, but I just said, 'Look, that's not the way I feel at all. Not at all! That was the first time since I was married to Ted that I felt so strong a feeling.' "

Mary Jo's parents were quite upset about the allegations made against their daughter's moral conduct. In an interview printed in *McCall's* September 1970 issue, Mary Jo's mother, Mrs. Joseph Kopechne, stated:

"Among Mary Jo's boy friends there was *not* one named Senator Edward Kennedy. All these stories about a romance between the two of them are just plain silly. She got to know him only after Robert Kennedy's death; and even then, she rarely saw him. She was better acquainted with Senator Kennedy's wife, Joan, because she often took her children to the Robert Kennedy house while Mary Jo was helping Ethel with her correspondence.

" 'Joan Kennedy is such a beautiful girl,' Mary Jo once said to me. When I asked her about the Senator, she said, 'I only know what I hear; that this one is the politician, the real politician ...

"In June, when Matt Reese sent her back to Jersey City for the runoff in the Whelan campaign, she agreed to on one condition: that he pay her plane fare back to Washington each weekend, so she could be with this young man, a foreign-service officer with whom she was in love. Mary Jo had been seriously dating two young men before him, but neither of them was settled, and she didn't want to give up her career for them. But now, she told us, she had found the man she wanted to marry ...

"The judge concluded that Senator Kennedy had lied when he told the court that he and Mary Jo had been driving toward the ferry for a return to Edgartown. This conclusion, by a man who didn't know Mary Jo leaves a bad taste in our mouths, and we absolutely reject it and any implications that flow from it.

"In May, my husband and I talked to most of the girls who were at the party, and we now believe that Mary Jo did leave to go home. As I've already said, one of the girls definitely heard her ask for a ride to the ferry. Why didn't she say good-by to everyone? Simply because she didn't want to break up the party. Many thoughtful people leave a party inconspicuously so that everyone else won't also start to leave. As I've said, even in Washington when Mary Jo was bored or tired at a party, she had no qualms about walking right out.

"The Judge's conclusion that Mary Jo did not intend to return to Edgartown was partly based on the fact that she left her pocketbook at the cottage. Well, could this not have been one of the few times when she simply forgot it upon leaving? My husband and I believe so."

There is one very convincing argument in favor of Mary Jo having accidentally forgotten her purse and that is that any woman will take her purse with her no matter where she is intending to go. If Mary Jo had been anticipating more than an innocent ride home she certainly would have wanted her comb so that she could repair any damage done to her hair. It simply is not logical to assume that she purposely left her purse behind for any reason.

Aside from the nice things Mrs. Kopechne has to say about Mary Jo's character, the fact that she was in love with a young man whom she evidently intended to marry makes it difficult to imagine her considering sexual relations with Senator Kennedy. Very few young women, especially one with a good reputation, would be willing to risk losing a prospective husband by taking a fling in the back seat of a car with a married man.

Officer Look's observation of the occupants of the car he encountered at the intersection is also noteworthy. "When the automobile passed in front of me and also when I was walking towards it there appeared to be a man driving and a woman in the front right-hand side ... "

The "right-hand side" seems like an unusual place for a girl anticipating a sexual encounter. One would expect to find her sitting right next to him unless they were not intending to play around.

Perhaps he really was giving her a ride back to the motel. Stranger things have happened. No matter what his motives were, the motel was the logical place for him to be going.

People who insist that there was a sinister cover-up point out that Mary Jo left her purse at the cottage and say that the reason the purse was not immediately returned to her parents, was that Kennedy did not want it known that the purse had been left behind. If this was so, it is hard to understand why the purse did not disappear entirely. It would not have been difficult for someone to toss it into Poucha Pond, a logical place for it to have ended up. Miss Nance Lyons, Mary Jo's roommate, explained to the court what happened to the purse:

Q. Did you take her purse back with you?
A. Yes, sir.
Q. Where did you find it?
A. In the living room in the cottage.
Q. Let me ask you something else. When you examined the purse were her keys in it?
A. I didn't examine the purse. I opened it at one point to take out her address book so I could call her parents and I packed her suitcase and I left out her bathing suit and at another point I opened it and just put her bathing suit in and her pocketbook.
Q. Did you return the items back to Mrs. Kopechne?
A. Yes.
Q. On the return trip to Washington?
A. No, sir. I brought them to Wilkes-Barre with me with the intention of turning them over to the Kopechnes. However, it didn't seem appropriate, so I brought them back to Washington with me and one of the Kopechnes came to collect Miss Kopechne's belongings.

There has also been speculation that Kennedy and Mary Jo were not alone in the car. Since Officer Look testified that he saw an object or a person in the back seat of the car, Rosemary Keough's purse was recovered from the vehicle, and Mary Jo was found in the back seat, some investigators think that Mary Jo was tired or perhaps intoxicated and went to sleep in the back seat of Kennedy's car. Later Kennedy and Miss Keough decided to drive down to the beach and went off the bridge. Kennedy and Miss Keough escaped unharmed. Not knowing that Mary Jo was still in the submerged vehicle, they left the scene and did not report the accident.

The theory nicely explains the failure to report the accident and Kennedy's subsequent strange behavior. However, it does not do well under close examination. The largest flaw is that Miss Keough and Charlie Tretter were inseparable all evening, running errands together, taking walks together, and even sleeping next to each other on the floor. It hardly seems reasonable that Kennedy would run off with Charlie's girl, or even that she would want to go. Miss Keough explained in court why her purse was found in the vehicle.

Q. Did you miss your purse sometime during the day?
A. I missed my purse after I knew it was there.
Q. You left it in Senator Kennedy's car?
A. Yes, sir.
Q. What time did you do that?
A. Approximately 9:30. We (Charlie and she) left the party to go to the Shiretown Inn to get a radio.
Q. That evening?
A. Yes, sir.

During questioning, Officer Look decided that whatever it was he saw in the back seat of the car was probably not a person.

A. ... there appeared to be ... either another person or an object of clothing, a handbag or something, sitting on the back. It looked to me like an object of some kind. I couldn't say what it was.
Q. Do you know what side this object was on, left or right?
A. It was on the right-hand rear.
THE COURT: Now, I am speculating a little bit, but it looks as though this car in the rear has, as many cars do, sort of a little shelf?
THE WITNESS: Yes, sir.
THE COURT: And I take it it was on that shelf where you saw what you thought might be a person or a bag or some clothing?
THE WITNESS: Clothing on that side of the car, yes, sir.
THE COURT: A sweater or clothing or a bag upon the seat, you wouldn't be able to see?
THE WITNESS: No, sir.

Finally, the back seat is the logical place for Mary Jo to have ended up. The car landed upside down with its trunk elevated. Mary Jo would have been thrown to the ceiling. Since her feet were under the dash board, her head would have been toward the rear of the car. As she tried to escape she would have moved upward toward the trunk, which would have put her in the back seat, whether she had started out there or not.

The Katama Shores Motel on Martha's Vine Yard where the women who attended the Chappaquiddick reunion stayed. (Willis February 1980)

Attorney Richard McCarron of Edgartown, Mass. represented Senator Edward Kennedy at the July 25, 1969 hearing. (UPI July 21, 1969)

CHAPTER IV
HOW COULD KENNEDY HAVE MADE THE WRONG TURN?

Various friends of the Senator came forward after the accident and said that Ted Kennedy has a terrible sense of direction. He has been known to get lost within a couple of miles of home. One wonders how anyone with so bad a sense of direction has managed to avoid being lost at sea.

Virtually everyone who is familiar with the intersection in question has flatly stated that a wrong turn was out of the question. Although the cross-road is a convergence of four roads, only the two on which Kennedy should have traveled are paved. The following is Judge Boyle's description of the intersection:

"Chappaquiddick has few roads. At the ferry slip, begins a macadam paved road called Chappaquiddick Road, the main road of the island, with a white center line which is partly obliterated at the curve. The road is approximately twenty feet wide, running in a general easterly direction for two and one-half miles, whence it curves south and continues in that direction past the cottage to the southeast corner of the island. Chappaquiddick Road is sometimes referred to in the testimony as Main Street and, after it curves, as School Road or Schoolhouse Road, because a schoolhouse formerly stood on that portion of it.

At the curve, and continuing easterly, begins Dyke Road, a dirt and sand road, seventeen to nineteen feet wide, which runs a distance of seven-tenths miles to Dike Bridge,* shortly beyond which is the ocean beach.

Cemetery Road is a single car-width private dirt road, which runs northerly from the junction of Chappaquiddick and Dyke Roads.

The Lawrence Cottage (herein called the Cottage) is one-half mile from the junction of Chappaquiddick and Dyke Roads and approximately three miles from the ferry slip.

Proceeding northerly from the Cottage, on the east side of Chappaquiddick Road, a distance of one-tenth mile before the curve, is a metal sign with an arrow pointing toward the ferry landing."

What the judge did not say was that the curve which went through the intersection was slightly

---

* The people who originally lived in Dyke house misspelled the name and called it Dike house. The bridge took this spelling.

Chappaquiddick Road

Ferry

Lawrence Cottage

Cemetary Road

Dyke Road

August 1969, Aerial view of the intersection where Kennedy turned right onto Dyke Road instead of bearing left toward the ferry. (John Hubbard, Black Star)

banked the way the pavement went. In order to make the wrong turn, Kennedy would have deliberately driven over a slight, gravely hump and looked for the dirt road on which to turn. Not only this, but he would have had to ignore the sign pointing to the ferry. The most trusting soul might still give him the benefit of the doubt except for the fact that both he and Mary Jo had been driven to the beach on Dyke Road and knew full well where it went.

In the first statement Kennedy gave to the police, he said he made a wrong turn. He evidently realized the weakness of that claim and deleted the idea from his televised version. However, when questioned later at the inquest, he had to stick with his previous claim of having made a wrong turn or admit to supplying false information to the police. Judge Boyle didn't buy it. In his report Judge Boyle says:

> "I infer a reasonable and probable explanation of the totality of the above facts is . . . that Kennedy did *not* intend to drive to the ferry slip and his turn onto Dyke Road was intentional."

Judge James A. Boyle presided over the July 25, 1969 hearing and the January 1970 inquest. (UPI August 28, 1969)

33

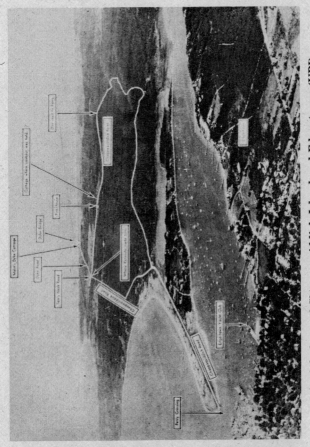

Aerial photo of Chappaquiddick Island and Edgartown. (UPI)

CHAPTER V
WAS KENNEDY DRUNK?

Many people subscribe to the theory that Kennedy was drunk. The assumption is that he drove down to the intersection, inadvertently or purposely turned right on Dyke Road and drove off the bridge. The reason the accident was not reported right away was that his friends were trying to sober him up.

The court very thoroughly went into the question of whether or not Kennedy was driving under the influence of alcohol. Kennedy voluntarily admitted to consuming a beer during the race in the early afternoon, part of a beer about 5:30 p.m., which he shared with Mr. John Driscoll at Ross Richards' boat, a third of a beer at his room at 6:30 p.m., a rum and coke about 8:00 p.m. at the cottage and one more rum and coke after dinner, probably within an hour of leaving. Assuming that Kennedy is being truthful, he should not have been affected by that amount of liquor spread over a nine or ten hour period. The others who attended the party were unsure of the amount that the Senator had to drink, but all insisted that he appeared sober the last time they saw him.

Many are unwilling to accept the statements of Kennedy and the party members as to his sobriety. However, there is a substantial amount of other evidence to support his claim. Before passing judgment, a scrutiny of Ted Kennedy's drinking habits during the period between Robert Kennedy's death in June of 1968 and the accident is in order. In his book *The Bridge at Chappaquiddick,* Jack Olsen, a former senior editor at *Time, Inc.,* says:

> "His worst enemies did not claim that he was a heavy drinker. Washington correspondents who had followed him around for seven years searched their memories after the accident and except for rare periods of let-down like the flight home from Alaska, were hard pressed to remember a single example of heavy drinking.

Even in his own home, at parties where liquor flowed in generous amounts, Kennedy had remained sober and composed. One correspondent remembered an Irish stag party, like most such affairs almost consecrated to intoxication, where Kennedy had sung a few ballads and gone home, completely steady on his feet. Some of the newsmen's memories stretched back through the histories of three Kennedy brothers, and the expert concensus was that none of them had been a two-fisted drinker. JFK had enjoyed an occasional scotch and water, and RFK had sipped politely at parties, and Ted had had his occasional airborne pillow fight and vaults into the swimming pool, but generally speaking one did not associate alcohol with the Kennedys as one associated it with certain other nationally known politicians."

While rumors of Ted Kennedy being seen drunk about town are rampant, one is hard pressed to locate reports of specific instances. Apparently, during that year after RFK's death, the Senator drank more heavily than before or since. Burton Hersh interviewed a close friend of Ted Kennedy in regard to his drinking habits during the summer of 1968.

" 'It's inaccurate to say he was drunk most of the time,' a confidant of the summer commented afterwards. 'It's also inaccurate to say he wasn't drunk at all.' There was a pause, an exceedingly thoughtful pause. 'He never drank on the boat, though . . .' "

After Kennedy unseated Russell Long as Senate Whip in December of 1968, one Senator commented, "At least Ted Kennedy never drank on the Senate Floor. Long, he . . . he reeled in sometimes. His friends finally had to vote against him."

At this time, Ted Kennedy's friends and associates were evidently becoming concerned about his increased drinking. On one occasion a friendly group was discussing Kennedy's uncanny ability to absorb information, interrelate it and then use it. Someone commented that Kennedy's mind is like a computer, to which another was heard to reply, "A computah?

Well, maybe that's what we need now in the Presidency. A computah ... a computah with alcohol in all its circuits."

Other than these general references to his increased drinking during the '68-'69 period, the author has been able to verify only two specific instances. One was a lighthearted spree in Hyannisport with Joey Gargan and a dozen Green Berets they had latched onto somewhere. However, it is difficult to determine if he was drunk or just having a good time. Most people, when they see a United States Senator running around with a lively group of service men, climbing up and repelling off of the Ambassador's roof, naturally assume that he is intoxicated. But Ted Kennedy does not always behave as a dignified statesman. With his personality, he would be just as likely to do it completely sober. On the other hand, later that same day the group was seen at a local restaurant offering toasts, drinking the contents and then breaking their glasses with the pledge, "No one shall drink from this glass again."

"Tip" O'Neill once made an interesting observation about Kennedy to Lester David:

> "Ted's personality has always been a great deal more outgoing than Jack's and certainly more than Bobby's, which could lead people to assume a great deal more about him than is actually the case. Let me illustrate what I mean:
>
> "When Jack Kennedy gave a cocktail party, the invitations would set a time limit: 'From six to eight p.m.' and he meant it. Promptly at eight, the guests would be expected to pick themselves up and go, and the party would be over.
>
> "After his election to the Senate, Ted gave a cocktail party at his Georgetown home and the invitations, as usual, read the same as Jack's — six to eight. When the guests rose to leave, Ted asked in astonishment: 'Where you fellows going?' He was told what the invitations said

and that his brother had expected his guests to stick to it .

" 'Well,' he answered, 'I'm not my brother! Take off your coats. Besides, we've got all that food.' And so we all stayed there, swapping stories until 3 a.m.

"This kind of convivial nature can easily be translated into playboyishness. Just that one party, for instance, could have been blown out of all proportion by gossipers: 'Hey, did you hear about the blast at Ted's house the other night? Boy, I heard a half-dozen congressmen got plastered and Ted himself was lit up like a Christmas tree and . . .' You can fill it all in yourself.

"This is an in-bred, gossipy kind of town. We love to swap tidbits even more than other towns because the important people are here. The stories that used to go around about Estes Kefauver, God rest his soul, would curl your hair."

As if to bear out O'Neill's observation, most of the stories of Kennedy being seen drunk turn out like the one Jack Olsen checked on in Edgartown.

"One also heard about a night when Kennedy had hosted a small delegation to the Seafood Shanty, on Edgartown Dock Street, and regaled the group with songs and jokes and impressions of Richard Nixon and Everett Dirksen and other GOP luminaries until the small hours. 'Drunk!' a cantankerous old man confirmed the next morning, but those who had been closest to the scene in the restaurant, including the owner himself, took violent exception to the sidewalk opinion. They protested that there had been drinking, but no drunkenness. The Senator had simply been enthusiastic and ebullient in that Irish way of his, and even some of the stiffest Edgartown conservatives had had to laugh at his table remarks, and the way he went through the scullery afterward, shaking hands with the workers and cracking still more jokes."

The only truly concrete instance that I have been

able to locate of Ted Kennedy having tied one on is the infamous plane ride home from Alaska in April of 1969. The newsmen on board did not report the incident because it was the first time such a thing had happened and from the comments he was making during the trip it was obvious that Kennedy was drinking because he was having difficulty coping with RFK's death and threats against his own life. So they all agreed to let the incident go unless he did something like that again. However, after Chappaquiddick the reporters who had been on the flight began talking about Kennedy's antics on that occasion. One remembered:

"He started whackin' the bottle in Fairbanks. He'd had nothing to eat, and it was drink, drink, drink, drink, *drink*, no sleep at all. He was all over the place, weaving up the aisle, chanting Es-ki-mo Power, pelting one of his guys with pillows, y'know 'C'mon, wake up, you're not supposed to sleep on these goddamned trips!'"

Another reporter observed:
"Ted was celebrating the fact that he had escaped for a few days from David Burke."

Kennedy was well potted when they landed at Dulles Airport in Washington, D.C. There was a delegation of newsmen waiting to welcome them with cameras ready. The reporters on board the plane figured the jig was up for Ted Kennedy and by the morrow the world would know he had been drunk ... but the luck of the Irish prevailed. One amazed reporter described the ensuing performance:

"We started to get ourselves together. I looked out and everybody was there all right, the TV cameras, the whole world. I left behind Kennedy, and he did look awful, his eyes were like oysters on the half shell. Joan saw him and her jaw dropped four feet. I remember thinking, that's all for you, buddy. Then little Patrick rushed over to him, and Kennedy picked the little boy up and kissed him and Patrick's head blocked off the cameras, and Kennedy was home free. The kid stole the show."

Kennedy's political opponents would like the public to believe that he was practically an alcoholic, but this is not what the verifiable facts bear out. While there is some evidence that during this period Kennedy might have been drinking more than he usually did, there was only one definite instance of his actually being seen drunk in public. In addition, according to his health history report (released November 7, 1979 when he declared his candidacy for President) as early as 1968 Kennedy was under a doctor's care for a duodenal ulcer. Although the ulcer has long since healed, due to its location, a duodenal ulcer is especially persistent because it is continually irritated by the passage of food, gastric juices and stomach acid over it. Therefore, it is probable that Kennedy was still being troubled by the ulcer in 1969.

Alcoholic beverages are detrimental to anyone who is suffering from an ulcer and in many instances consuming alcohol can make the victim quite ill. This is not to say that a heavy drinker cannot have an ulcer, for there is some evidence that suggests alcohol can contribute to the development of an ulcer. However, since Kennedy's ulcer occurred in 1968, it was more likely to have been caused by the stress of his brother's campaign — compounded by the emotional shock of Bob's death — followed by demands that he take RFK's place and run for President himself in 1968 — plus well-founded fears for his own life. No matter what the cause, the usual effect of such an ulcer is to cause the victim to avoid alcohol because the combination of liquor and the ulcer is painfully unpleasant. The fact that Kennedy's condition had been serious enough to require a doctor's care would make it unlikely that he had been drinking as heavily as rumors suggested.

In view of Richard Nixon's vigorous attempts to discredit his leading opponent, if there had been any instances (other than the infamous Alaskan plane ride) of Kennedy having been drunk in public they most certainly would have been exposed. Therefore, it would seem that stories of Kennedy's supposedly heavy drinking have been exaggerated. It is only fair to point out that after Chappaquiddick and in the past decade, Ted Kennedy has drunk less and less, reportedly even giving up alcohol altogether for a full year in an attempt to help his wife solve her problem. Complete abstinence apparently was not difficult for him but unfortunately Joan could not seem to do without.

The coroner's office tested Mary Jo's blood for alcohol and determined that her blood contained 0.09% ethyl alcohol at the time of death. The State Police Chemist, John J. McHugh, testified under oath that, "assuming the party is 110 pounds or thereabouts, it would be consistent with about 3.75 to five ounces, 80 to 90 proof liquor within one hour prior to death. Now, let me put that another way. It could result from that or it could result from higher amounts of liquor over a period of two hours prior to death."

From this testimony one can assume that Mary Jo probably had two or possibly three drinks (one jigger equals one and one-half ounces) within the last hour she was at the party. She was feeling fine but she wouldn't have been drunk. In all likelihood, she appeared happy and relatively sober, as the other party goers testified.

Legally speaking, according to Massachusetts law, a breath, blood, urine or saliva test must read 0.10% or higher before a person is considered legally intoxicated. Mary Jo was still 0.01% under the limit. Legally, her alcohol reading was low enough to allow her to drive a vehicle, provided she appeared otherwise in control. She was still rational and probably capable of using good judgment. Would she have been willing to climb into a car with a person who tended to drive too fast and was roaring drunk? In addition, there were no alcoholic beverages or containers found in the wrecked car, which would seem to indicate that what drinking there was probably did not take place in the vehicle.

If Kennedy wasn't inebriated, it wouldn't have

taken ten hours to sober him up, especially considering the physical exertion he went through, which would have burned off some of the alcohol. At the very least, he had to walk a mile back to the cottage to get his friends.

The court carefully questioned each witness as to Kennedy's state of sobriety. Officer Look said that the driver of the car he observed at the intersection seemed to be in complete control of the vehicle. Every person at the party declared that the Senator acted sober. Russell E. Peachey, the innkeeper with whom Kennedy had a conversation at 2:25 a.m., did not notice anything unusual about him at that time. Kennedy wasn't showing any sign of a hang-over early the following morning when he chatted with Ross Richards, Stanley Moore and Mrs. Steward. Police Chief Arena claims to have consciously observed the Senator for signs of alcohol use and noted that while he seemed depressed, he did not appear to be hung-over.

From these facts, one can conclude that Kennedy was probably relatively sober at the time of the accident. Alcohol might have contributed to the accident, but it certainly does not account for the ten hour delay in reporting it.

CHAPTER VI

WHO DID OFFICER LOOK SEE
AT THE INTERSECTION
AT 12:45 a.m.?

Kennedy claims to have left the party at 11:15 p.m. His testimony is as follows:

Q. Did you at any time drive into Cemetery Road?
A. At no time did I drive into Cemetery Road.
Q. Did you back that car up at any time?
A. At no time did I back that car up.
Q. Did you see anyone on the road between the cottage and the bridge that night?
A. I saw no one on the road between the cottage and the bridge.
THE COURT: Did you stop the car at any time?
THE WITNESS: I did not stop the car at any time.
Q. (By Mr. Dinis) Did you pass any other vehicle at the time?
A. I passed no other vehicle at that time. I passed no other vehicle and I saw no other person and I did not stop at any time between the time I left the cottage and went off the bridge.

Why the questions? Police Officer Christopher Look happened to be going home from work about 12:45 a.m. on the morning of July 19 and had a very interesting encounter with a strangely behaving vehicle at the intersection in question. Officer Look testified:

Q. Would you describe how you were dressed on the 18th when you reported to work at the Edgartown Yacht Club?
A. I had my deputy sheriff's uniform on which is a dark shirt, light tan pants with a darkish-brown stripe, badge on the left and name plate, and silver buttons down the front and on the lapels.
Q. And a patch also?
A. Yes, sir.
Q. Now, would you tell us what time approximately you were at Chappaquiddick Road at this juncture with School-house Road and Dyke Road?
A. Well, I have driven the road many times and I would say it would take me until approximately twenty minutes of 1:00 to reach the point, the corner and Dyke Road.
Q. So you say approximately 12:40 to 12:45 you were on that juncture?
A. Yes, sir, approximately.
Q. Did you see anyone or anything?

Diagram #3 of Police Chief Jim Arena's accident report depicting the intersection in question and the dark car observed by Deputy Sheriff Look.

A. As I approached it I saw a car coming from the right-hand side.

Q. Would that be Schoolhouse Road?

A. Yes, sir.

Q. Did you have occasion to notice anything about it?

A. You mean make?

Q. Make or size?

A. I noticed it was a dark car that passed in front of me.

Q. Where did it go when it passed in front of you?

A. It went onto a little dirt road maybe ten feet off the road that is commonly known, I believe, as Cemetery Road, and it stopped and as it stopped I proceeded around the corner and looked into the mirror of my car and noticed the car start to back up. Usually on Chappaquiddick people get lost quite often and I stopped in case they wanted to ask me which direction is the ferry or this way or that house, and I stopped when they started to back up towards me and got out of my car and walked back towards the car.

Q. How far were you from the intersection when you stopped?

A. Around 25 feet.

Q. All right. You stopped your car when you saw the light back up?

A. Right.

Q. Do you know how far this automobile, which you saw, entered into Cemetery Lane?

A. I would say that the back wheels just got off the macadamized road.

Q. And you saw the lights, you stopped and you got out?

A. Yes, sir.

Q. Tell us exactly what you did. You stopped your car and you got out:

A. I didn't stop at first. I almost came to a stop and I saw the lights coming from my right-hand side which would be in the direction of the fire station, coming towards me, and I practically came to a complete stop because the automobiles when they make that large corner usually cut it very close and I was afraid I might run into him and **the car passed directly in front of me about 35 feet away from my car, my headlights were on this car,** and right across and then stopped.

I continued around the corner and stopped and I noticed the car lights were backing up, and I said to myself, Well, they probably want some information, so I stopped my car and got out and started to walk back to them on Cemetery Road. I got about 25 or 30 feet when the car was backing up and backed towards the ferry landing on the macadamized road, and then it drove down the Dyke Road.

Q. Were there any lights either by your motor vehicle or that motor vehicle at that time. Were they on?

A. Yes.

- Car 1 (position 1a) crossed directly in front of car 2 (position 2a). Headlights of Look's car, 2, lit up interior of other vehicle and Look observed a man driving and a woman on front right side.
- Car 1 pulled onto Cemetery Road and stopped (position 1b).
- Car 1 backed up toward Ferry (position 1c).
- Look stopped station wagon, (position 2b) and got out.
- Look, on foot (position 3) approached car 1 (position 1c). Driver avoided police officer by taking off down Dyke Road. Look got part of the license number of car 1, L7 . . .7.

Q. And with reference to the motor vehicle you observed were its lights on?

A. Yes.

Q. Including its rear lights:

A. Yes, sir.

Q. And what did you observe about the car at that time, if anything?

A. That it was a dark car and that it was a Massachusetts registration.

Q. What did you notice, if anything, about the registration?

A. That **it began with an L and it had a 7 at the beginning and one at the end.**

Q. Did you observe anything about its occupants?

A. When the automobile passed in front of me and also when I was walking towards it **there appeared to be a man driving and a woman in the front right-hand side** and also either another person or an object of clothing, a handbag or something, sitting on the back. **It looked to me like an object of some kind.** I couldn't say what it would be.

Q. Now, as you approached, I asked you about the lighting conditions. Could you describe what they were?

A. Well, it was a moonlit night and my lights were on and the back-up lights of his car and the headlights and tail lights.

Q. With the lights on could you see reflections and shadows?

A. Yes, **on my body and uniform.**

Q. Now, Mr. Look, when you say you were about 25 feet from the car, it moved away from you?

A. Yes, sir.

Q. Would you describe how it moved away from you?

A. It just drove off.

Q. How long did you observe the car?

A. Just a matter of ten seconds.

Q. Well, how far did the car travel in distance during those ten seconds that you observed?

A. I wouldn't venture to say because the roads were dry and there was a lot of dust and all I could see was just the lights going on down the road, but I wouldn't know how many feet.

Q. You saw the lights going on down the road?

A. Yes, the rear of the car going down the road and the headlights and the dust. **I would say hurried moderately.** It didn't spin the wheels when it left.

Q. Was it on the macadam road when it left?

A. Yes, sir.

Q. Did you see the people in the automobile looking at you?

A. I didn't. I couldn't tell.

Q. Did you say anything to them, cry out?

Dukes County Deputy Sheriff Christopher S. Look, Jr., pictured with the station wagon he was driving when he encountered a strangely behaving vehicle closely resembling Kennedy's car over an hour *after* the Senator claimed the accident had happened. (July 1969, Wide World Photo)

A. No, sir.

Q. Nothing was said. What did you do next?

A. I walked back to my car and got in it and proceeded home.

Q. On the way did you encounter anyone or any other people?

A. Yes, sir.

Q. Could you tell us who you saw and when?

A. I met two women and a man. There was one tall girl. They were in a line going down the road . . . They were going the same direction I was.

Q. Which would be toward the Lawrence cottage, as you know it?

A. Yes, sir.

Q. [Please tell us] whether or not you had any conversation with anybody at that time?

A. I stopped my car and asked if they would like a lift.

Q. Was there a response made to you?

A. As I recall and to the best of my recollection, **the girl on the end said, "Shove off, buddy," or "Shove off, mister, we are not pick-ups,"** or something to that effect, and the man in front, I was about ready to get out and ask them if they wanted a lift, and the man in front said, "No, thank you, Sir. We are only going to this place over here," and he pointed in the direction of the cottage.

Q. The Lawrence cottage?

A. Yes.

Q. The next morning were you aware of the fact that there had been an accident on Dyke Road at Dike Bridge?

A. Yes.

Q. And in any capacity that you hold or for curiosity's sake did you go down to the scene?

A. My boy answered the telephone, one of my children, my oldest boy, I believe, I don't know if it was the Communication Center or who called, and they said there had been an accident and I may be needed to give Chief Arena some assistance, so I went down there.

Q. And was the car removed from the water in your presence?

A. Yes, quite a long while later.

Q. And what if anything did you observe at that time or say?

A. Well, **prior to the car coming out of the water, I had spoken to the Chief and also to Patrolman Robert Brougier about seeing people walking on the road and observing the car, and told them I hoped this wasn't the same one;** and about that time Chief Arena came up after they were still trying to get the car out and he asked me if I could give him a ride back to the point and I told him I didn't have my car; that I knew a doctor was there that would give him a ride back that lives on Chappaquiddick and he did; he took him down to the point. About a half hour elapsed and Chief Arena came back and told the patrolman and myself and said, gee, **do you know who was driving that car last night? I said, I hadn't the slightest idea,** only from what I told him it appeared to be a man and a woman and somebody else. He said, it is Senator Kennedy. I said, oh, my God!

Q. Did you look at the car?

A. The car was still in the water.

Q. Did you see the car at all?

A. You could just see the four wheels sticking up.

Q. Were you at the scene when it came out of the water?

A. Yes.

Q. What did you observe about it at that time?

A. As soon as they started to pull it out and it became visible, **I walked over and told Officer Brougier, gee, that is the car I saw last night.**

THE COURT: I want to ask you about the car that came out of the water. You said, I think, that the night before you saw a dark colored car?

THE WITNESS: Yes.

THE COURT: You said, as I understand it, that this car went by you and it was a dark colored car:

THE WITNESS: Yes, sir.

THE COURT: Could you be any more definite about its color other than it was a dark color?

THE WITNESS: No, sir, that it was either black, or deep blue or dark —

THE COURT: Or a dark green, any dark color?

THE WITNESS: Yes, sir.

THE COURT: You couldn't then, identify it as being the same color?

THE WITNESS: No, sir.

THE COURT: Definitely as the car that you saw taken out of the water?

THE WITNESS: No, sir.

THE COURT: And you recognized or you saw a letter, a seven, and then another seven at the end?

THE WITNESS: Yes, sir.

THE COURT: Do you remember how many numbers, letters and numbers there were on the plate ... Whether it was four numbers, five numbers, six numbers?

THE WITNESS: No, sir.

THE COURT: So that when you saw this number on this car that came out of the water, you can't identify that as being the same identical number that you saw the previous night?

THE WITNESS: In my opinion —

THE COURT: No, I'm talking about the positive identification.

THE WITNESS: No, I can't.

THE COURT: You can't identify the exact color?

THE WITNESS: No, sir.

THE COURT: Or the exact number plate?

THE WITNESS: No, sir.

THE COURT: Now, I am speculating a little bit, but it looks as though this car in the rear has, as many cars do, sort of a little shelf?

THE WITNESS: Yes, Sir.

THE COURT: And I take it, it was on that shelf where

you saw what you thought might be a person or a bag or something?

THE WITNESS: Clothing on that side of the car, yes, sir.

THE COURT: A sweater or clothing or a bag upon the seat, you wouldn't be able to see.

THE WITNESS: No, sir.

The court did make an attempt to check the license plate more closely. Judge Boyle wrote:

"During the inquest, a preliminary investigation was initiated through the Registry of Motor Vehicles to determine whether a tracking of the location on July 18 and 19, 1969, of all dark colored cars bearing Massachusetts plates with any and all combinations of numbers beginning with L7 and ending in 7, would be practicable. The attempt disclosed that it would not be feasible to do this since there would be no assurance that the end result would be helpful and, in any event, the elimination of all other cars within that registration group (although it would seriously affect the credibility of some of the witnesses) would not alter the findings in this report".

The license number of Ted Kennedy's car was L78207. Despite the court's ruling it is extremely unlikely that another car matching Officer Look's description and bearing a license number similar to the Kennedy Olds would be on isolated Chappaquiddick Island at that particular intersection on that particular night.

Officer Look still believes that he saw Kennedy's car at the intersection. In February of 1975 he told a *National Enquirer* reporter, "I know what I saw that night. And I know I wasn't wrong. One of us lied — Ted Kennedy or me. I told the truth then, and I'm telling the truth now. There is no way I'll ever change my claim ... It comes down to a matter of credibility. You either believe Kennedy or you believe me."

Like Ted Kennedy, Christopher Look has been continually harrassed by a curious public and a demanding press. He lamented that his life had become "a nightmare for me and worse yet for my whole family. Ever since that car went off the bridge we haven't been left alone. Questions all the time. Phone calls. People stopping us on the street. I want it to end."

51

The unfortunate Officer Look apparently became a pawn in the vicious political infighting that has surrounded the Chappaquiddick accident. He complained, "Investigators were asking about me all over Edgartown. Kennedy said he knew nothing about the questioning. But he had also said his aides may have been responsible. Whether he knew about it or not, they found nothing."

Deputy Sheriff Christopher Look attempting to ignore reporters as he makes his way to testify at the inquest into the death of Mary Jo Kopechne. (January 1970, Dennis Brack, Black Star)

Officer Look was justifiably upset over the efforts to discredit him. There were strangers asking questions all over Edgartown regarding Look's personal life. The investigators apparently even had nerve enough to ask Look's parents if he was an alcoholic and ran around on his wife. Virtually the entire community of Edgartown was furious with Ted Kennedy for the brazen attempts to dig up dirt on their well-liked deputy sheriff. The attitude was that if Kennedy thought he was going to get away with it, just wait until he was brought to trial and the Edgartown people who would make up the jury were able to sit in judgment of him!

In reflection, one has to ask oneself if Ted Kennedy would be so stupid as to try such underhanded tactics. With his political experience, he would certainly know that such a stunt would backfire on him. The Kennedys have had a wealth of experience dealing with that sort of discrediting — it is a common part of the "dirty tricks" aspect of campaigning.

In 1960, when JFK was running against Hubert Humphrey in the Wisconsin Democratic primary, according to Victor Lasky:

"In effect the Kennedys used anti-Catholicism to win votes. In the closing days of the Wisconsin primary, for example, vicious anti-Catholic pamphlets were circulated widely throughout certain areas of the state. They were mailed in the many thousands to Catholic homes and, as Marquis Childs reported at the time, 'often to individuals in care of the local chapter of the Knights of Columbus! While they seem to be originated with the lunatic fringes, the effect is naturally to create sympathy for Kennedy . . . And this may well be true not only among Kennedy's fellow Catholics in Wisconsin but among others who have all along felt the injustice of discriminating against a candidate for the Presidency because of his religion."

In this particular instance Robert Kennedy and Jack Kennedy were frantically trying to discover who sent the material out because they were certain it had come from inside of their own organization. Hubert Humphrey knew it too and was angrily trying to find out who it was in order to expose them. The Kennedys were attempting to stop the distribution before they were caught. Apparently neither side ever found the culprit, but many suspected Paul Corbin. Arthur Schlesinger reported that John Seigenthaler had said of Corbin, "He had a strange way about him. When he made up his mind to do something he'd do it." Schlesinger went on to say, "Robert Kennedy himself was defensive about him and on occasion exasperated by him. In later years, Robert McNamara, hearing of some Corbin mischief, suggested that he be given a lie detector test. 'A lie detector test?' said Robert Kennedy, 'Why, he'd break the machine!' "

Reverse psychology is a popular shenanigan used by rival politicians against each other. There is little doubt who was using it in the Edgartown incident. In the White House tape recording of the March 13, 1973 conversation between John Dean and President Nixon, Dean told the President:

"He [Tony Ulasewicz] was up there [in Edgartown]. He has talked to everybody in that town. He is the one who has caused a lot of embarrassment for Kennedy already ..."

Ted Kennedy had to have had a pretty good idea of what was going on, but there was absolutely nothing he could do about it. At that time, Richard Nixon was highly regarded by virtually everyone, whether or not they agreed with him politically, because this was prior to Watergate. If Kennedy had tried to say it wasn't he, but people out to do him harm, he would have been perceived as trying to shift the blame away from himself in a most underhanded manner. So Kennedy denied that he knew anything about the discrediting attempts, but he told the people what they wanted to hear — that somebody in his office could possibly be responsible and that he would look into it.

At the exhumation hearing, Officer Look testified that the driver of the vehicle appeared to be confused when he crossed in front of him and drove onto Cemetery Road, where the car remained for one minute. From the driver's actions, Look concluded that he was lost, so the officer stopped to offer assistance.

Not mentioned in the testimony was Look's very definite impression, which he related to reporters, that the driver of the vehicle recognized him as a police officer as he walked toward the car and that the driver was deliberately trying to avoid him, which is what prompted the officer to attempt to get the license number. Look reportedly said to himself, "Well, they certainly don't want to talk to me." In order to avoid the policeman, there was only one place for the car to go. The officer was standing in the road blocking the way back to the cottage. The rear of the car was toward the ferry. There was a "Private Drive" sign on the Cemetery Road, hardly the exit to use if one didn't want to arouse a patrolman. There was only one option open — Dyke Road.

Officer Look's impression of the occupants of the other vehicle was that they were lost, however, there is another, very logical explanation for the behavior Officer Look described. It is obvious that the driver of the strange car did not wish to go either to the ferry or to Dike Bridge for he turned neither right nor left. Nor was Cemetery Road his destination for he halted immediately upon entering the private drive and backed up toward the ferry. Perhaps he wished to return the way he had come.

In order to maneuver a U-turn in the cramped intersection one must pull to the far right so that the car's headlights shine up Cemetery Road — just as Officer Look described. However, as he slowed to observe the dark sedan, Look's car was blocking the intersection making it impossible for the other car to make a U-turn. Impatient and perhaps irritated by having to go back the way he had come, the driver decided to turn around by driving onto Cemetery Road and backing toward the ferry. Upon half-completing the maneuver, he discovered a deputy sheriff approaching his car blocking the way he wanted to go. Perhaps, in order to avoid conversation with the officer the driver simply detoured down Dyke Road. It should be noted that Ted Kennedy had a very good reason for wishing to return to the cottage where the party was being held — Mary Jo Kopechne had forgotten her purse and motel key.

People have asked why Kennedy would have wanted to avoid a police officer. After all, they say, he never has been very discreet about chasing women. Why would he care about a small town cop catching him with a girl? From all the stories floating around about him, one can assume that a few might be based on fact. However, the Senator has always been plagued by gossip-hungry reporters looking for any wild tale that will sell their magazines or newspapers.

The latest incident of this nature was reported by *Look* Magazine, April 30, 1979:

"... the recent blast of negative publicity (was) caused by newspaper photos of the senator and an attractive young blonde at the White House dinner celebrating the peace treaty between Israel and Egypt. It turned out the photos were deliberately cropped to show Teddy exiting from the party with the girl, when in reality she was trailing six feet behind. Kennedy was actually accompanied that night by Monsignor Lally, and the girl turned out to have been an uninvited guest."

Nor was the sniping at Kennedy confined to the press. H. R. Haldeman, in his book, *The Ends of Power,* says:

"One of Colson's first successes was very dear to the President's heart. It stuck a knife into Kennedy. One hundred points on the Oval Office chart. Somehow Colson obtained a picture of Teddy Kennedy leaving a night club in Paris with a beautiful woman not his wife in the small hours of the morning. He then arranged for the picture to be published in a gossip-type newspaper. The President loved that picture. From then on, as far as the President was concerned, Colson was Mr. Can-Do."

The list of incidents such as these are endless. How frequently Ted Kennedy actually lives up to the charges is certainly subject to question. He can hardly enjoy the publicity. Since he was having difficulty with such reports at the time, it seems unlikely that he would cheerfully invite a small town cop over to his car at 12:45 in the morning on a lonely road and introduce him to the attractive young blonde who was alone with him in his car. All he had to do to avoid it was to make a slight detour down Dyke Road. Why shouldn't he have done it? To sit there would have been inviting more gossip. Why set yourself up for bad publicity if the situation can be so easily avoided?

Kennedy may have had an even better reason for wishing to avoid a uniformed police officer. As detailed in the last chapter of this book, the Senator had reason to believe that there was a mafia hit contract out on him and this knowledge was weighing heavily on his mind. A technical writer and researcher who was involved in the early private investigation of the Warren Commission strongly believes that Ted Kennedy avoided the police officer because, under the circumstances, he feared the man might be an assasin. The investigator explained to the author, "Knowing what I know, if I was Ted Kennedy and I saw a man getting out of a private car and believed he was carrying a gun, I wouldn't care if he was dressed like a local police officer, J. Edgar Hoover or Santa Claus, I'd get the hell out of there!"

Kennedy contends that he couldn't have been at the intersection at that time because he left at 11:15 p.m. After all, the ferry closes at 12:00 midnight. 12:45 a.m. would have been too late for him to have caught the ferry. Many have pointed out that Kennedy had to have known that the ferry could be summoned at any time for a fee. Not being there at midnight does not mean one cannot cross. His cousin, Joe Gargan, inadevertently finished off Kennedy's argument when he said under oath:

> "We had a conversation about the ferry prior to his (Kennedy's) leaving ... Mr. Crimmins at 11:15 was somewhat agitated by the fact that we were all there, that we weren't moving out, and Mr. Crimmins pointed out that it was 11:15 and we ought to get everybody towards the ferry, we ought to think about leaving because the ferry did leave at 12 o'clock and that was the last ferry.
> "I indicated to Mr. Crimmins that I had a conversation with the ferryman in which I had asked the ferryman whether or not we couldn't possibly have it later. **The ferryman indicated to me that he would possibly keep the ferry going until one o'clock.** However, this would cost,

I forget whether he said 50 cents a person or a dollar a person after 12 o'clock."

According to ferry-owner, Jared Grant, who testified at the inquest, he closed down the ferry at a quarter to one but remained in the area and was readily available until 1:20 a.m. The point is that Kennedy knew the ferry would be available until 1:00 a.m. or so, and his being at the intersection at 12:45 a.m. would have coincided very nicely with catching it.

There is yet another problem with Kennedy's time schedule. It is not consistant with the statement given by the occupants of Dike House, located only 150 yards from the bridge. Miss Sylvia A. Malm, Mrs. Malm's college age daughter, was awake until midnight and gave Jim Arena the following statement, which was read in court.

"On Friday night, July 18, 1969, I read in bed underneath an open window which faces east from 11:00 p.m. to **12:00 midnight, looking at the clock just before I turned my light out.** Between 11:15 and 11:45 I heard a car going fairly fast on the Dyke Road. I didn't look out the window, so

Dike House is located a few hundred feet from Dike Bridge. According to witness depositions the bedroom window was left open all night and a light was shining in it until midnight. (August 1969, John Hubbard, Black Star)

I am uncertain of the direction, but thought at the time
it was heading toward the Dyke. I heard nothing further
that night."

Sylvia Malm did hear a car, but heard no splash
even though her window was open and faced toward
the bridge only 150 yards away — so close she could
hear fish jumping in Poucha Pond at night. From
the condition of Kennedy's vehicle, it had to have
made quite a splash when it hit the water. Neither
did she hear Kennedy loudly calling for Mary Jo in
hopes that she had escaped, nor did she hear Kennedy, Markham or Gargan calling back and forth
later as they attempted to rescue the girl. Surely she
would have heard something if she hadn't been sound
asleep when the accident occurred, but not even their
dogs were disturbed. It was regatta time, and the island traffic was greatly increased. The car she heard
probably was not the Kennedy car. Mrs. Malm supported her daughter's statement The following is Jim
Arena's testimony of what Mrs. Malm told him.

Q. And did you ask her whether or not she had seen or
heard an automobile?
A. Yes, she said she had heard a sound of an auto engine
close to around midnight. That is what her best recollection
was. That is the only thing she said. She never — **I asked
her if she had heard any sound of anything hitting
the water or anything like that. She said No.**

Assuming Mrs. Malm and her daughter are being
truthful, there seems to be little doubt that the accident must have occurred after they were asleep,
which would have been well after midnight.

Kennedy made a feeble attempt to verify the time.
When asked what time it was when they were all
at the bridge attempting to save Mary Jo, Kennedy
said, "I think it was 12:20, Mr. Dinis, I believe that
I looked at the Valiant's clock and believe that it
was 12:20."

The problem here is that the rented Valiant does
not have a clock and there are no bored holes on
the dashboard indicating that it ever did. When the
discrepancy was pointed out to the Senator on November 4, 1979 in an interview by Roger Mudd, Kennedy rapidly conceded, "If there wasn't a clock in

the car, there wasn't a clock in the car." However, he maintains that he definitely saw the time somewhere and says he must have looked at Mr. Markham's watch.

Kennedy said that they spent about forty five minutes trying to rescue Mary Jo. They never saw another soul. One has to ask what happened to the car Officer Look saw heading toward the bridge at 12:45? There was no place for the vehicle to go except to the two houses next to the bridge or the beach, yet Kennedy never saw it. None of the people who live near the bridge have a vehicle which matches the description of the one Look described. Did it just disappear?

Kennedy has still another problem verifying his time table. He stated that,

> **"I was swept along by the tide that was flowing at an extraordinary rate** through that narrow cut there and was swept along by the tide and called Mary Jo's name until I was able to make my way to what would be the east side of that cut, waded up to about my waist and started back to the car."

> Q. How far were you swept along by the current?
> A. Approximately 30-40 feet.
> Q. Now, in order to get back to the car was it necessary for you to swim?
> A. I couldn't swim at that time because of the current.

The Senator inadvertently proved that the accident did not happen when he said it did, for the fact of the matter was that there was very little if any current flowing under Dike Bridge at 11:20 p.m.

John Farrar, the scuba diver who removed Mary Jo's body from the vehicle, testified:

> A. ... the tide at that time was approximately four knots at the time of recovery; 8:55 a.m., was approximately four knots. It later slacked up and, of course, went completely slack with the change of tide which was approximately 11:30 a.m.
> Q. And if you know, how often does the tide change in that area?
> A. Well, of course, every six hours is the oscillation of the tide.

From this testimony one can easily deduce that exactly twelve hours earlier, at 11:30 p.m. when Kennedy claims to have been fighting a swift current, the tide was completely slack, and there was no current. One can arrive at the same conclusion by studying the tide tables and characteristics of the area. Low tide at Edgartown on July 18, 1969 was at 9:45 p.m. If one reads the official tide publication one would assume that the tide would be running fast under the bridge at 11:20 p.m., but such was not the case. The tide in Poucha Pond runs 45 minutes to two hours behind those at Edgartown, due to the geography of the island. The sea water must take a roundabout path before it enters Poucha Pond. The tide rises at Edgartown, forcing water through the narrow opening called Cape Poge Cut, which then fills Cape Poge Bay, eventually pushing the water up the narrow inlet to Poucha Pond, hence the long delay. The amount of time the process takes varies with the phase of the moon, the ocean currents and the winds. Low tide in Poucha Pond had to have occurred between 10:30 p.m. and 11:45 p.m. Experienced island dwellers familiar with the tides checked the level of the tide at Dike Bridge the morning after the accident, then calculated backward and pinpointed dead low tide as having occurred between 11:00 and 11:30 the night before. In other words, there was no current at the time Kennedy claims to have been swimming. However, by 12:45 a.m. the tide was well up and coming in fast, creating a very strong current under the bridge which would have pushed the car around and would have given Kennedy the trouble he has described.

From the combination of known facts, it is difficult to accept Kennedy's estimate of the time, even though virtually every party member swore he left the cottage sometime between 11:15 and 11:30 p.m. The curious thing here, besides the fact that everyone was so sure of the time even though there was no reason for them to be paying close attention, is that their estimates became more certain as the days passed.

A few days after the accident Esther Newberg was

interviewed by several reporters who wrote the following accounts.

The *New York Times:* "Miss Newberg described it as an informal group, with no one keeping particular track of who was there or who wasn't there at any given time. Thus, she said, no one specifically missed either the Senator or Miss Kopechne or noticed what time they had left."

The *Chicago Tribune:* "Miss Newberg said she was very vague about time during the evening, partly because her watch was a psychedelic one and 'you couldn't read it' and because no one was sitting around watching the clock ... 'At no time were we aware of time,' she explained."

The *Worchester Evening Gazette:* "Miss Newberg said she did not notice when Senator Kennedy and Miss Kopechne left the party ... She said she did not know the time accurately because her Mickey Mouse watch — which had been a topic of joking conversation — was not working properly."

However, under oath, six months later she testified:

> Q. ... did you become aware that Mr. Kennedy left at a certain time?
> A. Yes.
> Q. Can you tell us when?
> A. 11:30.
> Q. What makes you say 11:30?
> A. I have a rather large watch that I wear all the time and I looked at it.
> Q. Now, your watch said 11:30?
> A. That is correct.

Despite the backing of his friends, it does appear that Kennedy left the party later than he has indicated and that it was he who Officer Look encountered at the intersection.

CHAPTER VII
HOW DID THE CAR
GO OFF THE BRIDGE?

Since publication of the controversial *Reader's Digest* study of the Chappaquiddick accident in their February, 1980 issue, the question of exactly how the accident occurred and specifically how fast the Senator's car was traveling as it approached the bridge, has become a serious matter of contention.

The following is Judge Boyle's summation of the accident:

"Kennedy stated he drove down Chappaquiddick Road toward the ferry, that when he reached the junction of Dyke Road, he mistakenly turned right onto Dyke Road, realizing at some point he was on a dirt road, but thought nothing of it, was proceeding at about twenty miles per hour when suddenly Dike Bridge was upon him. He braked but the car went off the bridge into Poucha Pond and landed on its roof. The driver's window was open and he managed to reach the surface and swim to shore."

The approah to Dike Bridge. (July 1969, John Hubbard, Black Star)

The conditions at the scene were also summed up as follows:

"Dike Bridge is a wooden structure ten feet, six inches wide, has timber curbs on each side four inches high by ten inches wide, no other guard rails, and runs at an angle of twenty-seven degrees to the left of the road. There are no signs or artificial lights on the bridge or its approach. It spans Poucha Pond.

"The Kennedy Oldsmobile is eighteen feet long and eighty inches wide. Poucha Pond is a salt water tidal pond, and has a strong current where it narrows at Dike Bridge."

The following is the exchange between Kennedy and Judge Boyle concerning how the Senator drove off of the structure.

THE COURT: You are driving along the dike sandy road and you are approaching the Dike Bridge. Now, can you describe to me what you saw, what you did, what happened from the point when first you saw the bridge?

THE WITNESS: I would estimate that time to be fractions of a second from the time that I first saw the bridge and was on the bridge.

THE COURT: Did you have on your high beams, do you remember?

THE WITNESS: I can't remember.

THE COURT: Is it your custom to use high beams when you are driving?

THE WITNESS: I rarely drive. I really couldn't tell you. I may have.

THE COURT: It is recommended.

THE WITNESS: It is recommended, but sometimes if there is a mist, you see better with low beams.

THE COURT: Did you see the bridge before you actually reached it?

THE WITNESS: The split second before I was on it.

THE COURT: Did you see that it was at an angle to the road?

THE WITNESS: The bridge was at an angle to the road?

THE COURT: Yes.

THE WITNESS: Just before going on it I saw that.

THE COURT: Did you make any attempt to turn your wheels to follow that angle?

THE WITNESS: I believe I did, your Honor. I would assume that I did try to go on the bridge. It appeared to me at that time that the road went straight.

THE COURT: Were you looking ahead at the time you were driving the car, at that time?

THE : WITNESS: Yes, I was.

THE COURT: Your attention was not diverted by anything else?

THE WITNESS: No, it wasn't.

At the exhumation hearing held October 20, 1969 at the Luzerne County Court House in Wilkes-Barre, Pennsylvania, Police Chief Arena described what he saw at the scene of the accident.

"The motor vehicle was overturned in the water . . . the nose of the car pointing towards the bridge, it was a very slight angle . . . the car was completely covered except for a minute portion of the . . . left rear tire of the car . . . the windshield was smashed, but not out, the **car window on the driver's side had been rolled down,** however the **two windows on the right side had been shattered out** . . . there was a dent on the roof and there were some dents on the right side also . . . the front end of the car was no more than six or seven feet away from the actual closest point of the bridge . . . I have taken measurements and I believe . . . it was about 23 feet seven inches . . . from the gouge on the wood of the bridge . . . **it landed in the water about 23 feet up and about 5 feet out from the exit point on that bridge,** that gouge in the wood . . . there were scuff marks . . . they weren't really what you would call skid marks, they were marks that would probably . . . be brought about by **a tire going sideways,** sliding a bit, more than skidding into something."

Police Chief Arena presented to the Court a diagram of the accident scene which is a permanent part of the exhumation hearing record, and may be obtained (along with the complete accident report) with the transcripts of the hearing. Included on "Kennedy Accident Diagram #2" are all of the important measurements necessary to analyze the accident. Arena testified:

"I made the measurements after the car had been removed from the water, but I was given measurements from the Registry Inspectors who were at the scene conducting a simultaneous investigation and **their measurements were approximately the same as mine.**"

John Farrar, the scuba diver who removed the body from the submerged vehicle, supported Police Chief Arena's representation of the accident scene. John Farrar's testimony regarding Arena's measurements is as follows:

Q. Will you describe to the Court as well as you can the position of the automobile with reference to Dike Bridge?

A. Well, **Chief Arena gave that very clearly,** I would, although I don't have the footages, it was perpendicular —

* * *

Q. Now, did you make any measurements?

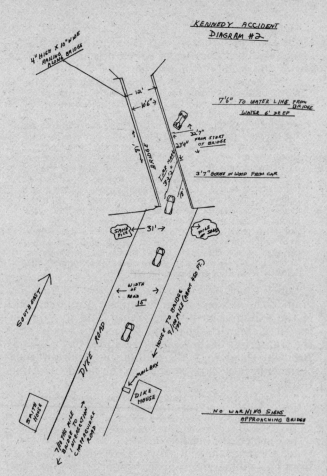

KENNEDY ACCIDENT
DIAGRAM #2

4" HIGH X 10" WIDE RAILING ALONG BRIDGE

12'

10'6"

7'6" TO WATER LINE FROM BRIDGE

WATER 6' DEEP

BRIDGE

2'7" FROM START OF BRIDGE

23'4"

8'

TIRE MARKS 31'/2"

3'7" GOUGE IN WOOD FROM CAR

15'

SAND PILE

31'

PILE SAND

SOUTHEAST

WIDTH OF ROAD 15'

DYKE ROAD

HOUSE TO BRIDGE 9/100 MILE (ABOUT 450 FT.)

MAILBOX

DIKE HOUSE

SMITH HOUSE

7/10 THE MILE BRIDGE TO INTERSECTION CAMPGROUND ROAD

NO WARNING SIGNS APPROACHING BRIDGE

Diagram #2 of Police Chief Jim Arena's accident report.

A. **I did not make any measurements at that time.**
Q. Did you make any later?
A. Yes, sir, I did.
Q. When did you make them?
A. Approximately **a week after.**
Q. The car was not there?
A. The **car was not there,** no.

66

John Farrar went on to say:

"... the automobile would be perpendicular to your passage over the bridge ... upside-down ... resting on the hood ornament and what I would call the brow of the windshield ... the front bumper of the car was approximately five, six feet from the bridge ... the windshield had been shattered, the glass had been shattered, however, the windshield was in place, by that I mean the safety film was holding the windshield in place, **the two right windows** were knocked out, completely ... they **were entirely shattered**, obliterated, there was just tiny pieces of glass left around the edge of the windows. This I take it would have been on impact. The top was crushed in a rather broad area and **the right side was crushed** ... I observed the ignition to be on, the car was in drive and the brake was off, and the lights were on. Now, let me qualify that the light switch was in the on position. **The car was as well, I might add, full of glass ... The driver's door ... was locked."**

Two and a half months later, at the inquest into the death of Mary Jo Kopechne held January 7, 1970 before the Honorable James A. Boyle in Edgartown, Police Chief Arena presented the same information regarding the accident as he had at the exhumation hearing, although not in as much detail. His inquest and exhumation hearing testimonies were reinforced by that of George Kennedy, Inspector for the Registry of Motor Vehicles, who had investigated the accident for the Motor Vehicle Department and who had also taken photographs and made diagrams of the accident scene. Inspector Kennedy testified that he and his assistant, Inspector Molla, carefully measured the skid marks on the bridge and found the right one to be eighteen feet long and the left one to be thirty-three feet, two inches long. Inspector Kennedy testified under oath that there were *no* skid marks visible in the dirt and gravel of the road approaching the bridge. Assistant District Attorney Armand Fernandes, who was conducting the questioning, pursued the matter vigorously as is evident in this exchange between Armand Fernandes, Inspector Kennedy and Judge Boyle:

Q. (Fernandes) Are you able to measure your skid marks on gravel?

A. (G. Kennedy) Not very well.

Q. A lot of traffic in the area of the bridge when you arrived?

A. That is correct.

Q. In any event, what you could measure was on the wooden structure?

A. Right.

* * *

Q. Could you tell us what your opinion was as to the speed of the car?

A. Approximately around **20 to 22 miles per hour —**

* * *

Q. Mr. Kennedy, your opinion is based on the skid marks that you observed at the scene, isn't that so?

A. To a certain degree, yes, and conditions.

Q. And what else you saw, but with reference to these skid marks, did you not also say earlier to the Court, and correct me if I am wrong, that you couldn't measure if there were any skid marks on the dirt road that preceded the bridge.

A. That is correct.

Q. And that would affect any opinion you have?

THE COURT: (Judge Boyle) Now, look. Now you are going into something that may not exist.

MR. FERNANDES: He doesn't know, your Honor.

THE COURT: He said **he didn't see any evidence of skid marks on the gravel, am I correct?**

THE WITNESS: (G. Kennedy) **That is correct,** your Honor.

THE COURT: Let's not go into conjecture now.

MR. FERNANDES: I think he said because he couldn't measure any he didn't know if there were any .

THE COURT: He said he didn't see any, is that correct?

THE WITNESS: (G. Kennedy) That is correct, your Honor.

According to Police Chief Arena's exhumation hearing testimony, corroborated by John Farrar, Arena's inquest testimony, and Inspector George Kennedy's inquest testimony, the following description of the accident can be drawn.

1. The bridge sits at a 27° angle to the road.

2. The left skid mark on the bridge was thirty-three feet, two inches long.

3. The right skid mark on the bridge was eighteen feet long.

4. There was a three-foot, seven inch gouge in the rub rail, left by the drive line of the vehicle as it went over the side.

Gouge marks left on Dike Bridge when Kennedy's Olds plunged into Poucha Pond. (July 1969, Dennis Brach, Black Star)

    5. The car left the structure approximately twenty-four feet, three inches from the start of the right side of the bridge.

    6. The front of the car came to rest twenty-three

feet, four inches away from where the vehicle departed the structure. (In his exhumation hearing testimony, Arena refers to this distance as twenty-three feet, seven inches, however, he made it clear that he did not have his notes and the distance was written on the diagram. On the diagram the distance is recorded as twenty-three feet, four inches)

7. The car was on the right side of the bridge, upside down with the front right corner being closest to the bridge — approximately six feet out from the bridge pilings.

8. The rear of the car was toward the beach. The car was resting where the bottom begins to slope. The rear was slightly elevated. It was between fifteen and twenty-five feet from the beachside (east) shore. (No. exact measurement was taken)

9. The depth of the pond at 8:55 a.m. July 19, 1969 varied from six to seven feet around the vehicle.

10. The distance from the bridge to the surface of the pond was between six to seven feet.

11. Dike Bridge is eighty-one feet long, ten feet, six inches wide plus parallel rub rails four inches high and ten inches wide, for a total width of twelve feet. (The rub rails were described as being two 2 x 10's nailed on top of each other. The *Reader's Digest* article claims that the rub rail was five and one-half inches high. Due to the fact that the 2 x 10's were rough cut and the surface of the bridge is uneven, the four-inch height measurement is not exact. However, the five and one-half inches claimed in the article is probably in greater error.)

12. The front bumper of Kennedy's car was fifty-two feet, seven inches from the beginning of the Edgartown (west) end of the bridge. (Kennedy Accident Diagram #2 shows this distance to be thirty-two feet, seven inches. This was apparently a copying error for that distance is not consistent with other available information. The distance of fifty-two feet, seven inches is consistent. In view of the fact that handwritten 5's often look like 3's, the error was most likely made by misinterpretation of handwriting.)

13. Dyke Road's average width is fifteen feet, but it was widened to thirty-one feet just prior to the bridge to allow for ease of passing and parking.

14. Dike House was located 450 feet from the start of the Dike Bridge.

Unfortunately, the facts have been muddled by the January 7, 1970 testimony of John Farrar. As noted elsewhere in this book, John Farrar has been inconsistent with his testimonies and interviews. His observations as recorded by various newspaper and magazine reporters have changed repeatedly, especially in regard to the time in which he says he could have rescued the girl. It was pointed out by Farrar's lawyer at the exhumation hearing that the press had "referred to him as being prejudiced, biased and anti-Kennedy, which he emphatically and unequivocally denies ..." Farrar might deny these assertions but from his various statements concerning Senator Kennedy and the accident, it is obvious that John Farrar does not like Ted Kennedy. This fact has been noted by most who have investigated the case, including Robert Sherrill, whose book *The Last Kennedy* is very unfavorable toward Kennedy. Whether or not personal considerations had anything to do with the difference between the sworn testimonies John Farrar gave at the exhumation hearing on October 20,

1969 and the inquest on January 7, 1970, only he can tell. However, the variation is serious. The portion of Mr. Farrar's inquest testimony in question is as follows:

Q. (Mr. Fernandes) Now, with reference to measurements at the water, did you make any measurements on your own or at the request of anyone?

A. (Farrar) I made some measurements on my own as to the position of the car from the point of impact, the height of fall and the height of the water.

Q. Could you give us those measurements?

A. My measurements were the fact—

THE COURT: (Judge Boyle) These were measurements taken at what time?

THE WITNESS: The measurement of the water was at the time of the accident when I was in the water. **The measurement as to the footages on the bridge were within two hours after the accident.**

* * *

THE COURT: I see. Well you had better give us the times when you give us those measurements. All right.

Q. (Mr. Fernandes) What time did you make the measurements of the depth of the water?

A. My time observation of the water depth was at the time of recovery of the body.

THE COURT: Which was?

THE WITNESS: Which was, I believe as I previously stated, at 8:55. I found the water at that time between six and seven feet, depending on where you were. In other words, around the car there was a variance within briefly a foot. The measurements of the position of the car with relationship to the bridge and the marks **I found to be a projectory or a distance from the point of impact to the car of approximately 36 feet** and a drop of approximately eight feet.

* * *

Q. (Mr. Fernandes) The 36 feet, would you tell me where that is from, for my own purposes?

A. That would be the point measured from approximately the two marks on the bridge to the perpendiculary in front of the car.

Q. All right. Now, did you make any other measurements at that time?

A. No, I did not, sir.

The court records prove that on October 20, 1969, John Farrar testified that he made measurements one week after the accident and he did not disagree with Police Chief Arena's twenty-three foot, four inches measurement. On January 7, 1970, John Farrar testified that he took measurements within two hours after the accident and said the projectory that he measured was thirty-six feet, as opposed to the twenty-three feet, four inches measured by Police Chief Arena. The question is, whose measurement is the accurate one? It is difficult to give credence to a man who changes his sworn testimony so drastically. In addition, Mr. Farrar's estimate of the distance does poorly under scrutiny. If we assume that Mr. Farrar meant he was measuring to the front bumper when he said "the perpendiculary in front of the car", the mathematics are as follows:

24 feet, 3 inches. . . .where right tire left structure.

2 feet, 6 inches. . . .from right tire mark to end of gouge.

36 feet. . . . . .Farrar's measurements of projectory.

12 feet. . . . . .Estimate of distance taken up by the 18-foot vehicle as it lay at an angle to the bridge.

74 feet, 9 inches . . .Total distance from beginning of bridge to rear bumper of vehicle.

81 feet. . . . . .length of bridge.
-74 feet, 9 inches

6 feet, 3 inches . . . .Approximate distance from beachside shore of Poucha Pond to rear bumper of Kennedy car.

According to Farrar's own testimony, Kennedy's car, while fairly close to the beachside shore, was resting where the bottom of the pond begins to slope upward. While no exact measurement was taken of the car's proximity to the beachside shore, estimates based on witness observations and photographs place it between fifteen and twenty-five feet out. All agree

Ted Kennedy's car resting in Poucha Pond at low tide, July 19, 1969. (John Hubbard, Black Star)

February 1980 photo of Dike Bridge illustrating where John Farrar's measurements would have placed the car in relation to the bridge. (Willis Photo)

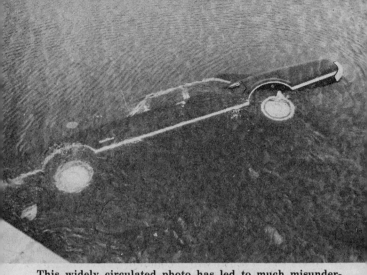

This widely circulated photo has led to much misunder-standing. It was taken at low tide after the car had been hoisted on its side by a tow truck prior to removing it from the pond. (July 19, 1969 John Hubbard, Black Star)

February 1980 photo of Dike Bridge illustrating where Po-lice Chief Jim Arena's measurements would have placed the car in relation to the bridge. (Willis Photo)

that it was in the channel and not on the sloping bank as Farrar's thirty-six foot estimate would place it. On the other hand, Police Chief Arena's measurement of twenty-three feet, four inches places the rear bumper about sixteen feet, five inches from shore, which agrees with the estimated location of the car.

Due to the fact that none of the exhibits and diagrams presented at the inquest are part of the transcript, the only estimate of the distance traveled by the car after leaving the bridge found in the inquest transcript is the thirty-six feet to which Farrar testified. To obtain Police Chief Arena's estimate one must read the Exhumation Hearing Transcript. This problem undoubtedly led to Tedrows' assertion that Senator Kennedy's car had been traveling between forty and fifty miles per hour, and the inaccurate *Reader's Digest* study which concluded the Senator's car approached the bridge at a speed of thirty-four miles per hour (give or take four mph).

The Tedrows conclude in their book *Death at Chappaquiddick* "[T]he Kennedy car had to be going at least forty to fifty miles per hour when it went off the bridge. It had to be going that fast for that heavy car to turn a rolling flip, hit the water on its top and right side, smashing in the passenger windows and coming to rest upside down on the bottom of the pond [34 feet from where it left the bridge]. If the car had been going twenty miles per hour it would have nosed off the bridge landing in an upright position on its right side on the bottom."

The Tedrows are in error when they say it is more likely for a car traveling fast to flip than one going slowly. Anyone who has watched movies realizes that it takes a high rate of speed to launch a stuntman off a ramp so that the car lands upright on target. Dike Bridge is built like a ramp. If Kennedy's vehicle had been traveling between forty and fifty miles per hour when it jumped the four-inch rub rail it would have sailed neatly off, landing upright on its undercarriage and traveling through the water as it sank. Its driveline would never have gouged the rubrail because at that speed the auto would have been over the water before it dropped that low. It would have continued forward under its own momentum and, with the help of a four knot current, it would have come to rest much farther out, with the rear of the vehicle toward the bridge. Since the car probably would not have turned over, Mary Jo, in all likelihood, would have survived because the landing would have been easier, her disorientation less severe, water would not have been pouring in through the windows immediately, and the car would not have sunk as rapidly as it did.

The *Reader's Digest* article by John Barron (senior editor), published in February of 1980 is also in serious error. Not only did the author use Farrar's faulty estimate of the distance traveled after the vehicle left the structure, he also had the car landing facing the **wrong direction.** The diagram printed in the *Reader's Digest* shows the vehicle upside down but with the front bumper pointing toward the beach when in fact the front bumper was toward the bridge because the car had somersaulted into the water.

In order to receive an accurate answer from a computer one must insert accurate figures into it. Since the *Reader's Digest's* figures on which their answer was based are faulty the answer is, of course, wrong. However, with a bit of rough adjusting one can see that the *Digest's* findings actually support Senator Kennedy's claim that the Olds had been traveling about twenty miles per hour as it approached the bridge. Using Farrar's faulty estimate, modified to thirty-five feet, the *Digest's* expert, Raymond R. McHenry, "one of the nation's foremost experts in automobile-accident analysis", concluded that Kennedy's vehicle was traveling between twenty-two miles per hour and twenty-eight miles per hour when it left the bridge. Because the distance traveled was actually 23.33 feet instead of thirty-five feet, one can multiply 23.33/35 times their estimated speed and roughly figure the answer they would have gotten if they used the proper figures. The results show a speed between 14.7 miles per hour and 18.7 miles per hour, which indicates that Kennedy's estimate of twenty miles per hour and the Motor Vehicle Inspector's estimate of between twenty and twenty-two miles per hour are fairly close.

The *Reader's Digest* was not content with the finding that the car left the structure at between twenty-two and twenty-eight mph — and added speed. Referring to McHenry's study, the article states, "driving on the wrong (left) side of the road, Kennedy approached the bridge at approximately 34 m.p.h. ...." There is no "wrong" side of Dyke Road; the average width of the poorly maintained dirt road is only fifteen feet, although it does widen to thirty-one feet just prior to the bridge to allow cars to pass easily and to provide parking. When traveling down such a rough country road, as long as visibility is good and there are no oncoming cars, any prudent driver will drive in the center, steering from side to side to avoid chuckholes. In addition, Dike Bridge is a single lane bridge ten feet, six inches wide between rub rails, which leaves only twenty-three inches on either side of Kennedy's car once it was on the structure. To say that the car started onto a one lane bridge from the "wrong" side of a narrow dirt road is ridiculous.

The article further states, "At least 17 feet from the bridge, he slammed the brakes down hard — 'panic braking', which locked the front wheels. Propelled by the high speed, the car skidded 17 feet along the road, about another 25 feet up the bridge, jumped a 5½ inch rub rail and hurtled approximately 35 more feet into the water."

The 35 foot measurement is inaccurate, and the 5½ inch rub rail measurement is in disagreement with expert testimony. A Department of Motor Vehicles Inspector testified that he looked for and found *no* visible skid marks on the road leading up to the bridge. A heavy vehicle going 34 miles per hour with the wheels locked would surely leave deep skid marks on a sandy dirt road. Although there had been some traffic on the road before the inspector arrived, signs of such a skid would not have been completely obli-

Dike Road is a mixture of sand and pea gravel. This vehicle
was skidded to a halt from a speed of 17 mph (half the speed
Reader's Digest charges Kennedy was traveling). It left deep
skid marks which would be visible even after being passed
over by other traffic.

terated. The claim made ten years later that such
a skid existed, is clearly in error, and suggests deliberate misrepresentation. (It is a disturbing coincidence
that Melvin R. Laird, President Nixon's Secretary
of Defense and Counsellor to the President while the
Nixon Administration was making maximum use of
Chappaquiddick in an effort to eliminate Ted Kennedy as a presidential contender, was the Senior
Counsellor for the *Reader's Digest* at the time the
very damaging article was published.)

A careful examination of the measurements accepted by the court and facts surrounding the accident
clearly shows that the car approached the bridge
going about 20 mph. The driver apparently did not
notice that the bridge was at an angle to the road
and continued in a straight line, not turning onto
the bridge. As a result, the front right wheel dropped
off of the structure approximately 24 feet, 3 inches
from the start of the bridge, thus lowering the undercarriage which came in contact with the bridge —

gouging out a deep three foot, seven inch cut in the rub rail as the vehicle continued forward. The driver braked and turned the wheels to the left in an attempt to regain the bridge but by that time it was too late, for the momentum of the car continued to carry it off the bridge and the weight of the engine and the rest of the car caused it to slide sideways leaving scuff marks of wheels skidding sideways on the bridge as it toppled off. Because of the slow rate of speed and the weight of the vehicle, the car turned on its right side as the heavy engine pulled it, front-end-first, seven feet to the pond below. Contact with the water slowed the forward momentum of the front-end but the rear-end continued forward causing the car to somersault and land on the right corner of its roof, buckling the doors, blowing in the right-hand windows and crushing the roof and windshield. The car still had a little momentum and continued in the direction it had been traveling a few feet more as the weight of the engine sent the hood to the bottom of the channel while the air trapped in the trunk of the car held the rear up temporarily as it filled with water. The combination of the somersault, the forward momentum and the four-knot tide hitting the side of the vehicle as it submerged caused the back end of the car to end up away from the bridge (more or less in line with the current) at an eastward angle to the structure.

The bridge is obviously dangerous. The width of the bridge and the width of Kennedy's car would leave twenty-three inches on either side of the vehicle before it would go off the edge. There were no guard rails. The bridge is low and if one is casually traveling down the road in the dark, conversing with a passenger and not paying close attention, one might be upon it before realizing it was there. Furthermore, it sits at an angle to the road. The vehicle must be deliberately turned onto it. If one continues to travel in a straight line the vehicle will travel off the bridge at the exact place Kennedy's car left the structure. The surprising thing about the accident was that it was the first time such a thing had happened at Dike

Bridge.

On the other hand, the reason there had never been an accident at Dike Bridge is that the road is poorly maintained and full of chuckholes, which effectively slows down would-be speeders. In addition, there are ruts leading up to the bridge, worn by use from other vehicles. The approach to the bridge is flat and the structure is clearly discernable in the car's headlights at distances estimated from 150 to 300 feet, depending on the headlights themselves and weather conditions.

That the Kennedy car missed the bridge cannot be entirely explained away by the fact that the bridge is hazardous. From the evidence at the scene and the condition of the road, high speed was not the cause. Other evidence would lead one to believe that Kennedy should have been sober enough to have maneuvered the bridge. Examination of the vehicle showed that the car itself was in good working order. However, something had to have been amiss within the vehicle, because the driver was obviously not in complete control or the accident would not have occurred.

Judge Boyle recognized that there had to be some explanation and concluded:

> "From two personal views, which corroborate the Engineer's statement (Exhibit 20) and other evidence, I am fully convinced that **Dike Bridge constitutes a traffic hazard,** particularly so at night, and must be approached with extreme caution. A speed of even twenty miles per hour, as Kennedy testified to, operating a car as large as this Oldsmobile, would at least be negligent and, possibly, reckless. If Kennedy knew of this hazard, his operation of the vehicle constituted criminal conduct.
>
> "Earlier on July 18, he had been driven over Chappaquiddick Road three times and **over Dike Bridge twice.** Kopechne had been driven over Chappaquiddick Road five times and over Dyke Road and Dike Bridge twice.
>
> "I believe it probable that Kennedy knew of the hazard that lay ahead of him on Dyke Road but that, for some reason not apparent from the testimony, he failed to exercise due care as he approached the bridge. I therefore, find there is probable cause to believe that Edward M. Kennedy operated his motor vehicle negligently on a way or in a place to which the public have a right of access and that such operation appears to have contributed to the death of Mary Jo Kopechne."

It is interesting to note that no formal accusation

or indictment based on that finding was brought against Kennedy. His lawyers protested the damaging finding but Kennedy was never given the opportunity to challenge it in court. Judge Boyle was obviously not convinced that his finding contained the sole cause of the tragedy, for in his statement he referred to the bridge as a traffic hazard, particularly at night. A finding could have been made that the County maintained the bridge in a hazardous condition, without protective guardrails, approach warnings or reflectors — which would have made the county liable for damages had either Kennedy or the Kopechnes sued. Had Kennedy been tried on negligence, his inexperience with regard to driving over the hazardous bridge and his speed of 20 mph would have exonerated him from criminal blame.

There is yet another curious thing about Kennedy's tale of how he went off the bridge. In the first statement he gave to Police Chief Arena he said, "After proceeding for approximately one-half mile on Dyke Road, I descended a hill and came upon a narrow bridge." Descended a hill? What hill? The only incline in the area ends 600 feet short of the bridge.

Photo taken at spot where Kennedy claims to have descended a hill. (February 1980, Willis Photo)

The slope there is 1%. Traveling 100 feet to drop one foot in elevation is hardly a hill. The final 400 feet to the bridge itself is perfectly flat.

It would be absurd to assume that Kennedy purposely lied about the topography. After all, Police Chief Arena was familiar with the road and he would have noticed the error immediately. It is much more likely that Kennedy and Markham were trying as best they could to remember the approach to the bridge. They didn't do a very good job for two men who claim to have been back and forth so many times. Perhaps a passenger in a vehicle breaking out of the brush into the open would have the sensation of going down a hill, but the person driving would certainly realize that there was no hill — and Kennedy claims to have driven to the bridge.

Dike Bridge took its spelling from the way Dike House is spelled on Mrs. Malm's mail box. (Willis, 1980)

Police Chief Jim Arena who was in charge of the original investigation of the accident and whose accident report shows the car traveled 23 feet 4 inches after leaving the bridge. (UPI, July 24, 1969)

John Farrar, shopkeeper and scuba diver, who claims his measurements show the car traveled 36 feet after leaving the bridge. Farrar points from the place Kennedy's car left Dike Bridge. This photo was taken in July, 1973 after the railing had been raised in hopes of preventing future accidents. (UPI)

84

CHAPTER VIII
HOW DID KENNEDY GET OUT OF THE CAR?

How Kennedy got out of the car is a mystery not only to the public but to the Senator as well. When questioned, the following exchange occurred:

A. Well, I remember the vehicle itself just beginning to go off the Dike Bridge and the next thing I recall is the movement of Mary Jo next to me, the struggling, perhaps hitting or kicking me and I, at this time opened my eyes and realized I was upside-down, that water was crashing in on me, that it was pitch black. I knew that I was able to get a half a gulp, I would say, of air before I became completely immersed in the water. I realized that Mary Jo and I had to get out of the car.

I can remember reaching down to try and get the door-knob of the car and lifting the door handle and pressing against the door and it not moving. I can remember reaching what I thought was down, which was really up, to where I thought the window was and feeling along the side to see if the window was open and the window was closed, and I can remember the last sensation of being completely out of air and inhaling what must have been a half a lung full of water and assuming that I was going to drown and the full realization that no one was going to be looking for us that night until the next morning and that I wasn't going to get out of that car alive and then somehow I can remember coming up to the last energy of just pushing, pressing, and coming up to the surface.

Q. And did you go through the window to get out of the car?

A. **I have no idea in the world how I got out of that car.**

Q. Do you have any recollection as to how the automobile left the bridge and went over into the water?

A. How it left the bridge?

Q. Yes. What particular path did it take?

A. No.

Q. **Did it turn over?**

A. **I have no idea.**

Many people have seriously questioned whether or not it was possible for Kennedy to have gotten out of the car at all. He had to have escaped out of the window next to the driver's seat, which was rolled down to within ¾ of an inch of the bottom. The opening was not very large to accommodate a 220 pound man wearing a back brace. Not only that, but he evidently had his seat belt on and would have been hanging upside down with water churning into his face. It would have been nearly impossible to have forced himself out of the window while the water was pouring in. If either person was to get out of the car, it should have been Mary Jo. Both windows were blown out on her side. She was very slight and would have fit out easily once the water equalized. In addition, she was an excellent swimmer. The crash did not knock her out — as was proven by the fact that she was found clutching the underside of the back seat.

Either Kennedy was extremely lucky with his escape, or he wasn't in the car when it went off the bridge. As a matter of fact, according to Judge Brominski who presided over the exhumation hearing:

"It was assumed [before Kennedy turned up at the police station and announced that he had been driving] **Mary Jo was not only the driver of the car, but its sole occupant.**"

It is interesting to note the concurrence of opinion among those who have made studies of the Chappaquiddick accident in this regard. Jack Olsen, author of *The Bridge at Chappaquiddick*, Zad Rust, author of *Teddy Bare*, and Malcom Reybold, author of *The Inspector's Opinion — The Chappaquiddick Incident*, all conclude that Kennedy was not in the car when it left the bridge. Olsen says he was in the brush, Rust says he had jumped out onto the bridge, and Reybold says he was standing near the bridge when the accident occurred. Robert Sherrill, author of *The Last Kennedy*, isn't sure where Kennedy was and hedges, "[O]ne is left to choose between unlikely alternatives; either Kennedy pulled a Houdini-like escape, or he wasn't in the car. Even if Kennedy was in the Oldsmobile, he will never convince a great many people of it. And if he wasn't, no amount of explaining will get him off the hook." The Tedrows, authors of *Death at Chappaquiddick* agree that it would have been impossible for Kennedy to have escaped if the car was completely up-side-down; however, they have decided that the vehicle must have sunk on its side, leaving the driver's window above water for awhile and Kennedy used Mary Jo to springboard his way out. Judging from the damage done to the center of the car's roof on impact, the idea that the car was on its side is simply not plausible.

Although the authors disagree on where Kennedy was at the time of the accident, they do agree that it was extremely unlikely, if not impossible, for Kennedy to have escaped from the submerged vehicle. But if Kennedy wasn't in the car, where was he? Jack Olsen, in his book, *The Bridge at Chappaquiddick,* suggests that he may have gotten out of the car prior to arriving at the bridge. His reasoning is that Kennedy had indeed avoided the police officer at the intersection and was afraid the officer might follow him, so he got out and hid in the brush while Mary Jo drove on alone. Being unfamiliar with the large car, not having the seat adjusted to fit her, being excited by the police officer and having consumed a few drinks, Mary Jo was not in complete control of the vehicle and miscalculated the bridge. This idea has been loudly rejected by many who again say that Kennedy wouldn't have gone to those extremes to avoid an encounter with the police officer. Besides, if he hadn't been operating the vehicle, what would possess him to say that he was?

Perhaps he did step out of the car. If he had gone down Dyke Road to avoid the officer in the first place, it would seem logical that he would not want to be caught in the car with Mary Jo after running away, should the officer decide to follow. Officer Look has said that his suspicions had been aroused enough that he considered giving chase, but it was late and he was off duty so he didn't bother. Kennedy did not know the man was off duty and would have realized that his actions might cause the officer to investigate further. Kennedy also knew that Dyke Road was a dead end. If the officer had decided to check him out there would have been no way to escape. Why take a chance as long as he had gone that far? All he

87

had to do to be in the clear was to calmly step out of the car for a few minutes.

In view of his family history and recent threats against his own life there is also the strong possibility that Kennedy had perceived Officer Look as an assassin and was genuinely fearful of being trapped in his car on a dead-end road. The expert on the Warren Commission is convinced that this is what happened and explained, "If I wanted to protect the person who was with me from danger, I'd put as much distance as possible between the two of us. I would have gotten out of the car too. That was the only safe thing to do. No professional killer would have bothered Mary Jo when he found out Kennedy had gotten away."

It is hard for those of us who do not live with the constant threat of assassination to understand that the Kennedys have been conditioned to react instinctively to situations of potential danger. Only the year before, Bobby and Ethel had been standing together in the back seat of a convertible when a string of firecrackers went off. Ethel dove away from her husband and curled up into a little ball in the corner of the back seat while Bobby remained standing and appeared to be intentionally drawing fire away from his wife. Given his background, it is entirely possible that Ted Kennedy's gut reaction to the circumstances presented to him that night on Chappaquiddick were, (1) the officer might be an assassin, (2) don't become trapped in the car on a dead-end road, and (3) get away from Mary Jo so she doesn't get hurt.

Halfway between the intersection and Dike Bridge is a lovely Oriental garden known as Maitoi Park. The park is conspicuous because it is hardly the type of landscaping one expects to find in the brushy woods of Chappaquiddick Island. Yet 0.4 mile from the intersection and 0.3 mile from Dike Bridge, is a picturesque, high-arching footbridge leading to an island in a beautifully landscaped pond which is fed by a gurgling brook. Comfortable benches are scattered around and there is a convenient turn-out

Maitoi Park is located halfway between the intersection and Dyke Bridge. (February 1980, Willis)

where vehicles can be parked off the road. The three-acre retreat was constructed in the early '60's, well before the Chappaquiddick accident, and should have been noticed by Ted Kennedy and Mary Jo Kopechne, who had both passed it twice earlier in the day. Maitoi Park would have been an inviting haven for an anxious politician who wished to disappear from his vehicle for any reason.

It should also be noted that Burton Hersh, in his book, *The Education of Edward Kennedy,* reports that, as a youth, Kennedy had an experience running away from a pursuing police officer. Hersh states that according to Thomas Whitten, the police lieutenant who nabbed Kennedy eleven years earlier, in March of 1958, the carefree college student zoomed past him doing ninety miles per hour. Needless to say, the officer gave chase. Kennedy decided to outrun him, going through a red light in the process. The incident occurred late at night. When Kennedy was well ahead of the officer he switched off his lights and turned down Barracks Road where he lived, got out of the car and disappeared. Eventually Lieutenant

Whitten pulled up, looked at the car and left. The following Saturday night Kennedy pulled the same stunt, but this time the patrolman knew where he was going and wasn't fooled when Ted switched off his lights. Not having time to escape from the vehicle, he lay down on the seat. Much to his chagrin the ploy didn't work. He ended up very embarrassed — with two tickets; running a red light and reckless driving — and fifty dollars in fines.

On Chappaquiddick Kennedy hadn't broken any laws, but if he was concerned about being followed and identified by the officer it would seem reasonable that he would draw on past experience, and Kennedy's past experience clearly proved that it wouldn't do one bit of good to run away from a police officer if he didn't get out of his car.

The prosecutor might have had the possibility in mind that Kennedy was not the driver during this exchange with Esther Newberg:

Q. (by Mr. Fernandes) Miss Newberg, could Mary Jo drive that car?
A. Could she have? Certainly.
Q. So, could she drive, she could operate a motor vehicle?
A. **Yes, yes.**
Q. This is a large car, is it not?
A. It is no larger than the car my father had and she is not any taller than I am.
Q. Could she drive a vehicle of that size?
A. Could she have or did she?
Q. Did you see her drive the car ever, first of all?
A. That particular car?
Q. That particular car.
A. No.
Q. **You didn't see her take the car that night?**
A. No.
Q. Have you ever seen her drive a car of that size?
A. You can ask Miss Lyons later; she had a rather large car.
THE COURT: I don't think size has anything to do with it.
MR. FERNANDES: I am just curious just in light of what she said that she believed that Miss Kopechne drove the car [back to the motel].
THE COURT: Let's leave it there. This is her opinion, so she states.

Of course Mary Jo could have driven Kennedy's car. However, she owned and drove a Volkswagen, so she would have been unfamiliar with a big powerful Oldsmobile with power steering and power brakes. In addition, the seat was adjusted for Kennedy who is 6'2", whereas Mary Jo was 5'2". If she was, in fact, the driver, it is not at all difficult to see how she could have dropped a wheel off the side of the bridge.

Several other factors indicate that Mary Jo could have been the driver. The door on the driver's side was locked. Why would Ted Kennedy bother to lock his door? Locking doors is usually a habit. Kennedy rarely drives himself, but is chauffeured. He is used to traveling with male company. It hardly seems likely that locking car doors is a personal habit of his. On the other hand, Mary Jo, being a woman who was used to driving home alone in the evening, would be very likely to have developed such a habit. In addition, if she was anticipating a talk with a strange man on a lonely road late at night, by herself, she most certainly would have locked the door. No woman would feel secure under the circumstances, even if it did appear that the man was a police officer.

Even more convincing is the fact that Mary Jo was not injured. The only mark on her was a "slight abrasion" on her left knuckle. **Had Mary Jo been on the passenger's side, it seems likely she would have been badly hurt,** for the car landed on that side, blowing the windows in. Whether or not her seat belt was fastened, she would have been slammed into the door and broken glass would have been driven into her body, not to mention the fact that if Kennedy was not wearing a seat belt, a 220 pound man would have come hurdling down on top of her. However, if she was the driver, she would have been desperately clinging to the steering wheel. Even if her grip was broken it would have reduced the violence of impact and by the time she landed on the passenger's side the glass would no longer have been flying.

In addition, no one, other than Markham and Gargan, saw Ted Kennedy in wet clothing. Upon returning to the cottage, Kennedy stopped in the darkness of the parking area outside the yard fence where he called to Ray LaRosa to get Gargan and Markham.

He then got into the Valiant and waited for his friends. Thus none of the other party goers could say what condition Kennedy's clothes were in when he summoned assistance.

There is also widespread belief on Chappaquiddick Island that Ted Kennedy was not in the car when it went off the bridge. A local resident who visited with the author at Dike Bridge declared, "I'll tell you right now, Kennedy was *not* in that car! Two friends of mine were standing right here when it was pulled out of the water and they told me that the window on the driver's side was all the way shut. When Police Chief Arena got back from seeing Kennedy at the station he went immediately to Kennedy's car and rolled the window down."

When pressed as to why this had never been told to the authorities or reporters, the gentleman explained, "Well, we didn't know it was important until later. By the time we found out that Kennedy was supposed to have gone out the window, reporters had been crawling all over the place, harassing everybody and making life miserable in general. Nobody wanted to make more waves and draw attention to themselves. We just decided to skip it. Besides none of those reporters ever get anything straight. They come down here with a story already made up, ask a few questions about it and then say we told it to them. It makes everybody mad. We wouldn't mind if they reported what we actually said ... but they never do. They twist everything you say, so nobody around here talks to reporters any more ... that is except Farrar."

While the local's story is very interesting, there is no way to confirm it because the witnesses, whose names he provided, have long since moved and were unavailable. Kennedy himself has repeatedly declared that he has no idea how he escaped from the car and can't remember whether or not the window was open prior to the accident. On the other hand, both Police Chief Arena and John Farrar testified under oath that the window was found down when the vehicle was removed from Poucha Pond. Even so, it is noteworthy that many Chappaquiddick Island dwellers who were living on the island at the time of the accident believe otherwise.

In view of these facts it is very possible that Kennedy did step out of the car and Mary Jo drove off down the road to her death. The idea is not at all illogical. But again, we are back to the question — why would he claim he was driving if he wasn't?

The court never attempted to prove or disprove that Kennedy was the driver of the car because he immediately confessed to the crime of driving off the bridge and leaving the scene of the accident. He was quickly sentenced, and as far as the court was concerned, that particular aspect of the case was finished.

Had Kennedy claimed he was not the driver, the investigation would have changed radically. The time of the accident and Officer Look's testimony would have been closely examined. If the grand jury found cause to believe that he had been the driver, which was most likely, he would have been charged with leaving the scene, and perhaps with manslaughter. Thus charged, he would have been tried publicly. In addition to the known facts surrounding the accident, the court would have closely scrutinized Kennedy's past drinking and driving habits as well as his general social conduct, in an attempt to determine his guilt or innocence. The proceedings would have been zealously reported by the press, which of course would pick out the most sensational, though probably not the most relevant, aspects of the testimonies in order to provide the public with the most exciting reading material — which naturally sells papers and magazines. Such a public trial never came to pass because Kennedy quickly volunteered all of the evidence against himself and admitted that he was indeed guilty of the crime as charged.

Edgartown landing for the Chappaquiddick ferry (February 1980, Willis)

Edgartown Police Station (February 1980, Willis)

CHAPTER IX
DID KENNEDY TRY
TO SAVE MARY JO?

Three years after the Chappaquiddick accident William H. Honan reported in his book, *Ted Kennedy: Profile of a Survivor,* the following incident.

"Since the plane crash in June, 1964, in which Kennedy suffered a severe spinal injury, he has had to wear a cumbrous plastic back brace, and while he can still sail (his favorite sport) and even play a little tennis and touch football, his dauntless days are behind him. Even so, he is still possessed of instant physical courage. One day not long ago, for example, Kennedy was sailing in a small boat off Bermuda with his old Harvard football teammate, Congressman John C. Culver, and his wife. The wind was up and they were boiling along. Suddenly — a strong gust; the boat heeled sharply and Culver's wife fell into the water. In a flash, Kennedy went in after her, back brace and all. 'He hadn't even a moment's hesitation', Culver recalls. 'Just zip! And he was swimming along beside her'. It was precisely the reverse of the sort of conduct of which he is remembered at Chappaquiddick, and yet, those who know Kennedy well insist that the way he acted that day off Bermuda is characteristic of him."

When questioned about his actions after the accident at Dike Bridge, Kennedy testified:

A. Well, I was fully aware that I was trying to get the girl out of that car and I was fully aware that I was doing everything that I possibly could to get her out of the car and I was fully aware at the time that my head was throbbing and my neck was aching and I was breathless, and at the time, the last time, hopelessly exhausted.

Q. You were not confused at that time?

A. Well, I knew that there was a girl in that car and I had to get her out. I knew that.

Q. And you took steps to get her out?

A. I tried the best I thought I possibly could to get her out.

Q. Mr. Kennedy, how many times, if you recall, did you make an effort to submerge and get into the car?

A. I would say seven or eight times. At the last point, the seventh or eighth attempts were barely more than five — or eight — second submersions below the surface. I just couldn't hold my breath any longer. I didn't have the strength even to come down even close to the window or the door.

Q. And do you know how much time was used in these efforts?

A. It would be difficult for me to estimate, but I would think probably 15 to 20 minutes.

Q. And how long did you spend resting?

A. Well, I would estimate probably 15 to 20 minutes trying to get my — I was coughing up the water and I was exhausted and I suppose the best estimate would be 15 or 20 minutes.

Q. Now, following your rest period, Senator, what did you do after that?

A. After I was able to regain my breath I went back to the road and I started down the road and it was extremely dark and I could make out no forms or shapes or figures, and the only way that I could even see the path of the road was looking down the silhouettes of the trees on the two sides and I could watch the silhouette of the trees on the sides and I started going down that road walking, trotting, jogging, stumbling, as fast as I possibly could.

Q. Did you pass any house with lights on?

A. Not to my knowledge, **never saw a cottage with a light on it.**

Q. And did you then return to the cottage where your friends had been gathered?

A. That is correct.

Upon his return to the cottage, Kennedy says he got Paul Markham and his cousin, Joe Gargan, to go back with him and try to get Mary Jo out.

Q. And what happened after the three of you arrived there?

A. Mr. Gargan and Mr. Markham took off all their clothes, dove into the water, and proceeded to dive repeatedly to try and save Mary Jo.

Q. And they were unsuccessful in entering the car?

A. Well, Mr. Gargan got half-way in the car. When he came out he was scraped all the way from his elbow, underneath his arm was all bruised and bloodied, and this was the one time that he was able to gain entrance I believe into the car itself.

Q. And did he talk to you about his experience in trying to get into the car?

A. Well, I was unable to, being exhausted, to get into the

water, but I could see exactly what was happening and made some suggestions.

Q. So that you were participating in the rescue efforts?

A. Well, to that extent.

Q. And now may I ask you, Mr. Kennedy, was there any reason why no additional assistance was asked for?

A. Was there any reason?

Q. Yes, was there any particular reason why you did not call either the police or the fire department?

A. Well, I intended to report it to the police.

THE COURT: That is not quite responsive to the question.

Q. Was there a reason why it did not happen at that time?

THE COURT: Call for assistance.

THE WITNESS: I intended to call for assistance and to report the accident to the police within a few short moments after going back to the car.

District Attorney Edmund Dinis (L) with Assistant District Attorney Armand Fernandes. (UPI March 10, 1970)

The Chappaquiddick firestation as viewed from the parking area in front of the Lawrence cottage where the cook-out was held. (February 1980, Willis)

Russell E. Peachy, co-owner of the Shiretown Inn, on his way to the inquest where he testified that he had a conversation with Kennedy at 2:25 a.m., shortly after the Senator returned to Edgartown following the accident. (UPI January 6, 1970)

CHAPTER X

WHY WASN'T ADDITIONAL ASSISTANCE SUMMONED TO TRY TO SAVE MARY JO?

One of the most serious flaws in Kennedy's testimony is his claim that he saw no houses with lights on. There was an available phone at Dike House, which was rented by Mrs. Sylvia R. Malm, who had been at home with her daughter that night. Dike House sits immediately on the road between the bridge and the cottage and is located about a hundred and fifty yards from the bridge itself. Police Chief Arena questioned Mrs. Malm at length about her knowledge of the accident. Under oath, he testified as to what he learned from the woman who had reported the car under the bridge.

A. **She said that she had a light on in her house.** I think her daughter was in her room reading, **which Mrs. Malm said reflected on the roadway.**

Q. Until what time?

A. The daughter gave a statement. I think if I remember right, **until some time after midnight.** I'm not really sure. I think I have it.

Mrs. Malm submitted a written statement which was read in court. In it she says:

"I think I went to sleep sometime between 11:30 and 12:00 midnight, but I do not know the time. **I heard nothing during the night. We have two dogs and a night light was burning all night.**"

Kennedy claims to have sat on the bank resting for 15 to 20 minutes. There is just no way that he could have missed seeing Miss Malm's second story bedroom light which shone toward the bridge. However, if the accident occurred after midnight, that light would have been off and only a smaller, less visible night light, would have been burning elsewhere in the house.

Not only did the Dike House have a light on, but there was a night light burning in the house diagonally across the street, occupied by Mrs. Smith. Police Chief Arena also spoke to her.

The Smith house is located approximately 600 feet from Dike Bridge and within 30 feet of Dyke Road. (February 1980, Willis Photo)

"I had a conversation with Mrs. Smith and she stated **she had a night light** in one of her children's rooms which she left on all night. This was **on the road side** of the house."

According to Kennedy's own testimony, he had to have walked right by these two occupied houses on his way to get Paul Markham and Joe Gargan. Unless he really didn't see the houses, which seems unlikely, it is hard to imagine why the Senator would pass up two available telephones which could have been used to summon help. His actions have mystified everyone, for they were as completely out of character for him as they would have been for virtually anyone whose friend was trapped in a car nine feet under water. Kennedy should have rushed to the Dike House and called for help. Yet, he claims he never saw it. If the accident happened when he said it did, he would have had to walk through the shaft of light which shone onto the road. If it happened later, after Officer Look saw the mysterious car, there was still a night light on in the house.

Kennedy had behaved totally different in 1964, even though seriously injured and in great pain fol-

Wreckage of 1964 plane crash. Two persons were killed and Kennedy sustained a broken back. (June 20, 1964, U.P.I.)

lowing a plane crash. In his book, *Ted Kennedy: Triumphs and Tragedies,* Lester David reports:

"Scheuer took off his raincoat and covered Kennedy who, though dazed and in considerable pain, was asking about Marvella and the others. 'See that she is taken care of,' he told Scheuer. 'Kennedy asked for water, a sign of approaching shock ... He was lying there in the wet grass,' Scheuer remembers, 'cool as a cucumber, worrying about Mrs. Bayh and the others and asking us not to move him until help came.'"

Rose Kennedy reports in *Times to Remember:*

"Ted was very badly injured. As we learned later, he had sent all the others ahead in the first ambulance that arrived — while he lay stretched out on the ground with no more than first aid — and waited for the second one to take him to the emergency ward. Once in the hospital, it was touch and go for a while as to whether he would live; and after that, if he lived, whether he would be able to walk and lead a normal life again, since several of his vertebrae were fractured and there was a possibility his spinal cord had been damaged."

In 1964, according to all who were involved and observed the Senator's behavior the night of the crash and subsequently in the hospital, he was very heroic. However, in 1969, according to his own statement, he fell apart completely. He says that the car accident shook him up and he hit his head. He hit his head and a great deal more in the plane crash five years earlier, and though he went into shock he was still concerned about the safety of his friends.

Upon returning to the cottage where the party was in progress, Kennedy summoned Gargan and Markham to help. He completely ignored Ray LaRosa, his personal friend who was a fireman trained in rescue and who also happened to be a very good skin diver. Why was LaRosa left out? Kennedy spoke to him; he asked LaRosa to get Markham and Gargan, but didn't tell him about the accident. The Chappaquiddick Fire Station was across the street from the cottage, as everyone at the party knew. A red light was burning on it all night, and several of the party-goers mentioned that fact at the inquest, yet Kennedy and

Kennedy walked past the Chappaquiddick Fire Station when he returned to the cottage after the accident. (February 1980, Willis Photo)

his two helpers totally ignored the fire station where help was readily available.

According to Jack Olsen, "[O]ne of the girls had said [to reporters] that Kennedy returned to the cottage after midnight with a story that **his car had run off the road and Mary Jo was sitting in it.**" However, Kennedy denies having said anything to anyone other than to ask LaRosa to get Gargan and Markham.

Although the participants claim that Kennedy offered no explanation to LaRosa regarding why he needed to see Gargan and Markham, Maryellen Lyons described a very interesting conversation involving Ray LaRosa which took place immediately following Gargan's and Markham's departure to help Kennedy.

Q. (Dinis) What did he say, Mr. LaRosa, to you about that particular question?

A. He just said that the Senator had — that he was sitting out front and the Senator had come back and asked for Mr. Markham and Mr. Gargan. That is all.

Q. Was there any talk about Mary Jo at that time?

A. No, we were speculating whether a car had been caught in the sand or how do you put that, and we —

Q. You were speculating with whom about the sand and the car?

A. **Mr. LaRosa** and others.

Q. Who were the others?

A. Talking about how it had happened before, **the cars got stuck in the sand.**

Q. Cars got stuck in the sand before that same night?

A. Oh, no, not that night.

Q. Well, what then? Will you tell the Court what about this incident, your experience with being stuck in the sand with an automobile?

A. It wasn't my experience, Mr. Dinis. We were speculating whether or not a car had been stuck in the sand and they were saying that another year when they had been there a car was stuck in the sand and they came back and called for another car and by the time it ended there were three cars stuck in the sand. So that is essentially what we were speculating about. Another car stuck in the sand and another one up and was that now stuck in the sand, too.

Q. Was there any conversation as to why these automobiles were in the sand?

A. No, we didn't know that they were in the sand. The cars were gone and we were just saying, you know, where is everybody? The only thing we could think of was that

Aerial view of Dike Bridge and the ocean beach beyond. The gravel ends where the two vehicles are parked. Beyond that point the sand is loose and suitable for off road vehicles only. (August 1969, Fred Ward, Black Star.)

a car was stuck in the sand and Mr. Gargan and Mr. Markham had taken the other car to get the first car out of the sand . . .

The three "rescuers" claim to have gone back to the bridge to try to save Mary Jo on their own. When unsuccessful, they say they gave up and went off, leaving their friend who they assumed had drowned by then, in the car at the bottom of the pond. Although they had intended to report the accident, they were so overcome with emotion and exhaustion that instead they went home and went to bed.

The District Attorney didn't like their story and pressed them about it. He asked Kennedy about LaRosa.

Q. How long had you known Mr. LaRosa prior to this evening?
A. Eight years, ten years, eight or ten years.
Q. Were you familiar with the fact or — strike that — did you have any knowledge that Mr. LaRosa had some experience in skin diving?
A. No, I never did.

When grilled about why he didn't get additional help Kennedy responded:

". . . at some time, I believe it was about 45 minutes after

Sandy Trail at the end of Dyke Road. Motorists frequently get stuck here when turning around. (February 1980, Willis)

Gargan and Markham dove they likewise became exhausted and no further diving efforts appeared to be of any avail and they so indicated to me and I agreed. So they came out of the water and came back into the car and said to me, Mr. Markham and Mr. Gargan at different times as we drove down the road towards the ferry, that it was necessary to report the accident."

The District Attorney also questioned Mr. Gargan about the failure to summon additional assistance.

Q. Did you make any effort to obtain additional assistance?

A. No, we did not .

Q. Was there a particular reason?

A. Not a particular reason, no. I mean, I dove into the water, I felt — at that moment when I went down — I felt there was only one thing to do and that was to get into that car and as quickly as possible, because I knew if I did not there wasn't just a chance in the world of saving Mary Jo. You must realize that Mary Jo was a very good friend of mine, a person that I hold in great esteem, great affection, and I had lost a friend. She was in the water in the car and I thought at that time the only thing to do was to get in that car and get her as quickly as possible. When we failed in that, Mr. Dinis, I didn't think that there was anything more that could be done.

According to his own testimony, after dropping the Senator off to swim across the channel, Mr. Gargan and Mr. Markham went back to the cottage and Gargan fell right to sleep on the floor. This is indeed strange behavior for someone whose "very good friend" was still at the bottom of Poucha Pond.

How did Mr. Markham respond to the question of why no help was summoned?

A. . . . the girl was apparently gone. We had to get help and we had to report that.

Q. Who said that?

A. Joe and myself.

Q. So I understand it, you and Mr. Gargan suggested that you get help and report it?

A. That is correct. Report the accident.

CHAPTER XI
WHY WASN'T THE ACCIDENT REPORTED TO THE POLICE IMMEDIATELY?

In a November 2, 1979 interview with Tom Jarriel on "20/20", when asked this same question Kennedy replied, "I wish that I had. I will always wish that I had. It was a serious mistake that I didn't."

All three men testified that they left the bridge with the intention of immediately reporting the accident. Nevertheless, they did not go to the fire station; they did not go to the nearest telephone; they did not use the pay phone at the ferry house. Instead, they all went to the ferry landing, had a short discussion and Kennedy decided to swim across and report the accident directly to the police in Edgartown, while Joe and Paul went back to the cottage to get some sleep. Gargan and Markham both say that they didn't report the accident that night because they assumed that Kennedy would. Kennedy wholeheartedly agreed that he was the one who fell down on the job and has been adamantly insistent on taking the entire blame.

If Kennedy was intending to report the accident, one must ask why he would bother to swim the channel. After all, he must have realized that he would have to come back with the officers to show them where the car was, especially since Mary Jo was still in the vehicle. It would have been much more logical for him to call from the pay phone and await their arrival at the ferry landing.

It also seems reasonable that Gargan and Markham would expect a visit by the police yet they made no attempt whatsoever to dispose of the liquor bottles lying around the cottage.

The swim across the channel between Edgartown and Chappaquiddick is quite dangerous. When the tide is coming in, as it was that night at that time, the current is fast and there is a strong undertow.

Kennedy is no stranger to the sea; he was well aware of the difficulty of the swim. Even so, he allegedly jumped in fully clothed and swam across, very nearly drowning in the process.

Robert Sherrill, in his book *The Last Kennedy,* examined the question of whether or not Kennedy could have made the swim:

"Kennedy's television appearance had hardly ended before the channel between Edgartown and Chappaquiddick Island, which Kennedy claimed he swam to return to his motel after the accident, was filled with swimmers seeing if it could be done. The next day Farrar, the professional swimmer and diver for the local rescue squad, made the crossing to test Kennedy's story and found that it took him between five and six minutes in his clothes. But Farrar was fresh and very well trained. Kennedy, although a good swimmer, not only had come to the island exhausted from his work in Washington but had also worn himself out that evening running around to get help for Mary Jo and diving for her himself — at least, 'exhausted' was the word he, himself, used to describe his condition that evening.

"The distance between the two islands is about 500 feet, considerably more than the length of a football field. Even if the water were calm, that is a pretty good piece for a tired man to swim in his clothing. The currents in that channel are said to be moderately swift when they are not dangerously swift. Some local residents with intimate familiarity with the currents doubted that Kennedy could have done it. Dick Hewitt, whose work on the ferry would certainly make him familiar with the currents, was quoted as saying, 'If he were here right now, I'd call him a liar to his face.'

"On the other hand, some of the Saturday morning detectives who gave the channel swim a test did make it, so that portion of Kennedy's

The ferry crossing the channel as viewed from Edgartown looking toward Chappaquiddick. Kennedy began his swim in front of the ferry house to the left of the landing. (August 1969, Dennis Brack, Black Star)

story could not be written off as an impossibility."

Even stranger than Kennedy attempting to make the swim in his exhausted and confused condition is that Gargan and Markham willingly went along with the idea. The District Attorney questioned them about it.

Q. In time, Mr. Markham, approximately how long did it take you in observing him in the water?

A. Approximately three or four minutes or so.

Q. Were you concerned with the fact of whether or not he would arrive safely on the other side?

A. No, I wasn't.

Mr. Gargan gave a very firm answer.

Q. Weren't you concerned about his —

A. No.

Q. — ability to make it?

A. No, not at all. The Senator can swim that five or six times both ways. That may seem unusual, Mr. Dinis, except I have been with the Senator 30 years swimming and sailing and I don't know if you know the breakwater, off Hyannisport, but we used to swim every day around that, the breakwater, and it is the only thing the Senator has done since his back injury, besides skiing. The real form of exercise for the Senator since the back injury is swimming.

Q. Notwithstanding the back injury?

A. No question about it. I assume he had his back brace on that night. I was not concerned about his ability to make it to the other side.

Gargan might not have been concerned about Kennedy's ability to make the swim but Kennedy was.

"[A]s I looked over that distance between the ferry slip and the other side, it seemed to me an inconsequential swim; but the water got colder, the tide began to drag me out and for the second time that evening I knew I was going to drown and the strength continued to leave me. By this time I was probably 50 yards off the shore and I remembered being swept down toward the direction of the Edgartown light and well out into the darkness, and I continued to attempt to swim, tried to swim at a slower pace and be able to regain whatever kind of strength that was left in me. And some time after, I think it was about the middle of the channel, a little further than that, the tide was much calmer, gentler, and I began to get my — make some progress, and finally was able to reach the other shore . . ."

When one stands on the beach at night at the point from which Kennedy began his swim, it is easy to see why no one was concerned about the current.

View of Edgartown from Chappaquiddick where Kennedy claims to have begun his swim. Note the ferry landing on the right which acts as a breakwater. (February 1980, Willis Photo)

The ferry landing has solid walls which run out into the channel about 50 feet. These walls form a very effective breakwater and the water behind it remains calm even when the tide is running swiftly in the channel. Because it was dark, Kennedy could not see that the current was swift in the middle of the channel. He had to have been out at least 50 feet before the tide caught him and by then Gargan and Markham could not have seen him clearly enough to realize what had happened.

During the inquest a few of the party-goers indicated that they had been under the impression that Gargan and Markham had impulsivey jumped into the channel in an effort to stop Kennedy from making the dangerous swim. However, neither Gargan nor Markham said that they did this and both were wearing dry clothing when they returned to the cottage. When asked to explain why they did not get wet during their rescue attempts they explained that they had removed their clothes when attempting to rescue Mary Jo so that they could swim more easily and because they feared their clothing might catch on the submerged vehicle.

During his Presidential campaign, Kennedy's statement that he was caught in a strong current and swept toward the Edgartown lighthouse was questioned. According to a February, 1980 *Reader's Digest* article by John Barron:

"Storms and shifting sands have changed the topography of Edgartown Harbor in the years since 1969. So it is impossible today to take measurements in the channel that would scientifically ascertain the precise velocity of the current between 1:35 a.m. and 1:45 a.m., July 19, 1969, the time Kennedy and his friends claim he made his swim. But other data, including tidal elevation differences did enable Bernard LeMehaute to calculate the relative strength and direction of the current. 'Around 1:30 a.m., the current flowed southward toward Katama Bay at an increasing velocity until approximately 4 a.m.' Thus, had Kennedy encountered any current at all, it would have swept him not northward toward the lighthouse, as he says, but *southward,* in exactly the opposite direction." However, Jerome Milgram, a professor of oceanography at MIT, said that the *Reader's Digest* scientist based his information on studies made in November of 1979, while government publications — including tide charts — prepared in 1969 when the accident occurred, "confirm Senator Kennedy."

Also in early 1980, the *Washington Star* announced that they had discovered that the channel at the south end of Edgartown had been virtually closed by a fill at the time of the accident, thus eliminating the normal tidal currents. This has been proven untrue by Lawrence Hoch, an admiraty lawyer from Boston, hired by Senator Kennedy. Mr. Hoch found absolute proof that the channel was not closed until November 5, 1969 — four months after the accident occurred. The lawyer also located people who had sailed through the channel at the time of the 1969 Edgartown Regatta. As an expert in legal matters pertaining to the sea, Hoch declared:

"It is my strong opinion that if Senator Kennedy entered the water between 1:00 a.m. and 1:30 a.m. on July 19, 1969, he was swept the way he said he was swept and there was no other way he could have gone."

Besides the fact that the findings of the *Washington Star* and the *Reader's Digest* are in conflict with each other, at the time of the accident the knowledgeable residents of Edgartown and Chappaquiddick Island did not question Kennedy's statement as to the current but vigorously debated his ability to have made the difficult and dangerous swim at all. None of the ferry operators, including Jared Grant, who made a run across the channel at 12:45 a.m., July 19, 1969, about 45 minutes before Kennedy says he made his swim at the same place, and Officer Christopher Look, who was ferried across the channel in the Edgartown Yacht Club launch at 12:25 a.m., ever questioned Kennedy's evaluation of the direction and strength of the current. These people were extremely interested in the case, and Grant and Look both testified that they had crossed the channel that night. In fact, Look told Jack Olsen that the current was running strong when he crossed. If Kennedy's testimony had been as far out of line as the 1980 absentee investigators claim, John Farrar, Christopher Look, Jared Grant or Dick Hewitt, all of whom testified at the inquest, or some of the townspeople, would have called attention to it back in 1969.

The local people of Edgartown and Chappaquiddick Island were angered by the *Washington Star* and *Reader's Digest* reports, and the harbormaster, Robert T. Morgan, was moved to call his own press conference in January of 1980 to personally refute the allegations. Morgan told the Vineyard Gazette:

"The tide that night could not have been other than what Mr. Kennedy testified and said it was ... I know the tide facts and I know the facts are contrary to everything they are writing about ... I didn't feel at any time up to now — until the reports in the (Washington) Star and the Reader's Digest — that it was ever necessary for me to speak out after Ted Kennedy said he drifted toward the lighthouse. This was the way somebody would drift. That was the direction somebody would go ... The tide couldn't be otherwise." Morgan went on to say that he knew how the tides ran the night of July 18-19, 1969 because he had been out in the channel at 1:30 a.m. answering a distress call from a crippled boat.

Another long-time island dweller, angry about the allegations made by the two recent articles, told the author in February of 1980:

"Those articles are *wrong* and everybody around here knows it! I don't know how Kennedy got across that channel but I do know that the tide runs exactly like he said it did — fast in one place and hardly at all in another. That tide can easily run 20 miles per hour. I've seen it faster than that ... Right after Kennedy said he swam the channel two friends of mine who are excellent swimmers decided to try it while the tide was running. Let me tell you — they almost didn't make it! When they finally did get to the other side, they just collapsed on the beach for fifteen minutes and couldn't move. They told me later the swim scared them half to death — it was a stupid thing to try and they were never going to do a thing like that again."

There have been those who say that Kennedy did not swim, but found a boat and had Gargan and Markham ferry him across and the reason he says he swam and nearly drowned in the process is to provide himself with some sort of excuse for not reporting the accident. Since no one other than Gargan and Markham observed Kennedy making the swim, no one in Edgartown saw the Senator in wet clothing and the local police never thought to ask to see his wet clothes, there is absolutely no way to either prove or disprove the theory. Ted, himself, has lamented this fact and asked, "Why would I say I had if I didn't?" It is true that he has never used the episode as an excuse. Instead he says the reason he did not report the accident after he recovered from his swim was that "I just couldn't gain the strength within me, the moral strength to call Mrs. Kopechne at 2:00 o'clock in the morning and tell her that her daughter was dead." Kennedy seemed to think that this was his personal responsibility and was, in fact, the person who did call the Kopechnes and gave them the sad news.

It is also true that he is the one who had to tell his father that Jack was dead, and five years later that Robert was going to die. He was present when his parents learned of Joe Jr's death. Because he knew first hand the anguish such news would cause the Kopechnes, it is reasonable that he would find informing them very difficult. A few months earlier, on November 26, 1968, Rose Kennedy was quoted by *Look,* "I don't believe in telling people bad news at night; it only robs them of sleep and strength.

Better to wait for daylight." Perhaps, knowing his own mother's attitude, he delayed the chore of informing Mary Jo's parents. However, this does not totally explain why he did not report the accident to the authorities. Since he was positive she was dead (and in fact she was), in his distraught state it is not beyond the realm of possibility that he did delay the report to insure that the Kopechnes did not hear about their daughter's death until morning. This is what he claims he did. He now admits that it was not a rational thing to do and was a terrible mistake on his part.

Besides the fact that he never used his nearly drowning as an excuse for failing to report the accident, it is perfectly within Ted Kennedy's personality to have made the reckless swim across the channel without giving it a second's thought. From the time he was a child he has been a bit of a dare-devil. His mother reminisced:

"I remember an incident on the Riviera at Eden Roe, a beautiful hotel with grounds that end abruptly on a twenty — or thirty — foot cliff with the Mediterranean below. The water below is deep, so it is a great place for high diving, provided one knows how to do it. And I remember Teddy up there on the cliff and Joe Jr. and sometimes Jack yelling up to him to jump in. And he did. To my consternation and concern he kept doing it, egged on with great applause. I didn't interfere because the big brothers wouldn't be putting him up to it unless it were safe. And he seemed to be having a great time."

Over two decades later, he was challenging John Tunney to jump off some towering French cliffs into the sea below, happily bailing off himself and yelling up to the terrified Tunney, "Come on! Come on! When the going gets tough, the tough get going." Tunney eventually closed his eyes and complied.

But perhaps the most revealing statement about this trait of his is told by himself in a little story he wrote for his mother's book *Times to Remember:*

It was rather like Jack saying, when someone asked him about being a war hero, "It was unintentional. They sank my boat." I went to a ski-jump event near Madison because there was a big crowd there, eight or ten thousand people, and the idea was that somebody would introduce me on the public-address system and I would say a few words about the election and vote for my brother, and then go around and shake hands. Someone in charge said I should go to the platform at the top of the jump and be introduced from there. So up I went and there were several people waiting and one fellow with an official's badge introduced me and ended by adding, "Maybe if we give him some encouragement, he'll jump." The crowd applauded.

I had on ski clothes, more or less, so I would blend into the scene of the day. I could ski pretty well. I should've by that time because my parents, Mother in particular, started me out when I was six or seven, and Dad was in the embassy and Mother took us over to Switzerland for the Christmas and New Year holidays. And I remember seeing my brother Joe go down that dangerous one-man bobsled run, and skiing with him and Jack — they were trying to teach me — and I twisted my knee, and they took me down to the hospital, and I was laid up for a while. But I had done a lot of skiing later and I was pretty good at the usual things, though I hadn't jumped. I knew the principles.

This was an Olympic-size jump, but I thought I'd try. Somebody was kind enough to offer to lend me a pair of skis. So down I went. In the circumstances, it seemed I should. I didn't show the grace of an eagle, but I managed to keep everything going in the right direction and landed upright about seventy-five feet or so away and skied on down the slope and was very happy still to be alive. There was applause. Maybe there were some extra votes for Jack ...

I certainly never went around looking for things like that. But I did find myself involved in a similar situation later on during the general election. They put me in charge of the campaign in the mountain states, so one day I was at a big rodeo in Miles City, Montana. I was there with the same idea, to be introduced and say something about my brother and shake some hands. But they said no political figures were going to be introduced. They said, "If you want to ride, you'll be introduced like everybody

Ted Kennedy "Comin' out of chute 4" at the Miles City, Montana Rodeo in 1960 after being told that was the only way a politician would be introduced. (1960 Wide World Photo)

117

else." Which would be like, "Ted Kennedy, now comin' out of chute 4."

I knew how to ride a horse. I never had been on a bronco. But if that's the way it had to be ... so I got on the bronco and we went out the chute, and I think I may have lasted six seconds — it seemed like an hour before I was thrown. No real damage, no broken bones. People seemed to think I had done all right for an amateur. They like to test you in that part of the country. Possibly I had conveyed something about our family — about Jack — that resulted in a few more votes.

"Jack called me shorty after that to say that he had just talked with the state chairman in Wyoming, who told him I was coming to Rock Springs the next Saturday night. They were arranging to have a sharpshooter shoot a cigarette out of my mouth at twenty yards. Jack said, casually, that he didn't think I had to go through with that if I didn't want to, but ...

Rose commented, "Teddy was always stalwart, and optimistic from the time he was a little child. I think none of us were greatly surprised by his ski jumping and bronco riding."

The point of all this is that Ted Kennedy does rise to challenges. The idea of swimming the channel between Chappaquiddick and Edgartown would not have bothered him at all.

During the questioning Kennedy went on to say that when he arrived at Edgartown he was totally exhausted and shaking with cold, and his neck and back hurt. He planned to go to his room to change and then go on to the police station, but ended up collapsing on the bed. The noise from a party next door woke him, however, and he got dressed and went out to see what time it was. He bumped into the innkeeper who informed him it was 2:25 a.m. Instead of continuing to the police station, he turned around and went back to bed. Why would he do that if he was already down the stairs on his way to report the accident? Kennedy flatly stated that he considered his actions "indefensible" and never tried to explain or excuse them, except to admit on television that, "I was overcome, I'm frank to say, by a jumble of emotions: grief, fear, doubt, exhaustion, panic, confusion and shock." This was certainly a remarkable confession for a politician with his eye on the White House to make.

Ted may have been grief-stricken but it is highly unlikely that he was in a state of panic and fear. Past history shows he does not react that way. Lester David reported:

> "While climbing the 14688-foot Matterhorn in the Pinnine Alps, he slipped and dangled for heart-stopping moments over a sheer precipice. In this state of suspension, he cooly peeled and ate an orange. He climbed back and went on to the top."

Granted, the Chappaquiddick situation differed in that it was highly emotional, but he handled the funerals of both brothers very well, even delivering a eulogy to Robert, which was a very difficult thing for him to do and required an impressive amount of self-discipline. Virtually everyone who knows him well comments that his reported actions the night Mary Jo died were totally out of character for the Ted Kennedy they know.

Dr. Donald Mills, associate medical examiner of Dukes County, Mass. who examined the body of Mary Jo Kopechne and ruled drowning was the cause of death. (UPI October 20, 1969)

John Farrar enjoys another interview with reporters during the January 1970 inquest. (Dennis Brach, Black Star)

CHAPTER XII

COULD MARY JO HAVE BEEN SAVED IF HELP HAD BEEN SUMMONED QUICKLY?

There has been a great deal of speculation as to whether Mary Jo might have survived if Kennedy had summoned professional help immediately. The general feeling is that if she could have been saved and Kennedy did not get additional help, he is guilty of far more than merely leaving the scene of an accident. Various interviews of John Farrar, the scuba diver who removed the body from the car, have done much to make it appear that Mary Jo could have lived. *Newsweek* summarized one such interview in their August 4, 1969 issue:

"John Farrar, the 33-year-old scuba diver who finally retrieved Mary Jo's body from the sunken car, thought there was a 'slim chance' that he and Chief Arena might have saved her. Mary Jo's position in the car suggested to Farrar that she might have found a temporary air pocket (though how long this would have lasted with water flooding in through an open window was problematical). Farrar feels Kennedy had no real chance to save her by himself; the water was too murky and the tide too strong for most fit men, let alone a dazed and injured accident victim with a chronically bad back. But Farrar said he and Arena, in diving gear, 'had the body out in half an hour after I was called ... Even working in the dark, I think we would have had her out in 45 minutes.' "

As the months wore on, John Farrar continued to talk about it and seemed to convince himself that he could have saved Mary Jo. By November his story had a decidedly different tune to it than it had three months earlier. *U. S. News and World Report* printed the following interview with the diver on November 8, 1969.

A. ... The girl was in the back seat of the car. Her head was cocked back, and her face was pressed upward into the foot well of the car, with her hands holding onto the leading edge of the back seat so that she could hold herself in a position to take advantage of the last bit of air in the occupant's section of the car.

Q. You are quoted as saying Miss Kopechne might have lived if a diver had been called in time. What were the odds she might have been saved?

A. I think the odds were rather good, for these reasons:

First, the way the car entered the water, which would have caused it initially to trap a large amount of air.

Second, the position of the car on the bottom. It was resting on the hood ornament and the brow of the windshield with the rear end just slightly below the surface of the water.

Third, the consciously assumed position of the victim, as previously described.

Fourth, the fact that air bubbles emanated from the car as it was removed from the water 10 to 11 hours after the accident was said to have happened, and

Fifth, the fact that there was a large air void and lack of water in the trunk of the car when it was removed.

Only recently there have been two incidents in New England in which people lived for some time by finding an air bubble in a submerged car. In one, a woman lived for two hours, and in the other a woman lived for six hours.

Q. But the windows were broken out —

A. The fact that the windows were knocked out does not mean that an air lock could not have been formed. The car was overturned, and the broken windows were on the low side, completely open to the sea, so the effective air lock could have remained.

Q. Where were you the night before, around midnight, when the accident was reported to have occurred?

A. At home in bed.

Q. How long would it have taken you to get to Dike Bridge?

A. No longer than it did the next morning.

Q. Doesn't the ferry quit running at midnight?

A. Yes, but the ferry operator is on our emergency radio frequency. He has a radio by his bed, just as I do. He would have been waiting for me by the time I had gone to the station to get my gear. I was at Dike Bridge in 20 minutes from the time I got the call that morning, and at the girl's side in another five minutes.

In three months, Farrar had reduced the rescue time by 20 minutes and was sure he could have saved her. Other island dwellers do not agree with Farrar's later estimate. An auto mechanic who frequently makes emergency crossings on the Chappaquiddick ferry and has lived on "Chappy" for over 30 years, told the author that, in his opinion, Farrar could not possibly have gotten to the girl in less than 45 minutes.

Even though he does not know the Kennedys any better than does the rest of the public, John Farrar has been very outspoken against them — before as well as after the accident. Robert Sherrill's book *The Last Kennedy,* is extremely critical of the Senator and is designed to present Kennedy in a very poor light, yet even this author questioned the reliability of Farrar's claim.

"Farrar was manager of the Turf and Tackle Shop in Edgartown and captain of the Edgartown Fire Department Scuba Search and Rescue Division. When he is above water he is talkative, and when he is under water he knows what he is doing. His recollections of what he did and what he saw have to be considered technically authoritative, but his interpretations

123

and estimates of what *might* have been the situation *if* Kennedy had taken actions he did not take must be received with the understanding that **Farrar does not like Kennedy even a little bit."**

Sherrill also noted that Farrar "never ceased telling *his* story about how Miss Kopechne probably stayed alive for hours in an air bubble and very likely could have been saved if he had been called promptly."

As positive as he was about his rescue theory, when questioned under oath, Farrar did not seem interested in expressing his ideas to the judge, and although the District Attorney never brought the matter up when questioning Farrar, the scuba diver seemed happy with the way things went in court. As Sherrill reported:

"And yet even more baffling was the fact that after he had testified, Farrar seemed to be trying to give reporters the idea that he *had* been asked about his favorite theory. When he came out of the courthouse, he told reporters that 'we are satisfied we had the opportunity to give everything we had to offer,' and he called Dinis's questioning 'very fair and very thorough.'"

Once away from the courthouse, however, Farrar's tongue has continued to wag. Over the years he has regaled willing listeners with his tale of possible rescue and irritated Edgartown's year round inhabitants, many of whom openly refer to Farrar as a "bullshiter and an egotist." One of Farrar's critics alleged that in the summer of 1979, "Farrar grew a beard, then shaved half of it off down the middle of his face and walked around town that way to see what the reaction would be."

No matter what his post-Chappaquiddick accident motives may have been, in 1969 John Farrar seemed determined to cause Kennedy as much grief as possible. He made a statement to Ron Rosenbaum, who writes for *Esquire* magazine:

"She didn't drown. That's the point. She died

of suffocation in her own air void. Gene Frieh, the undertaker, has said to me and said to others that he feels she did not drown but died of suffocation in her own air void. He's done twenty-four embalmings on drowned victims and in every case they've been filled with water, every body cavity filled with gallons of water. Full of water from their assholes to their appetites, as Gene Frieh puts it. But Gene found about half a teacup in her. Half a teacup, that's all. She suffocated to death. But it took her at least three or four hours to die. I could have had her out of that car in twenty-five minutes after I got the call. But he didn't call."

What did the undertaker, Gene Frieh, actually say about it? Mr. Frieh was present at the scene when Dr. Mills examined the body. He testified at the inquest:

Q. And what did you observe when Dr. Mills performed his examination?

A. Well, the usual procedure of general examination of a body so found. Dr. Mills loosened up the front of the blouse, took his stethoscope and applied it to various sections of the thoracic region and the abdominal region. He also manipulated the thoracic region with his hands.

Q. Did this produce a flow of water?

A. It produced some water flow, water and foam, mostly foam.

Q. Some water and foam?

A. Yes.

At the hearing for the exhumation of the body, in Wilkes-Barre, Pennsylvania, Frieh testified:

Q. Did you manipulate the body in any way as to extract water from the body?

A. As is our custom on a drowning case, we usually use what is called a body block. May I go into detail?

Q. Yes.

A. A body block is placed under the abdominal area thereby compressing that area very precisely.

Q. Did you do this?

A. Yes.

Q. What did this produce, if anything?

A. A very little moisture, sir.

Q. Did you find this unusual?

A. I did raise an eyebrow, sir, in the sense that I expected much more moisture.

David Guay, Frieh's assistant, is reported to have said that he and Frieh obtained only 8 to 10 ounces of water from the body.

Doctor Donald R. Mills, an Associate Medical Examiner for Dukes County for over 20 years, is the person who made the diagnosis of death by drowning. His testimony at the inquest is as follows:

> Q. Now, Doctor, you say that you formed an opinion as to what the cause of death was?
> A. Yes.
> Q. Could you tell us how you formed that opinion and then tell us what the opinion was?
> A. I formed my opinion by the fact that this girl was completely filled with water; that is, her bronchial tubes were full, her mouth was full of water. There was water in her nose. This was clearly demonstrated by making just light pressure on the chest wall in which case the water would simply pour out of the nose and mouth. There was some foam about the nose and mouth which is characteristic of drowning.
> Q. And your opinion was that she had died of drowning?
> A. Yes.

Contrary to what Kennedy's antagonists would like the public to believe, the medical profession is in complete agreement that people don't always fill up with water when they drown. Dr. Arthur C. Guyton, Professor and Chairman of the Department of Physiology and Biophysics at the School of Medicine of the University of Mississippi and author of *Textbook of Medical Physiology,* described asphyxia in drowning in 1966:

> "Asphyxia in Drowning: Approximately 30% of all persons who drown do not inhale water, and even after recovery of the body from the water the lungs are still dry. These persons simply die from asphyxiation. The reason they do not inhale water is that water, in attempting to enter the trachea elicits a powerful laryngeal reflex that causes spastic closure of the vocal cords."

In reviewing the available information, it appears that Mary Jo did inhale some water and this caused the described laryngeal reflex. Being under water for several hours after death allowed some additional water to seep into the airways, thus, when the body was examined by Dr. Mills, water was produced when pressure was applied to the chest. Some of that water probably did come from the lungs, but much of it was also in the bronchial tubes and nasal cavities. If the lungs had little water in them, as might be expected, then Frieh is also truthful when he says he got less than a cup full of water from the body by using a body block. There is nothing at all inconsistent with the observations made by these three people in relation to a drowning case. According to Dr. Guyton's description, these observations would be expected in nearly one out of three cases.

If we re-examine what we know about the position of the body in relation to the car, we can conclude that Miss Kopechne lived at least a short while after impact, the fall did not knock her out, and she was conscious long enough to grab hold of the lower edge of the back seat while attempting to hold her head up. That she found much air is doubtful. For one thing, the car was upside down. The underside of any

The crash crushed the right doors of the vehicle and blew in the windows on the right side making it impossible for an air bubble to form in the passenger compartment. (July 19, 1969, UPI Photo)

car is not very air tight because there are many nuts and bolts as well as openings for pedals, wires and vents. The perimeter of almost any car door will leak and in this case the **doors on the right side of the vehicle were badly damaged,** as illustrated by photographs taken at the scene, and obviously incapable of forming any sort of an air lock.

The only possible place that a little air might have been trapped in the passenger part of the car would have been in a foot well. If the car was level, the very maximum amount of air would have been about three inches. But the car was not level. It was resting on the hood with the rear of the car elevated. Such a position would have reduced the amount of air in the foot well to practically nothing. Also, one must remember that there is no solid divider between the back seat and the trunk. Since the trunk was the highest part of the car, any trapped air would have ended up there, which is precisely what happened. As Farrar testified, . . . "we examined the trunk which we found remarkably dry." Air bubbles were released when the vehicle was turned over, which was the air escaping from the trunk. An air bubble in the trunk would not have done Mary Jo any good. She obviously could not have gotten into the trunk from the back seat of the car.

The accusations that Mary Jo might have lived had Kennedy summoned help quickly caused the Senator so much grief that he finally hired the Arthur D. Little Co. to make a study to determine the validity of the charge. The study concluded that water would have rushed into the car so quickly that Miss Kopechne could have remained conscious for only one to four minutes and that she could have been revived up to ten minutes after she lost consciousness, therefore she could not have been saved by help summoned from Edgartown.

Kennedy's critics have disregarded the study's findings charging that it was paid for by Kennedy money and is not to be trusted. Even so, it does not take much insight to see that the findings are probably accurate. At the very least, it would have taken a half hour for help to arrive even if Kennedy had run straight to the nearest phone. If Mary Jo was able to find an air bubble inside of the car, why would she sit there waiting to be rescued? She had to have desperately wanted out of that death trap. At first she would have been terrified. However, if she had presence of mind enough to find a shallow air bubble and make use of it, she would have had to hold still, and even though she would have been very frightened, she should have calmed down enough to search for a way out. Mary Jo was an excellent swimmer. Three windows were open and available to her for exits. (Her contorted body was easily removed through the right rear window.) Surely she would have eventually found a window and swum out. She would not have sat there playing Russian Roulette for up to six hours as some have charged — to see if she would be rescued before she suffocated — not when it would have been quite easy for her to save herself. It seems very unlikely that Mary Jo lived more than a few minutes after the car filled with water — not long enough to become oriented and find an open window. She certainly could not have survived long enough to be saved by a diver summoned from Edgartown.

It should also be noted that, although the car was badly damaged, Mary Jo had no visible bruises. It takes several minutes for bruises to form after receiving a blow. If she died within a few minutes of impact, even though she might have been injured, no bruises would have had time to form before the blood supply was cut off. It seems unlikely that in such an accident she would not have been bruised. It is more likely that she died too quickly for the bruises to form.

Mr. Joseph Kopechne embraces his wife, after the two day hearing ended on the exhumation of the body of their daughter, Mary Jo Kopechne. (UPI October 21, 1969)

CHAPTER XIII

WAS THERE AN ATTEMPT TO SNATCH THE BODY AWAY SO THAT THERE COULD BE NO AUTOPSY?

The fact that a full autopsy was not performed on the body has caused Kennedy a great deal of pain. He has been accused of snatching the body away and paying people off to prevent the discovery of the true cause of death. The speculation ranges from the idea that she suffocated to the preposterous charge that he murdered her. These accusations have all proved groundless. Kennedy had nothing to do with the decision not to perform an autopsy. Had he been asked, he most certainly would have requested one. He is experienced enough with political muckraking to know that failure to have an autopsy would leave him open to this sort of attack. The Senator was evidently not aware that the autopsy had been skipped until after Mary Jo was buried. Blame for this procedural omission can be placed on bureaucratic bungling by the authorities in charge of the case, but it is Kennedy who ended up taking most of the criticism.

Ted Kennedy truly felt miserable about the accident. It was all he could do to inform Mrs. Kopechne about it. When told, she became extremely distraught, as was Kennedy by the time he finished the conversation. Having lost four siblings himself, he was well aware of the trauma involved in taking care of the body of a loved one. He felt responsible, and wanted to help the Kopechnes all that he could. For this reason, he contacted his legislative aide, Dun Gifford, and asked him to see to it that the body was transported and cared for in accordance with the parents' wishes.

He also wanted to protect the Kopechnes as much as possible from the crass interrogation they were sure to be subjected to by the press. Only the year before, on the day Bobby died, his mother had gone to church to pray, where she had been pounced upon by excited reporters who wanted to know how she felt. Naturally, the incident was very traumatic, even for a strong person such as Rose Kennedy. It was obvious from the way Mrs. Kopechne reacted on the phone that she would not be able to stand such abuse. Therefore, Kennedy called William vanden Heuval, a close friend, and asked him to go visit the Kopechnes and help handle the press, preferably keeping most reporters away from the parents, and to help them make funeral arrangements. That Kennedy had any motives other than simply trying to help is most unlikely.

Once Kennedy had assigned William vanden Heuval and Dun Gifford their tasks he never thought about it again. He was terribly upset and had a tremendous amount of other problems on his mind, such as how he was going to explain the nine hour delay in reporting the accident. It probably never occurred to him that a full autopsy might be skipped or that he would be accused of body snatching, when he was merely trying to assist the bereaved parents.

The story soon circulated that Kennedy was afraid of what might be discovered and had his man, Gifford, take the body away before an autopsy could be ordered. Gifford, the story continues, went to Dr. Mills with a death certificate and pressured Mills into signing it. Then, without even waiting to obtain a coffin, had the body taken to the airport. In the meantime, District Attorney Dinis ordered an autopsy, but Gifford was racing to the airport with the body. Gifford's plane was grounded, and Dinis could have retrieved the body, but Gifford, it was alleged, had the mortician lie to the D.A. and say they had already left, when in fact they didn't take off for two more hours. Thus, Kennedy's man escaped with the body to another state which was out of the D.A.'s jurisdiction. This story is a sick twisting of the facts to make a purely humanitarian act take on the appearance of a sinister cover-up.

The District Attorney questioned both Dr. Mills and the mortician, Gene Frieh, in detail about the handling of the body.

Dr. Mills testified:

A. After I finished examining the body I released it to the undertaker ... Eugene Frieh, and I instructed him to hold it pending my notification of the District Attorney's office, particularly in connection with whether an autopsy should be performed.

Q. Did you ever speak with the District Attorney personally at that time about the autopsy?

A. No.

Q. As a result of a conversation with someone in the State Police, did you give any instructions to the mortician?

A. Yes, I — working through the State Police, which is my custom, I requested the officer to notify the District Attorney's office that such — that there was such a case, giving the details, such details as I had and asking if an autopsy would be done, requesting an autopsy if in the opinion of the District Attorney's office an autopsy was indicated. I received a reply back that the District Attorney himself was not available at that time, but his associate, Lieutenant George Killen, had stated that if I was satisfied that there had been no foul play, that **as far as he was concerned there was no need for an autopsy.**

Q. Did you receive instructions to take a blood sample?

A. Yes, thank you, I did.

Q. From Lieutenant Killen?

A. Yes, from Lieutenant Killen.

Q. And you related those instructions to the —

A. To the mortician.

Q. And then you released the body?

A. Yes.

Q. At that time the identity of the girl was still not known, is that right?

A. I didn't know who the girl was.

Q. And at the scene, Doctor, was there any mention of the fact that whether or not this girl had been alone in the car, were you aware — let me strike that — were you aware of any facts as to how the accident happened when you formed your opinion as to death? For example, did you know that she was alone in the car or that she was accompanied by somebody else?

A. No, I did not.

Q. Did you know whose car she was in?

A. No, I didn't know.

Q. So, at the scene, it is safe to say that facts surrounding the circumstances under which the car came into the water were not known?

A. Completely unknown to me.

Q. And also for the record, Doctor, when you say you

had your conversation with Lieutenant Killen or someone relaying a conversation with Lieutenant Killen at that time you did not know the facts surrounding the circumstances of this girl being in the car?

A. That is right, I did not.

Q. Did you at some time sign a death certificate?

A. Yes.

Q. Will you tell us when and where?

A. Yes. Mr. Guay (assistant to mortician) and Mr. Gifford came to my office that afternoon when I was attempting to hold office hours.

Q. Do you know what time that was, approximately?

A. 2:30 to 3 o'clock, with a certificate for me to sign, which I did.

Q. And you understood Mr. Gifford to be Mr. Kennedy's legislative assistant?

A. That is right. He introduced himself to me.

Q. And you signed it at that time?

A. I signed it at that time.

Q. And the death certificate indicated the cause of death?

A. As asphyxiation by immersion. In other words, by drowning.

The following is the testimony of the undertaker, Eugene Frieh.

Q. What did Dr. Mills say to you?

A. He had said to me that he would be in touch with the District Attorney's office and I can't recall whether he mentioned names or not, but that in his own words, as I recall, he said if I was perfectly satisfied with my diagnosis, that no further examination such as an autopsy would be necessary and just to go ahead and make arrangements.

Q. He also told you they wanted a blood sample, did he not?

A. He did at that time.

Q. And you produced a blood sample for the doctor?

A. Yes, we did. At the time of preparation it was taken from the axillary region.

Q. Now, how was it that you knew who this body was?

A. Through a call from the Kielty Funeral Home in Plymouth, Pennsylvania. **They had been authorized by Mrs. Kopechne,** the mother of this decedent, to take charge and see that the daughter was brought back to Plymouth for service and burial.

Q. You spoke with Mr. Kielty?

A. John Kielty.

Q. What exactly did Mr. Kielty tell you?

A. He told me he was authorized by Mrs. Kopechne to make arrangements; that he interrogated me as to the condition of the body and I told him that the body had been fully cleansed and properly prepared. So, **he told me to ship it down as soon as possible** to Pennsylvania, and

I asked him how; and he said, well, can you fly it down: I said, yes, we have arrangements. So, in due course it was flown down.

Q. Well, can you tell me how — could you tell me whether or not you had a conversation with Mr. Gifford?

A. Yes, that was in the middle of the afternoon, about 3:00 o'clock.

Q. Where did you see Mr. Gifford?

A. When he arrived at my office he entered my funeral home and apparently heard myself and Mr. Guay speaking in my office and walked directly into the office making himself known as being on the Kennedy staff.

Q. And at that time did he identify the girl?

A. He did not. We wouldn't allow him to go down to the prep room. No one has authority to go in there other than the personnel we authorize.

Q. And what did he say?

A. Well, he said he just had flown in from Nantucket and he wanted to make arrangements. I said, well, **you have no authority as far as I am concerned.** I'm taking all my orders from the Kielty Funeral Home down in Pennsylvania. So, **he let it go at that.** He asked me if he could use the telephone and he made some telephone calls and during his presence I had said to Dave Guay, I said, you had better run down and catch Dr. Mills on a death certificate if we have to ship this body down to Pennsylvania. So, when he heard that, he said to Dave, well, can I ride down and see Dr. Mills? Well, I had no authority to stop him, so he rode down and saw Dr. Mills.

Q. With reference to the body, when did it leave your funeral home?

A. The following day, which was a Sunday, and it was scheduled to leave at 9:30 but due to the fact of weather conditions and the breakdown of a particular plane that was to fly this young lady down to Wilkes-Barre, Scranton Airport, this Hathaway AFA, which is Air Funeral Arrangement Service, called up approximately about 9:00, 9:30 along in there on the Sunday morning mentioning the fact that they just couldn't fly this body down in the Comanche airplane they wanted to fly it down in, and the big twin that they have had some oil failure and just couldn't be used and they wondered if it would be all right if they could use Mass Airlines which could be converted for the carrying of the body.

Q. It is my understanding that they wanted a twin engine plane instead of a single engine?

A. Yes, due to the fact we were taking this Dun Gifford down, which was apparently authorized because **I asked Dave to call and see if it would be okay if Dun Gifford escorted this young lady down in the plane and the word came back affirmative and so we allowed him to fly down.** The fact still remains regardless of whether

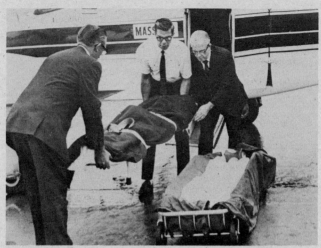

Mary Jo Kopechne's body being transported from Martha's Vineyard to Wilkes-Barre, Pennsylvania. Critics claim the body was secretly taken from the island to prevent an autopsy, yet a UPI photographer had no problem taking this picture. (July 20, 1969, UPI photo)

it was a single or twin engine plane it couldn't have been flown that morning with Mr. Gifford anyway unless we did go Mass Airlines.

Q. It was supposed to have left sometime 9:00, 9:30?

A. We were supposed to leave our funeral home at 9:30 and meet the plane between then and 10:00 o'clock.

Q. And in fact when did the body leave?

A. The body left at 12:30.

Q. Sunday morning?

A. Sunday morning.

The question remains, how could the District Attorney have failed to understand the significance and the need of a full autopsy? Frieh says that he was concerned about it and was "surprised that there was no post-mortem. I figured there should have been one for three reasons — the type of accident, the important people involved and the fact that insurance companies would be hounding officials over double-indemnity claims." Frieh went on to state that he could have shipped the body Saturday but delayed it because "I felt Dr. Mills might change his mind and order an autopsy, or that someone in higher authority might direct an autopsy."

Dun Gifford had not had much experience in this sort of thing, but he testified that he was concerned about the lack of an autopsy and made inquiries about it right up until the plane was ready to taxi down the runway, to be sure that Massachusetts didn't want to hold the body. He had asked the State Police several times and was told that no autopsy had been requested.

Doctor Mills caught much of the blame for the missing post-mortem and was unhappy about the accusations. He said that District Attorney, Dinis, apparently didn't want one done.

"I further feel that had Mr. Dinis considered an autopsy advisable after embalming, he would have ordered it. Certainly he knew of the Kennedy connection as soon as I did. I talked with Dinis and his aide several times in the following two weeks. It was crystal clear to me that the D.A. wished to keep out of the case completely.

"An autopsy would have done one thing: Saved me from being accused of being bought off by Kennedy money ..."

Dinis did apparently make a half-hearted attempt to have a last minute autopsy but when told by Lieutenant Killen that the body was supposed to have left the island at 10:00, he forgot the idea and didn't bother to see if the plane had actually taken off.

There is no way that responsible people can construe Kennedy's well-meaning attempt to help the Kopechnes as a cover-up, especially in view of the fact that the decision not to have a post-mortem was made by District Attorney Edmund Dinis, who was no friend of Kennedy, and in fact held a well-known grudge against the Senator, who had not supported him in the last election.

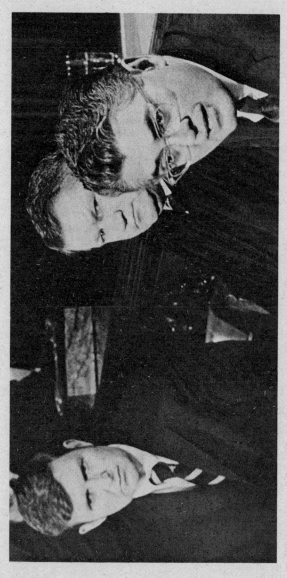

Participants in the exhumation hearing. Left to right: Joseph Flanagan (attorney for Mr. and Mrs. Joseph Kopechne), Judge Bernard Brominski (judge who presided over the hearing), District Attorney Edmund Dinis (D.A. who petitioned for exhumation.) (UPI August 15, 1979)

CHAPTER XIV

DID KENNEDY BLOCK THE EXHUMATION OF THE BODY FOR A BELATED AUTOPSY?

The charges which have been flung against Senator Kennedy in this regard are very unfair. He was not involved in the conflict. A hearing was held on whether to exhume the body for a belated autopsy three months after the girl was buried. The exhumation was fought by Mr. and Mrs. Joseph Kopechne, who did not want their daughter's body disturbed. The unhappy parents proclaimed that they were satisfied that their daughter had drowned. Their opposition to the exhumation was reported on front pages across the nation. They felt that Kennedy's political enemies were trying to exploit the tragic death of their daughter in an effort to destroy the Senator and did not want their daughter's grave violated to settle a political squabble. Joseph Kopechne testified:

"... [W]e feel now more than ever that we do not want an autopsy and it would be just like another funeral for us. We've had it. We feel that they had a chance at an autopsy, it wasn't performed and we absolutely do not want it now, we see no value in it at all."

It would have been much better for Kennedy if exhumation had been allowed, for it would have put a great deal of speculation to rest. He chose not to become involved in the hearing, and although he was obviously interested, he had no lawyers there to represent him in the case.

Some right-wingers have charged that Kennedy paid for the Kopechne's lawyers. Technically, his money did pay those attorneys. The $140,904.00 insurance settlement with the Kopechnes — of which Kennedy ended up paying $90,000.00 out of his own pocket because he had been carrying the standard $50,000.00 liability policy — was used in part to cover the Kopechne's legal fees. This turn of events is very ironic, for Kennedy's own money paid the lawyers who were responsible for the blocking of the exhumation, which would have helped clear him of many vicious and unfounded charges. What happened instead is that the Senator was immediately accused of having been in cahoots with the Kopechnes to block the autopsy so that the truth would never be known. Kennedy did not help himself any in this respect when he announced publicly that he was satisfied with the decision because of what it meant to Mrs. Kopechne. What he meant was that even though failure to exhume the body would hurt him, he didn't mind because of the further anguish it would have caused Mary Jo's mother. Mrs. Kopechne told reporters that she "could never have gone to that cemetery again if the grave . . . had been disturbed."

If the Kopechnes had wished to have the body exhumed, in all probability the judge would have called for it. However, since Mrs. Kopechne was very distraught, the judge carefully reviewed the evidence and decided that the possibility of Mary Jo Kopechne having died of anything other than drowning or that the autopsy would turn up anything conclusive was too remote to put the parents through the ordeal. Judge Brominski concluded:

> Even if we assume that an autopsy would reveal a broken neck or any other bone in the body, a fractured skull, the rupture of an internal organ, none of these would be incompatable with the manner in which the accident occurred . . . from the testimony before this court, every reasonable probability leads to a conclusion that supports the original finding of the cause of death of Mary Jo Kopechne, asphyxiation by immersion, i.e. death by drowning.

> In view of the testimony and law considered herein, and bearing in mind that courts are not reluctant to grant autopsies in given cases, we must be mindful that Joseph A. Kopechne and Gwen L. Kopechne, the parents of Mary Jo Kopechne, have indicated that they are unalterably opposed to exhumation and autopsy. Thus, it is incumbent that this court give weight to their objections. While their disapproval is not an absolute bar to an exhumation and autopsy, in view of the facts presented to this court, their objections are well taken.

> **It is the conclusion of this court that the facts presented herein are insufficient to support a finding of**

**the cause of death of Mary Jo Kopechne other than
asphxiation by immersion.**

Therefore, we enter the following:

ORDER

Now this 8th day of December, 1969, at 11:55 a.m., EST,
it is hereby ordered and decreed that the objections of Joseph
A. Kopechne and Gwen L. Kopechne, parents of Mary Jo
Kopechne are hereby sustained and the petitioner's request
for exhumation and autopsy of the body of Mary Jo
Kopechne is hereby denied.

BY THE COURT

**Judge Bernard Brominski of Luzerne County, Pennsylvania
denied the exhumation request. (UPI September 3, 1969)**

Wilkes-Barre, Pa: Gwen and Joseph Kopechne, parents of Mary Jo Kopechne, leave Luzerne County court house after two days of hearings regarding an autopsy on the body of their daughter. (UPI October 27, 1969)

CHAPTER XV
WAS THERE FOUL PLAY?

The possibility of foul play has repeatedly been brought up. "Enemies" of the Senator have done all they can to plant suspicion in the public's mind. Right-wing extremists have gone so far as to say they think Kennedy purposely killed Mary Jo. The fact that a full autopsy was not performed has added fuel to the fire, even though a grand jury, and two different hearings (the exhumation hearing and the inquest) under three different judges, in two different states, with scores of expert witnesses, did not turn up one piece of evidence that pointed to foul play.

Whether Mary Jo could have died from anything other than drowning was carefully gone into at both the exhumation hearing and the inquest. By the time the inquest was held, wild stories were rampant and the judge and prosecutors explored every angle. The reason for the inquest in the first place was to determine if there was cause to further prosecute Senator Kennedy. The inquest was convened to determine if Mary Jo's death could have been anything but accidental. It was not held to determine what kind of a party Kennedy had attended or what motives he might have had for being alone with her in the car or even to find out if he had indeed been the driver and left the scene. He had already pleaded guilty and had been sentenced for that crime. Instead, they were specifically looking for signs of intoxication, reckless or negligent driving or any purposeful harm to the girl on the part of Senator Kennedy. In the process, some very interesting facts turned up which were not pursued because they were not relevant to whether or not Kennedy was guilty of additional crimes. For instance, the exact time of the accident was not investigated vigorously because it would not alter the fact that he says he drove off the bridge and failed to report the accident.

Judge Boyle found no evidence whatsoever of foul play, and nothing that would indicate drunk driving.

However, he did not let Kennedy off the hook completely. The judge concluded his report by saying,

"I, therefore find there is probable cause to believe that Edward M. Kennedy operated his motor vehicle negligently on a way or in a place to which the public have a right of access and that such operation appears to have contributed to the death of Mary Jo Kopechne."

Needless to say, Kennedy was unhappy with the judge's conclusion. The Senator's friends and lawyers have expressed bitterness over the fact that the judge declared Kennedy to have been driving negligently, but no charges were ever filed against him — so Kennedy never had the opportunity to disprove the accusation, which was published world wide. As mentioned earlier, had such charges been brought, they certainly would *not* have been proved, for the evidence was very weak. Judge Boyle and the prosecutor were well aware of this fact, which is probably why the finding was left hanging.

Be that as it may, negligent driving is the worst finding that came out of the grand jury investigation, exhumation hearing and the four-day-long inquest — and that is a shaky conclusion at best.

The testimony concerning the cause of death leaves little question that Mary Jo did indeed drown. The following is the testimony of Dr. Ronald R. Mills, the Associate Medical Examiner for the County, who examined the body at the scene of the accident.

Q. Now, you say you made an examination of this body at the scene. Could you tell us exactly what you did, just for the record?

A. Sure, I would be glad to. I pulled back the blankets and saw the body fully dressed, **appropriately dressed,** of an attractive woman. I would say in her twenties, blonde, hair swept back, wearing some bracelets on her right wrist and arm. I believe there was a ring. She was in complete total rigor mortis.

Q. Did you find any external marks on the body?

A. No.

Q. You found **no incised wounds?**

A. No.

Q. **No other bruises?**

A. No.

Q. Did you receive instructions to take a blood sample?

A. Yes, thank you, I did.

Q. From Lieutenant Killen?

A. Yes, from Lieutenant Killen.

Q. And you related these instructions to the —

A. To the mortician.

THE COURT: Expert evidence already introduced has indicated that the white blouse was subjected to chemical analysis and shows evidence of blood.

THE WITNESS: Yes.

THE COURT: Now, assuming that the white blouse was the one worn by the decedent at the time you examined her, are you able to express a medical opinion with reasonable certainty whether the presence of that blood is consistent with your diagnosis of death by drowning?

THE WITNESS: Yes.

THE COURT: And what is that opinion, that it is consistent or that it is not consistent?

THE WITNESS: That it is consistent.

THE COURT: With your diagnosis?

THE WITNESS: With my diagnosis of death by drowning.

Q. Could you explain to the Court the reasons why you formed that opinion?

A. In a drowning case when a person drowns there is what we call an exacerbation of blood or a putting out of blood from the lungs in the violent attempts to gain air, and blood may and I believe usually perhaps more often than not, may be evidenced in the mouth and the nose of the decedent. Such blood might, in the efforts, the physical efforts to avoid drowning, might spread I suppose almost anywhere to the person's clothing.

Q. Are you able, Doctor, to render an opinion as to how much blood normally is released from this kind of death?

A. A very small amount. I mean, less than half a cupful, for example.

Eugene Frieh, the mortician who prepared the body for burial was also called to testify;

Q. In your preparation of the body, did you notice any external signs or marks or bruises or what did you observe?

A. Well, I assisted my own assistant in cleansing the body, soaping the body down with a germicidal soap and taking the spray and washing the body and I personally took charge of cleansing the hair which was impregnated with much salt water and a little seaweedage and things of that sort that we usually find on a decedent, and in so doing I thoroughly examined the scalp and manipulated it in my fingers to see if there were any fractures, feeling in my own mind going over a bridge of that sort and crashing there might be some fractures, but I didn't find any fractures.

Q. In any event you saw no marks or bruises or anything?

A. **The only bruising I saw was on the left knuckle. That was very slight. We call that a slight abrasion, that is all.**

145

Many people at the scene of the accident, including three police officers, saw the body. All were in agreement that they saw nothing which indicated violence. The body was still neatly dressed and unmarked by injury.

Mr. John J. McHugh, the State Police Chemist who did the analysis of the blood sample and tested the clothing, was called to testify. He tested the clothing for blood and got a positive reading off of the blouse.

A. . . . gross examination of this item under visible and ultraviolet light disclosed the presence of **reddish brown and brown washed-out stains** principally on the back and left sleeve surfaces. Most of these stains gave positive benzidine reaction indicating the presence of residual traces of blood . . . All of the tests on the rest of the submitted clothing were negative.

* * *

Q. All right. Now, Mr. McHugh, did you also perform a blood test or test with reference to certain items of blood that were received?

A. Yes, I did.

Q. And could you tell the Court what tests you performed on the blood sample received by you?

A. Yes, the sample is enclosed in here. There were a series of four tests run on this blood. Let's see if I might — the ethyl alcohol, carbon monoxide, barbiturate, and organic basis . . . the level of **ethyl alcohol in the blood was 0.09%.** The carbon monoxide content was less than 5%. That means, generally speaking it was negative, but, however, it is very hard to determine low amounts of carbon monoxide; but generally speaking anything below 5% would be considered negative. **The barbiturate was negative.** Anything along the line of sleeping pills. **The organic basis, there were none detected.** That would be amphetamines and that type of material. Those tests were negative.

THE COURT: I might ask, what is the purpose of determining the carbon monoxide in the blood?

THE WITNESS: Oh, to find if a person has been in any manner affected by significant amounts of carbon monoxide. The purpose of the carbon monoxide level is to find out if the person has been or the blood has been in any way affected by carbon monoxide of significant quantities. It is determined in automobile accidents to find if there was any possibility of carbon monoxide having affected the person's driving ability or passengerwise or have anything to do with the cause of death. In this specific case less than 5% means relatively speaking it is negative. It would have to be significant percentage to mean anything material.

THE COURT: Is that for instance, what one would get from a desire to commit suicide and turn on the motor and sat in the car and ran a tube up into the car, is that carbon monoxide?

THE WITNESS: That is right, sir, and if you wish, I can give you the level. There would be 70 to 80 per cent usually, unless the person has physical weakness.

THE COURT: How is carbon monoxide related to death by drowning in an automobile?

THE WITNESS: A death related to drowning in an automobile, we always run carbon monoxide to make sure the person has been all right prior to the death in the water.

THE COURT: There is no relation to drowning as such itself?

THE WITNESS: No, sir, there is not.

The possibility of foul play from outside sources was investigated also. George Kennedy, the supervisor of the Motor Vehicle Department, checked the car carefully and testified, "Immediately we checked the foot pedal of the car to see if the brakes were still serviceable, and they were."

Even though the court failed to turn up any evidence of foul play, Kennedy's enemies refused to give up. They immediately pounced upon the fact that traces of blood were found on the blouse and boldly proclaimed that Dr. Mills had been bought off by Kennedy to make it appear that the presence of blood was acceptable. Such an accusation is ridiculous. Dr. Mills was merely repeating a fact that is well known to the rest of the medical profession and was readily backed up by other physicians familiar with drowning cases. Both Dr. Werner Spitz, deputy chief medical examiner for the State of Maryland, and Dr. Henry C. Friemuth verified Dr. Mills' diagnosis at the hearing for the exhumation of the body. The following is an excerpt from Judge Brominski's opinion:

"Turning to the testimony of Dr. Werner Spitz, the pathologist testifying for the respondents, while his colleagues in his field did not attach particular significance to pinkish foam about the nose and mouth in drowning cases, he explained that when water enters the lungs under pressure, particularly salt water, the rupture gives the foam a pinkish appearance. Then when resuscitation stops, foam develops and being lighter than water, comes up. While there may be difference of opinion among pathologists, it would be illogical for this court not to accept that which is a logical explanation in view of all the attending circumstances. In addition, Dr. Spitz gave the only explanation as to the presence of blood on the back of the blouse of the deceased. He stated that when this pinkish foam begins to form, it runs down the face along the neck and makes a puddle behind the head and hence the blood on the back of the blouse. **He said he couldn't imagine a drowning victim looking any different.** He concedes that he would have liked to have had an autopsy when the body was first removed from the water, but that **an exhumation and autopsy would be of academic importance and added that, in his opinion, within medical certainty, Mary Jo Kopechne died from drowning.**

"The testimony of Dr. Henry C. Friemuth, a toxicologist, lends verity to the testimony of Drs. Mills and Spitz in that **the stains on the blouse of the decedent were characteristic of the stains produced by pinkish foam from drowning victims.**"

Dr. Arthur C. Guyton, author of the medical text, *Textbook of Medical Physiology,* states:

"If a drowning person inhales salt water instead of fresh water, osmosis of water occurs in the opposite direction (from the blood vessels into the lungs) through the pulmonary membrane because the crystalloid osmotic pressure of salt water is several times that of blood. Loss of water out of the blood causes marked hemoconcentration but not hemolysis or cardiac fibrillation. Instead, the person dies of asphyxia in five to eight minutes."

To explain this, if there is salt water in the lungs, the salt pulls the water out of the blood vessels lining the lungs. That, coupled with the dialation of the vessels in their attempt to absorb oxygen and ruptures of delicate membranes coming in contact with salt water, would cause blood to flow out of the circulatory system and into the lungs, hence the presence of blood in the water and froth expelled from the lungs. Since there was at least some salt water in the girl's lungs, there had to have been blood in the water and foam forced out during the examination.

It is obvious from the location of the blood stains on the blouse that the bloody water and foam which was expelled when Dr. Mills pressed on her chest, ran out of her mouth and nose, down her neck and onto the back of the blouse and sleeve, the only logical place for it to go.

Tedrow and Tedrow, in their book, *Death at Chappaquiddick,* actually declared the blood stains to be grass stains which they say proves that Kennedy and Mary Jo had been playing around before the accident. The Tedrows base this ridiculous assumption on the fact that green leaves and ordinary grass will give positive reactions to a benzidine test. Aside from the fact that a qualified State Police Chemist, John McHugh, testified that he was aware other substances would react so he performed the test in such a way there could be no doubt but that the stains were blood, the stains on the blouse were officially described as "reddish-brown, washed-out stains." It should be obvious to anyone that grass stains are not reddish-brown. This in itself demonstrates the validity of the Tedrows' book.

Even though the police lab tested for and found *no* seminal fluid on her clothing, much was made of the fact that it was never absolutely determined by examination of the body whether or not Mary Jo had intercourse or was pregnant. The court was not concerned with the question because such a finding would have had no bearing on the investigation or on the ultimate ruling. Even though the public was clamoring to know, it was none of the public's business. When the court refused to pursue the issue, a cry of outrage went up. Speculation was that if Mary Jo was pregnant, perhaps she was trying to blackmail Kennedy and he killed her to prevent her from talking. Kennedy would have been much better off if an autopsy had been performed because it would have put a stop to such cruel stories. Even then, a few die-hards would have said he paid off the medical examiner too.

The idea that Mary Jo might have been trying to blackmail Kennedy is preposterous. First, there was no external sign that she was pregnant. Second, even though the press investigated zealously, no evidence was turned up that Kennedy ever had any sort of private relationship with the girl. Third, it was well

149

known that Mary Jo was an extremely loyal Kennedy supporter, which is why she was at the party. Fourth, it would have been smarter and considerably less dangerous to buy her off. Fifth, driving a perfectly healthy young girl off a bridge is not a sure-fire way to do her in. Not even a mafia leader being blackmailed would finish the girl off personally in his own car. To suggest that Kennedy would, shows faulty reasoning and demonstrates the unfeeling and ghoulish use of a tragic accident by those who can gain from it.

At the exhumation hearing, Dr. Spitz also showed that Mary Jo had to have been very much alive when the car left the bridge.

> Dr. Spitz: That foam is the combination of water and protein that is being shaken, and the shaking action is the breathing action.
> D.A. (Dinis): So she breathed?
> Dr. Spitz: That girl, she breathed.
> D.A. (Dinis): She was not dead instantaneously?
> Dr. Spitz: That can be eliminated. **You won't find a case of instantaneous death, whether you exhume or you don't.**

There is no question that Mary Jo was alive and well at the time of the accident. She had to have lived a short time or she could not have assumed the position in which she was found. There is no way that she could have been put into that position prior to the car turning over. That the mishap and subsequent death of Mary Jo was anything but accidental is inconsistent with the evidence and can be discounted.

CHAPTER XVI

WAS KENNEDY, MARKHAM
OR GARGAN INJURED
IN THE RESCUE ATTEMPT?

The car involved was badly damaged by the fall off the bridge. The windows were smashed, the roof was caved in and the doors were buckled. It had to have hit the water with great impact. Mr. Frieh, the mortician, testified that he purposely examined Miss Kopechne for fractures because he expected to find some due to the severity of the crash. If Kennedy was in the car during the accident, it is unlikely that he would have escaped unscratched, especially since his back is very easily injured.

Kennedy does claim to have been hurt in the accident. Upon his return to Hyannisport, he was examined by the family physician, Dr. Robert Watt of Hyannis, who told reporters that Senator Kennedy had "a possible concussion and an acute cervical strain. His back condition, chronic since he suffered a spinal fracture in an airplane crash, was aggravated. I had him on an oral muscle relaxant, heat, and bed rest. He was in bed all weekend, and I had to put a neck collar on him to get him up Monday."

At the inquest, X-rays along with an affidavit from Dr. Watt, and a certificate from Dr. Milton F. Brougham, who examined Kennedy on July 22, 1969, were submitted.

Affidavit of Doctor Robert D. Watt (read by the D. A.):

On July 19, 1969, I was called to see Edward M. Kennedy at his home. His chief complaints were headache, neck pain, generalized stiffness and soreness.

The history of the present illness was as follows: He stated that he had been in an automobile accident last night on Martha's Vineyard.

The car went off a bridge. There is a lapse in his memory between hitting the bridge and coming to under water and struggling to get out. There was a loss of orientation — at the last moment he grabbed the side of an open window and pulled himself out. He was not clear on the events following but he remembered diving repeatedly to check for a passenger — without success. He went for help and returned. Again, effort to rescue passenger was without success. He was driven to the ferry slip and swam to the main body of land. He went to his hotel where he slept fitfully until 7 a.m.

Diagnosis: Concussion, contusions and abrasions of the scalp, acute cervical strain. The contusion of the vertex was demonstrated by tenderness and a spongy swelling at the top of his head. The abrasion over the right mastoid was obvious. The acute cervical strain was substantiated by X-ray studies which showed a loss of the normal cervical lordosis, which was due to spasm of the cervical musculature. The diagnosis of concussion was predicated upon the foregoing objective evidence of injury and the history of the temporary loss of consciousness and retrograde amnesia. Impairment of judgment, and confused behavior are symptoms consistent with an injury of the character sustained by the patient.

Certificate from Dr. Milton F. Brougham, chief of neurosurgery at the Faulkner Hospital, the Carney Hospital, the Jordan Hospital and the Cape Cod Hospital:
July 22, 1969   KENNEDY, Senator Edward

This patient was given a neurological examination in the presence of Dr. Robert Watt as a result of injuries which he sustained in an automobile accident which occurred on July 18, 1969. In describing his recollection of the events occurring at this time, he states that he can recall driving down a road and onto a bridge, and has some recollection of the car starting off the bridge which he thinks was a realization that the car struck a beam along the side of the bridge; however, he remembers nothing immediately following this; has no recollection of the car turning over or any impact of the car against water or any solid object. There is a gap in his memory of indeterminable length, but presumably brief and his next recollection is of being in the front seat of his car which was filling with water. He somehow escaped from the car, but does not know how he did this. He states further that he can recall making repeated efforts to get back to the car by diving. Subsequent events are recalled in a somewhat fragmentary fashion with an impaired recall of their exact time relationships.

Diagnosis: Cerebral concussion. Contusions and abrasion of scalp. Acute Cervical Strain.

Comment: This patient gives a history of loss of consciousness and retrograde amnesia sustained at the time of his accident, and the occurrence of the head injury is corroborated by the contusions of the scalp over the vertex and in the right mastoid area ... Examination of the scalp reveals a zone of tenderness approximately 3 c.m. in diameter.

At the time of this examination, the patient is alert and fully oriented.

Milton F. Brougham, M.D.

Judge Boyle summed up the two medical opinions as follows:

"Drs. Watt and Brougham examined Kennedy on July 19 and 22. Diagnostic opinion was 'concussion, contusions and abrasions of the scalp, acute cervical strain. Impairment of judgment and confused behavior are consistent with this type of injury.'"

It is interesting to note that Kennedy did not submit these doctor reports at the hearing where he pleaded guilty to the leaving the scene charge. They could have provided very solid grounds for a "not guilty" finding.

Dr. Brougham's examination was made three days after the accident. At that time the "zone of tenderness" was 3 c.m. or about 1 inch in diameter where Kennedy apparently hit the top of his head. It does not appear that the injury itself was very severe, however, there are a great many factors such as the location of the injury and the surface area that made contact, which would have had a bearing on the effect of the injury on the thinking process. Such an injury coupled with the trauma of the accident itself might very well have produced a state of shock. *Time* magazine went into the question of whether or not Kennedy was in shock in its August 1, 1969 edition.

"Questioned by *Time,* the three experts said, however, that Kennedy's behavior was not unusual for a person who had suffered such an experience. By simple definition, shock causes a person to dissociate himself temporarily from threatening circumstances. Subconsciously seeking the protective company of those he knew, Kennedy might thus have passed up nearby houses that could have offered help for the more certain, if more distant safety of his friends. 'No one knows what his own breaking point is,' says Dr. Max Sandove, professor at the University of Illinois Medical School. 'It is different at different times for different people.' Nevertheless, it remains somewhat difficult to accept the thought that Kennedy's state of shock could have allowed him the rational move of calling on his friends for help and giving them various instructions but would have prevented him from making the equally rational move of instructing them to call the police."

Kennedy himself did not emphasize his injury once it had been brought to the court's attention through the statements of the two doctors. One of the few times that he referred to the fact that he was injured was when describing his return to his motel. "... at this time I was very conscious of a throbbing headache, of pains in my neck, of strain on my back, but what I was even more conscious of is the tragedy and loss of a very devoted friend."

Kennedy is not the only one who says he sustained an injury that night. Both Mr. Gargan and Mr. Markham insist that they hurt themselves during the rescue attempt. Kennedy noted that, "Mr. Gargan got half-way in the car. When he came out he was scraped all the way from his elbow, underneath his arm was all bruised and bloodied ..."

The prosecutor asked Mr. Gargan if he did hurt himself.

Q. You didn't sustain any injuries?
A. I did.
Q. What injuries did you sustain?
A. My chest, my arm and my back was badly scraped.

Mr. Markham also claimed injury:

"I had banged my leg again. I had hurt my leg coming over the day before. That was one of the reasons I didn't sail that day."

The problem with everyone's injuries is that Kennedy, Markham and Gargan are the only ones who noticed they were hurt. By the time the court was in a position to question the injuries, six months had elapsed, which gave everyone time to completely recover — so we have only their words to go by. Charlie Tretter did comment on Markham's leg, "I asked him how he slept and I said 'I slept very badly on the floor, how did you sleep?' He said, 'I slept terribly, my knee bothered me.'"

The District Attorney asked Tretter specifically what he knew about the Senator's injuries.

Q. Did anyone or did Mr. Gargan mention anything about any injuries or the condition of the Senator?
A. Other than describing his condition of the night before, no.

The District Attorney carefully questioned Ross Richards who had gone for a walk and visited with Kennedy the morning after the accident.

Q. (by Mr. Fernandes) Now, what observations, if any, did you make of the Senator at this time as to any injuries, his appearance or attitude?
A. I didn't notice anything out of the ordinary.
Q. You noticed nothing out of the ordinary in his speech?
A. In his speech, no.
Q. In appearance?
A. In appearance, no.

155

Esther Newberg, who attended the Chappaquiddick party, was questioned about her observation of Joe Gargan the following morning.

Q. During any of the time that you have described, did you observe any injuries that he had received?
A. No.
Q. Was there any mention by anyone that he had received injuries anywhere in any manner at that time?
A. No.

The supervisor of the Motor Vehicle Department, George Kennedy, was very sure of what he saw.

Q. (by Mr. Fernandes) All right, now we are back at the police station. Now, you saw Mr. Markham and Mr. Gargan were there. Did you have occasion to observe these two men?
A. I did.
Q. Were you in close proximity to Mr. Gargan?
A. I was.
Q. Would you tell us what he was wearing as you best remember?
A. He was wearing a chino pair of pants and a short sleeved T-shirt sport shirt.
Q. Did you have occasion to see his arms?
A. I did.
Q. Did you observe any marks?
A. I did not.
Q. Did you have occasion to watch them walk and move around?
A. I did.
Q. Did you make any observations as to limping or any sign of injury on anyone?
A. No limping on anybody.

The ferry operator, Richard P. Hewitt, who gave Kennedy, Gargan and Markham a ride to and from Chappaquiddick the morning following the accident, was questioned.

Q. Do you recall whether or not any of them appeared to be injured in any way?
A. I didn't notice anything that would make me think that they were injured.

Police Chief Jim Arena didn't help Kennedy in this respect either.

Q. In your observation of Mr. Kennedy, did you make note of any injuries or bruises?
A. No injuries. He just appeared to be very depressed mentally, but **I noticed no physical injuries.**
Q. To Mr. Markham?
A. No, sir.
Q. To Mr. Gargan?
A. No, sir.

Even the Kennedy's employee Nance Lyons who attended the party, couldn't support the injury claims.

Q. Did you make any observation with reference to injuries?

A. When Mr. Gargan came to pick us up?

Q. At any time?

A. No, sir.

It is interesting that even the Senator's friends said they saw no signs of injury on any of the three. Failure to support Kennedy, Markham and Gargan on this point hurt their credibility with many people.

The only person who seems to have noticed Mr. Gargan's injury was Rita Dallas, who observed him the next day at Hyannisport and wrote in her book *The Kennedy Case:*

"The next afternoon Joe Gargan was at the house talking with his sister, and I noticed he was moving his arm rather stiffly. It was especially noticeable, for he was wearing a long-sleeved shirt, something seldom seen around the Cape. When I asked him what was wrong, he raised his brows and said, 'Oh, haven't you heard? I scraped it trying to save Mary Jo.'"

In view of the fact that virtually no one noticed Senator Kennedy acting stiff and sore, it is hard to believe that he suffered so severe an injury that he was bed ridden for two days and forced to wear a neck collar for his strain. He is either unbelievably tough and able to tolerate a great deal of pain, or he wasn't injured as badly as his doctors seemed to think he was. A slight cut and bruise less than an inch across on a Kennedy is hardly unusual. The entire clan is known for its roughhousing and Ted Kennedy is one of the most rambunctious. James MacGregor Burns related a college day incident involving John Tunney:

"One day between classes he and Tunney were tossing a football around when Kennedy had a new idea, 'Let's play tackle'. When the boxer's son took the toss and tried to make a run around Kennedy, he was hit by a flying tackle. 'I couldn't believe it,' Tunney said.

'There we were in our street clothes, with no padding, supposed to be doing full tackles on each other!' "

Such behavior was not the least bit unusual for Ted Kennedy. It is true that the 1964 airplane crash slowed him down, but by 1969 he had made great progress and was able to participate more actively in his favorite games. He'd spent the day running around with his buddies, especially Joe Gargan who, being a Kennedy cousin and raised with Ted, is also disposed toward the rougher side of play. Kennedy had been swimming and sailing and had enjoyed a rather loud party. It is not beyond the realm of possibility that he could have been injured somewhere other than in the accident. A likely place to have hit the top of his head is on the boom which controls the sail and which would have swung over him to catch the wind as he manned the tiller. Kennedy has had plenty of experience with injuries and knows how to act when hurt. It would not have been difficult for him to convince an agreeable doctor that he was more seriously injured than he actually was.

Ted Kennedy standing on his sailboat Victura. (Edith Blake, Black Star)

CHAPTER XVII

WHAT DID GARGAN AND MARKHAM TELL THE OTHER PEOPLE AT THE PARTY AFTER THE ACCIDENT?

Perhaps one of the strangest actions taken by Markham and Gargan was that they didn't tell anyone at the party about the accident even though one of the girls was Mary Jo's roommate and all were her close friends. Kennedy testified that they were merely doing what he told them to do.

Q. Now, Senator, in that televised broadcast, you said and I quote, "I instructed Gargan and Markham not to alarm Mary Jo's friends that night," is that correct?

A. That is correct.

Q. Can you tell the Court what prompted you to give this instruction to Markham and Gargan?

A. I felt strongly that if those girls were notified that an accident had taken place and that Mary Jo had in fact drowned, which I became convinced of by the time that Markham and Gargan and I left the scene of the accident, that it would only be a matter of seconds before all of those girls who were long and dear friends of Mary Jo's to go to the scene of the accident and dive themselves and enter the water with, I felt, a good chance that some serious mishap might have occurred to any one of them. It was for that reason that I refrained — asked Mr. Gargan and Mr. Markham not to alarm the girls.

Both Mr. Markham and Mr. Gargan agreed that this was the only reason they did not inform the other party members. It is rather amazing that Kennedy who was "overcome by a jumble of emotions: grief, fear, doubt, exhaustion, panic, confusion and shock", to use the Senator's own words, would even think about what was going to be said to the other party members, much less worry about their reaction to it. What Gargan and Markham told their waiting friends is also very odd. The judge questioned Charlie Tretter about everyone's reaction when Markham and Gargan returned.

THE COURT: Was there any unusual excitement when you got back to the cottage and found them all there?

THE WITNESS: No, I think it was just aggravation.

THE COURT: No indication that anything unusual had happened?

THE WITNESS: No.

THE COURT: Nothing said about anything unusual happening?

THE WITNESS: No.

Judge Boyle thought it was very strange that no one at the party was informed of the accident and pressed Esther Newberg about it.

THE COURT: Your original plan was to stay together. Suddenly you are left without transportation on an island and none of you girls said anything to each other?

THE WITNESS: We all wanted to go back that night.

THE COURT: None of you said, "What happened, what caused this; this isn't the plan?"

THE WITNESS: We wondered where Miss Kopechne was. We wondered where everyone was, but we made assumptions. In retrospect we were wrong. She was not back at the motel. We assumed that she was. We assumed the Senator was at the Shiretown Inn.

THE COURT: And you thought the other two men had gone back and deserted you?

THE WITNESS: It wasn't a question of desertion. We were on the island with two friends.

THE COURT: Well, you could think of no reason why the two men should leave you and take the last transportation available without saying a single word to you, not even a by-your-leave, didn't excite you at all, didn't seem to be at all unusual?

THE WITNESS: (No response)

THE COURT: I have no further questions.

Q. (by Mr. Fernandes) They have come back. Meantime, while they have gone, you wondered about where they went?

A. That is right.

Q. Mr. Markham sits on your leg or sits on a couch where you are or somehow you are injured or hurting and you ask him to get up. In the meantime, he says to you, if you knew what I have been in, you would let me lie down or words to that effect. Now, nothing was said after that; nothing was followed through in the light of the thoughts that you had in your mind before they returned?

A. Nobody volunteered any information. We may have questioned or may have said, what do you mean, Mr. Markham, or Paul, and nothing was volunteered at this time.

Q. No one asked?

A. No, and later in the other room **when Mr. Gargan said that the Senator swam across, it was almost as if we didn't need to know.** By that time we couldn't get off the island anyway, and we **assumed that Mary Jo was back in that motel room.**

160

Maryellen Lyons testified:

Q. Did they tell you more? Did you ask them any questions about this particular episode of the Senator going back and swimming back to Edgartown?

A. We, you know, when they arrived, we asked them, you know, where they had been; what had happened. Oh, it was just, oh, **don't even ask us, we have been looking for boats.** It was confused.

Q. That they had been looking for boats, they said that?

A. That was one of the things they said, and that somebody else said that **Miss Kopechne was back at Katama Shores and that the Senator was back at Edgartown.**

Q. Now, who said that Miss Kopechne was back at Katama Shores?

A. I believe it was **Mr. Gargan.**

Q. Mr. Gargan told you that Mary Jo was back at Katama. Did he say how she got there?

A. I assumed that — I can't remember that whether he said it, that **she made the last ferry.**

Q. That she had made the last ferry. Did you ask why the Senator decided to dive in or swim across the channel?

A. No, I didn't.

Q. Did anyone ask that at all?

A. No.

Q. Wasn't there any one conversation about that behavior?

A. Well, no one was concerned really about anything. When they got back, **we thought they had been stuck in the sand,** and where have you been, and that was about the size of it. It was confusing.

Q. Did anyone ask where the Senator's car was?

A. Well, **Mary Jo had taken the car on the last ferry.**

Q. Mary Jo had taken the car on the last ferry, and who told you that; was it Mr. Gargan?

A. Yes, as I remember, it was Mr. Gargan.

Maryellen's sister, Nance Lyons, backed up Maryellen's testimony.

Q. What did he (Mr. Gargan) say?

A. I don't recall the conversation. I can recall what I said. The first was, you know, it is late and you have to sail in the morning, let's, you know, let's get some sleep; and then I asked Mr. Gargan where Miss Kopechne was.

Q. What did he say?

A. **He told me she was at the Katama Shores.**

Q. Did you ask where Mr. Kennedy was?

A. He said he also had returned to his hotel — I am trying to recall — I think they stated that they had gone with the Senator to the ferry and the ferry wasn't there and the Senator had swam across.

Q. Did anyone say, where is the car?

A. Yes.

Q. Who?

A. I don't recall if it was myself or my sister.

Q. And what was the response?

A. That **Miss Kopechne had taken the car to the Katama Shores.**

Rosemary Keough testified that she asked Mr. Gargan about the Senator and Mary Jo.

Q. Now, had you heard any conversation concerning the whereabouts of Mary Jo or Senator Kennedy?

A. I did ask Mr. Gargan.

Q. And what did he tell you?

A. He said that not to worry about it, that Mary Jo and the Senator had probably taken the ferry.

Susan Tananbaum remembers observing Mr. Markham that evening.

A. I overheard Mr. Markham say he was very tired.

Q. I see. To whom did he say this?

A. I think he said this to Miss Newberg and to me.

Q. Did he give you any reason as to why he was tired?

A. No.

Q. What was his appearance? Was he excited?

A. **No, he seemed tired.**

Q. Just tired?

A. Yes.

In the morning, Markham and Gargan still weren't talking. They gave Charlie Tretter, Rosemary Keough and Susan Tananbaum a ride to the Shiretown Inn, but nothing was said about the accident. Later, about 9:00 a.m., Mr. Gargan returned to the cottage and, for the first time, told everyone that something had happened, yet he still didn't tell them that Mary Jo was dead, Nance Lyons testified,

Q. I take it you were walking back to the ferry?

A. We had waited a significant amount of time and begun to head toward the ferry.

Q. Did anyone ask him why he was taking you back to the cottage?

A. Yes.

Q. What was the conversation at this time, as best you can remember it, between all parties?

A. Well, I can only relate my reaction at the time and I knew that **looking at Mr. Gargan's face I knew that something was wrong** and I said, "Is something wrong?" and he said, "Yes, get in the car." And we got in the car and we all began asking, "What happened, what is wrong." and he said, "There has been an accident," and someone asked if the Senator had been hurt and he said, "No", and at that point I knew that something had happened to Mary Jo.

Q. When you returned to the cottage, what was said at that time?

A. We arrived at the cottage. We were all pressing Mr. Gargan, asking what had happened, and he asked us to go inside and sit down and he said that there had been an automobile accident and **Miss Kopechne was missing.**

Q. Did you say how he knew that she was missing?

A. It is all rather vague and it is sort of jumbled.

Q. Well, did anyone ask these questions?

A. I think they were asked, but I can't recall where or when they were asked because then we drove back to the Katama Shores and conversation continued during the car ride.

Q. What was the conversation as you best remember?

A. Just, you know, what had happened, where was the accident what had been done about it, had the Coast Guard been called, these kinds of questions.

Q. What was the answer?

A. I don't know. **Mr. Gargan kept repeating that he had no details.**

Nance Lyons also noticed a marked change in Mr. Gargan's behavior between the night before at 2:30 a.m. and the next morning at 9:00 a.m.

A. Well, **it was fairly obvious when he came to pick us up in the morning that something had transpired by the expression on his face.**

Q. You say it was fairly obvious when he came back to pick you up that morning that something had occurred?

A. Yes, sir.

Q. When you saw him or had that conversation with him that night when he returned from trying to get a boat, did you make any observations about him?

A. No, sir. **In retrospect I could compare the two and say that it appeared when he returned that he had no knowledge of what had actually transpired.**

Q. And you felt something was wrong by what observations or what appearances or what in fact made you conclude that something was wrong?

A. When he returned in the morning?

Q. Other than what he said, yes.

A. Just his face.

Maryellen's memory of the following morning was similar.

Q. When Mr. Gargan was asked about what happened, what did he say?

A. **He just said that he didn't know. He just said that there was an accident and she was missing.**

Q. And when did you learn that Mary Jo had died?

A. I think pretty soon after we got back to Katama Shores.

Q. And who told you?

A. I believe it was Mr. Gargan.

Q. Didn't Mr. Gargan, at Katama Shores after you arrived and went into Mary Jo's room, didn't he take you aside and tell you what happened?

A. He didn't come back with us to Katama Shores originally. He drove us to the ferry and we took the ferry over and took a cab from the other side back to Katama Shores and we were there, you know, by ourselves.

Q. Was there any conversation on the boat (home) about what happened?

A. Well, we didn't know what had happened. This was the big thing and at that time I felt — **I didn't know that Mr. Gargan and Mr. Markham had been at the scene until just prior to the Senator's address on television because Mr. Markham and Mr. Gargan came back to the cottage and appeared very normal.** Nothing was wrong. You know, we didn't, we weren't asking anything because there was no reason to ask anything. We didn't know anything had happened. We didn't know until the next day.

Q. Now, you say just prior to the Senator's TV address that you learned that Markham — Mr. Markham and Mr. Gargan were, had been at the scene; that is, the Dike Bridge?

A. Yes.

Q. Who told you?

A. Mr. Hackett, David Hackett, who worked with us in the campaign. He ran the boiler room as they call it.

Q. What did he say to you? What exactly did he say to you, Mr. Hackett?

A. We were on the Cape at our summer house and he came over I think before the address was going to be on to inform us of what it was going to be and he just thought we might like to know.

Q. Did you ever speak to Senator Kennedy about the accident?

A. No, I did not.

Nance and Maryellen weren't the only ones who didn't know that Markham and Gargan had been to the bridge. No one did. Not even Police Chief Arena was told.

Q. Mr. Kennedy never told you how the car went over the bridge?

A. No, he didn't; no, sir.

Q. Did he tell you that he had spent some time trying to remove the body?

Q. If I recall the statement, it was only — the only thing he even mentioned about the accident other than to say he was the driver, was in the statement.

Q. Did either Mr. Markham or Mr. Gargan indicate they, too, were at the scene?

A. **They never said anything that day, no, sir.**

164

Markham tried to explain the fact that they were not mentioned in the original story by saying:

"The Senator, that morning, I think when we were at the telephone booth or sometime that morning before we went to the station, he told us, he said, "Look, I don't want you people put in the middle on this thing. I'm not going to involve you. As far as you know, you didn't know anything about the accident that night.""

Shiretown Inn where Senator Kennedy and Joe Gargan were staying during the 1969 Edgartown Regatta. (UPI)

Paul Markham, Senator Edward Kennedy's close friend, who attended the cook-out and left the cottage to assist Kennedy after the accident, arriving at Woods Hole to board the ferry for Martha's Vineyard. (January 1970, Wide World Photo)

Joe Gargan, Senator Ted Kennedy's cousin, who put on the reunion cook-out and supported Kennedy's inquest testimony, on his way to Dukes County Court House, January 1970. (Dennis Brack, Black Star)

CHAPTER XVIII

WHAT DID KENNEDY DO THE FOLLOWING MORNING BEFORE HE REPORTED THE ACCIDENT TO THE POLICE?

Kennedy's behavior the morning after the accident was very odd for a person who knew one of his friends was dead in his car at the bottom of Poucha Pond. He got up around 7:30 a.m. and went for a short walk. He met Ross Richards and Stanley Moore, walked back to the motel with them and sat visiting on the balcony for a half an hour, giving all indication he intended to race that day. Kennedy recalls the conversation, "Mr. Moore was relating about how, I believe, some members of his crew were having difficulty with their housing arrangements."

The prosecutor questioned Mr. Richards in depth about Kennedy's activities that morning.

Q. What was the conversation at this time?

A. It was about the prior race the day before. I happened to win the race and he congratulated me on it and we discussed that back and forth for maybe ten or fifteen minutes.

Q. So, you walked and discussed this matter and then you went up to the porch or deck which is adjoining both rooms and you also discussed this?

A. Right.

Q. How long would you say you were in his company all told?

A. It was until 8:00 o'clock.

Q. So, would it be safe to say approximately half an hour?

A. Half an hour.

Q. And within this time you had conversation with him?

A. Yes.

Q. About the races and anything else?

A. And the weather. It was a nice day.

Q. Was there any discussion about Chappaquiddick Island?

A. There wasn't a word mentioned of Chappaquiddick.

Q. Were you joined by anyone during this conversation?

A. Stanley Moore followed behind us and he was sitting on the porch with us.

Q. Now, did anyone else join or come onto the deck during that time?

A. My wife came out around 7:50. She came out of our room. She heard us talking out there and we were about to go to breakfast, so she came out and sat for five or ten minutes.

Q. Did anyone else come?

A. No, sir.

Q. Were you ever joined or see Mr. Markham or Mr. Gargan that morning?

A. Mr. Markham, Mr. Gargan, I remember the bell at 8:00 o'clock, it rang and we asked the Senator if he would like to have breakfast with us and he said, no, he wouldn't, but **he may join us later,** and at that time Mr. Markham and Mr. Gargan —

Q. May I stop you?

A. Yes.

Q. You said the Senator discussed the possibility of joining you at breakfast later?

A. Later.

Q. And could you please describe to the Court what observations you made of these two gentlemen at this time?

A. Oh, **they were ruffled looking.** I would say **they looked damp.** Their hair hadn't been combed in some time.

Q. What happened when they came up on the deck?

A. They went directly to the Senator's room and opened the door and he followed them into the room.

After Kennedy, Markham and Gargan retired to the room, Charlie Tretter, who had come over with Gargan and Markham and then gone his own way, returned and visited them briefly. Charlie Tretter testified:

Q. And do you know what time you arrived at the Senator's room?

A. **Sometime between 8:00 and 8:30,** I guess.

Q. And what did you do there?

A. Well, I knocked on the door, knocked, looked in the window, and the Senator was sitting in such a position that he was, here to his right would be the window and I was looking in the window and I thought he motioned me in, not by his hand or anything, I just thought from his eyes he said, come in. I walked into the room and closed the door behind me and there was no conversation between the three and the Senator looked at me and said something to the effect of, this is going to be a private thing. Do you mind?

Q. How did he appear to you?

A. Well, I thought there was something bothering him because I was a little angry myself, having worked for him long enough, I thought I recognized the sign to come into the room and then when I got into the room, I was almost instantaneously told to get out in so many words and I

168

thought there was something wrong, but I thought he was angry or disturbed, but I didn't know whether it was at me for interfering with the conversation or what.

About 8:30, Kennedy turned up in the motel lobby. He visited with the clerk, Mrs. Francis Stewart, and asked if he could buy a couple of newspapers, a *Times* and a *Boston Globe*. He also borrowed a dime from her and tried to make a phone call but he couldn't seem to get through. Shortly after that, Kennedy, Gargan and Markham went back to Chappaquiddick. The ferry operators remember giving them a ride. Richard P. Hewitt testified:

Q. Now, where did you go; where did you take them?

A. They went to Chappaquiddick.

Q. And could you tell us where they went on Chappaquiddick?

A. They didn't go very far. They stood around the point over there.

Q. Well, how long were you in their company or in their vicinity?

A. Oh, I would say approximately 20 minutes or so.

Q. Do you know what they were doing?

A. They appeared to be just **milling around waiting for something or someone.**

Q. They were not in the telephone area?

A. They were in the telephone area.

Q. Did you have a conversation with Mr. Bettencourt?

A. Yes.

Q. What did he tell you?

A. He told me that the car that went off the Dike Bridge had been identified as Mr. Kennedy's.

Q. And then did anyone relay that to Mr. Kennedy?

A. Yes, or not to Mr. Kennedy, but to Mr. Markham.

Q. Who did that?

A. I did.

Q. What did you tell Mr. Markham?

A. I asked him if he was aware of the accident and he said, **"Yes, we just heard about it."**

Q. Those were his exact words?

A. Right.

Q. Yes, we just heard about it?

A. We just heard about it.

Where had they just heard about it? Between the time that Mr. Bettencourt told Hewitt about the accident and the time that Hewitt asked Markham if they were aware of it, Bettencourt talked to Senator Kennedy. He told him, **"Senator, they just took a dead girl out of your car. Do you want a ride**

up to the bridge?" To which Bettencourt says Kennedy replied, "No, I'm going over to town."

The second ferry operator, Steven Ewing, was not called at the inquest, however, Jack Olsen relates the following tale:

"Senator Kennedy and two male companions stepped aboard. 'Hi!' Kennedy said jovially to the young Ewing. The three men paid their fifteen-cent fares and sat on the side benches for the short trip and when they reached Chappaquiddick, they strode up the landing and into the ferryhouse, where there was nothing but a few wall benches and a pay telephone. Hewitt and Ewing figured the men were waiting for a ride."

However, according to Olsen, the three were acting quite differently on the return trip.

"Ewing and Hewitt returned to the ferry prepared to cast off, and they were quickly joined by the Senator and his companions. There were no cars on the trip and the three passengers took seats side by side on the bench reserved for those on foot. Kennedy sat quietly, his head slumped, while the tall man with the receding black hairline [Paul Markham] spoke softly but emphatically, sometimes waving his arms to make a point. When the *On Time* nuzzled its nose against the landing on the Edgartown side, Kennedy jumped off even before the cables were hooked up. Hewitt and Ewing watched as the heavy-set figure headed straight up the middle of Daggett Street, moving so fast that the tall, dark man was plainly having difficulty keeping up, and a photographer with a camera had to swing his body in a rapid arc to hold the vanishing image in his view finder. Two men strolling in the opposite direction jumped aside to keep from being bumped as Kennedy pushed doggedly on, his eyes fixed on the pavement and his deck shoes flashing in a style reminiscent of the Olympic walking event."

170

According to Robert Sherrill, in *The Last Kennedy,* "He arrived at the police station shortly before 10:00 a.m. The only person on duty, a policewoman, says — and she was the first to see him in this condition — that he appeared 'very shaken, and he looked concerned and confused. He seemed to think I knew all about what had happened, but I really didn't. I thought someone had taken his car for a joy ride. He asked if he could use the telephone and he looked as if he was really nervous."

Kennedy, Gargan and Markham did their best to explain away this erratic behavior. Kennedy testified.

Q. Can you give the Court what the conversation was? [In the motel room the next morning]

A. Well, they asked, had I reported the accident, and why I hadn't reported the accident; and I told them about my own thoughts and feelings as I swam across that channel and how I always willed that Mary Jo still lived; how I was hopeful even as that night went on and as I . . . tossed and turned, paced that room and walked around that room that night that somehow when they arrived in the morning that they were going to say that Mary Jo was still alive. I told them how I somehow believed that when the sun came up and it was a new morning that what had happened the night before would not have happened and did not happen, and how I just couldn't gain the strength within me, the moral strength, to call Mrs. Kopechne at 2:00 o'clock in the morning and tell her that her daughter was dead.

Q. Now, at some time you actually did call Mrs. Kopechne?

A. Yes, I did.

Q. And prior to calling Mrs. Kopechne, did you cross over on the Chappaquiddick Ferry to Chappaquiddick Island?

A. Yes, I did.

Q. And was Mr. Markham and Mr. Gargan with you?

A. Yes, they were.

Q. Did anything prompt or cause you to return to Edgartown once you were on Chappaquiddick Island that morning?

A. Anything prompt me to: Well, what do you mean by prompt?

Q. Well, did anything cause you to return? You crossed over to Chappaquiddick?

A. Other than the intention of reporting the accident, the intention of which had been made earlier that morning.

Q. But you didn't go directly from your room to the police department?

A. No, I did not.

Q. What was the reason?

A. It was to make a private phone call to one of the dearest and oldest friends that I have and that was to Mr. Burke Marshall. I didn't feel that I could use the phone that was available, the public phone that was available outside of the dining room at the Shiretown Inn, and it was my thought that once I went to the police station, that I would be involved in a myriad of details and I wanted to talk to this friend before I undertook that responsibility.

Q. Did you not reach him?

A. I did not.

Many people did not like the idea that Kennedy would have crossed back to the island to use a phone when there were several other pay phones available within a short walk of the Shiretown without the hassle of having to ride the ferry. However, Joe Gargan was adamant that that was the reason for the trip.

Q. Was there any particular purpose in crossing over on the ferry at that time in the morning. What was the purpose?

A. So he could make a phone call.

Q. And that was the only purpose that you had in mind at that time?

A. That is correct. You have to remember that I have been coming here and racing for thirty years and one thing you can't get in an Edgartown weekend, Mr. Dinis, is a telephone. I know all the telephones on this island well and where they are and you just can't get them. Certainly I wanted a place where the Senator could talk privately to tell exactly what had happened and then immediately report to the police station.

Even if Kennedy's explanation for returning to Chappaquiddick instead of going straight to the police station is acceptable, it does not explain his sudden change in behavior. Perhaps he thought he had been hallucinating about the happenings of the night before and put them out of his mind like a bad dream when he spoke to the Richards and Stanley Moore. But he had been reminded of the accident quite vividly by Mr. Markham and Mr. Gargan by the time he decided he would like to have a couple of newspapers to read. Why was he in such a good mood crossing the ferry to Chappaquiddick, and why the abrupt change of attitude on the return trip and at the police station?

CHAPTER XIX
WHAT ABOUT THE SEVENTEEN PHONE CALLS?

Muckraker columnist Jack Anderson and reporter Arthur Egan (of *Human Events* magazine) both claim to have information concerning seventeen phone calls made by Kennedy and associates during the night of the accident.

Tedrow and Tedrow, in their book *Death at Chappaquiddick* wrote:

"... the Senator and/or his associates made at least seventeen calls during the night while he was in shock, but none to report the accident. Perhaps the following record will help the Senator's understandably faulty memory.

"A very worried Senator Kennedy made five calls before leaving Chappaquiddick Island and twelve when he reached the Shiretown Inn. All seventeen were billed to Kennedy's credit card number through the Edgartown operator. More could have been made and either paid for, charged to another credit card, or placed collect.

"Although Kennedy has denied making these calls, it would have been to his advantage to have the phone company release his records if he was telling the truth."

Tedrow and Tedrow are wrong when they say that the phone company records were not presented. There was absolutely no cover-up here. In fact, Robert A. Malloy, the general accounting supervisor of the New England Telephone Company appeared at the inquest with the "records of telephone calls made with the credit card of Edward M. Kennedy on July 18th, and 19th, 1969." The Tedrows carefully avoided mentioning Mr. Malloy's testimony and exhibit number four, the list of calls, because that part of the inquest destroys their unfounded allegations. The list of calls presented to the court by Mr. Malloy is a long one, of every call placed from either Edgartown or Chappaquiddick Island — which Judge Boyle scrupulously went over.

The following is an excerpt from Mr. Malloy's testimony.

A. On the 19th the first one was at 10:57.
Q. And that call lasted 23 minutes?
A. Twenty-three minutes and 54 seconds, sir.
Q. It began at 10:57?
A. Yes, sir.
Q. Now, this is on the morning —
A. On the morning of the 19th, sir.
THE COURT: I ask this question now. You do not require the person initiating the call to identify himself or herself?
THE WITNESS: No, sir.
THE COURT: In other words, anyone can use my credit card if they know the number?
THE WITNESS: Yes, sir.

The prosecutor was well aware of Mr. Anderson's and Mr. Egan's accusations about the seventeen phone calls charged to Kennedy's credit card. There were many calls charged. However, the record undisputably proved that the first of the calls placed the morning of the accident was made at 10:57 a.m., which was probably from the police station. If Kennedy and company were frantically making calls all night long they were not billing them to Kennedy's credit card. The Tedrows attempt to further discredit Kennedy by saying that he could have made all kinds of undetectable calls by paying cash, calling collect, or using another credit card. It is more likely that the reason we don't have any evidence of such incriminating calls is that they were not made. Instead, the allegation of the seventeen phone calls appears to have been based on unfounded rumors. When querried as to the source of his information, Jack Anderson has failed to reply.

CHAPTER XX

WAS KENNEDY TRYING TO CREATE AN ALIBI WHILE GARGAN TOOK THE BLAME?

Kennedy's strange behavior has been neatly explained away by those who claim that the Senator knew he was in trouble the minute the car ended up in the water. They say he did not want to be implicated in the girl's death so he avoided the houses near the bridge and went straight to Gargan and Markham. They then returned to the bridge and tried to get her out but decided that she had drowned. The three of them supposedly cooked up a plan to keep the Senator completely out of it. Gargan would say that he had been the driver. They couldn't claim that Mary Jo was; for one thing, the seat wasn't adjusted for her, also it wouldn't make sense for her to have taken off alone in the car, leaving eight people with only one compact vehicle. Besides, since it was Kennedy's car and these questions would be raised, the public would immediately assume that he had been the driver unless there was a stand-in. Once the plan had been arrived at, the opponents say, Kennedy swam or was rowed across the channel so that the ferry operator would not be able to say what time he left the island. He then took pains to speak to the innkeeper and asked what time it was to establish that he spent the night at the Shiretown. The next morning he went out looking for people to play act to in order to convince everyone that he really didn't know anything about the accident. Everything went as planned until the police found the wreck too soon. Since they hadn't reported it, the theory goes, Kennedy was afraid that the plan would not work and chickened out. He decided to tell the truth and belatedly reported the accident.

Since Joe Gargan and Ted Kennedy are very close, there was little doubt that Gargan would have taken the blame if he had been allowed to — he wasn't in politics and he had nothing to lose by doing so. However, there is one glaring error in this theory. Why would Gargan fail to report the accident as soon as Ted was safely away? After all, if he was going to take the blame for the accident, why would he want to take a leaving the scene rap too? Being a lawyer who handled auto cases, he knew what the score was and he wouldn't have wanted to risk going to jail. There was no reason to, because everything would have been routine if he had reported the accident. There would have been little or no investigation because it would not have appeared that any laws had been broken.

It is also questionable that Kennedy would want to establish the fact that he had been up and around at 2:30 a.m. when he had to have known that coroners can quite easily approximate the time of death. It would have been much more logical for him to have quietly gone to bed while Gargan reported the accident and then been awakened from a sound sleep to be informed by the police that his car and his cousin had been involved in a fatal accident.

If Gargan was planning to take the blame, why would he act so innocent at the cottage afterward? Why would he be at the cottage sleeping? He wasn't even interested in cleaning up the liquor bottles. It would seem more logical for him to try to convince the others that somehow he had ended up driving Mary Jo around after Kennedy went back to the motel. In addition, Kennedy's personality does not fit the image of the self-serving, callused, cold-blooded politician interested only in saving his own skin. From past performance, Senator Kennedy is not the type who would fail to get help for Mary Jo just to save himself some embarrassment. He might have been willing to detour around a policeman to avoid adverse publicity but it is ridiculous to assume that he would let her drown simply to prevent some bad press. After all, his reputation was already tarnished, there was no point in hysterically protecting it. If he had behaved rationally and summoned help immediately or even reported the accident to the police that night, the incident would have shortly been forgotten and replaced when a more recent scandal was discovered.

Kennedy was greatly affected emotionally by the accident, a fact which was noted by virtually everyone who knew him or worked with him — even President Nixon, who commented "When I saw him at a meeting in the Cabinet Room a few days later, I was shocked by how pale and shaken he looked." Ted had not recovered completely, and never did, from Robert's murder and there had been a series of violent deaths within the family and among close friends — Kennedy couldn't help feeling overwhelmed. He had never acted cold-blooded about anyone dying before, why would he suddenly start with Mary Jo? By the end of the day of the accident, he was distraught. Four days later at her funeral he was in tears. He rapidly lost twenty pounds although he had always had a problem keeping his weight under control. His fellow Senators shook their heads, saying that it was a hell of a way to lose weight and all were concerned about the way he was taking Mary Jo's death. The Congressional Doorkeeper, "Fishbait" Miller, reported:

"I remember it was like a morgue on the Hill when Ted Kennedy suffered the tragic incident of Chappaquiddick. He didn't have a mean bone in his body. He just had suffered an attack of the dumbs. That's what bad judgment is called on the Hill. Even his enemies felt sorry for Ted — it was all too terrible for words. A girl lay dead in his car and he had not gone around the neighborhood screaming for help. There was almost the same sadness when his two brothers had been assassinated. Congressmen and Senators went around saying, 'Why? But Why?' And they still don't know, but every speculation has been made."

Rita Dallas, nurse for Joe Kennedy, Sr., made an interesting observation:

"After Chappaquiddick, I would see him [Ted] stumbling around the compound confused and alone, and I knew that his heart was broken. His hopes were dashed; his trust in human nature was shattered. I'm sure any doctor would have recommended hospitalization for Teddy, for he was apparently in deep emotional shock, but the 'advisers' decided not to enter him."

For weeks Kennedy couldn't pull himself together and concentrate on his job. Burton Hersh reports Kennedy saying shortly after returning to the Senate:

"Can you imagine how it feels walking down these corridors, and the tourists are staring at me? And I know what they're thinking ... I know what they're thinking. Can you imagine that, if I had in fact done what they think ... done what they think ... that I could hurt the Senate, that I would be here?"

Lester David remarks in *Ted Kennedy: Triumphs and Tragedies,*

"It was difficult for friends to talk to him. 'He would listen to you,' an aide recalls, 'and then begin an answer. Pretty soon you would see his eyes move from you to a corner of the room or a faraway point if we were outside, and his words would just fade away. You knew what he was thinking and it was hurting like hell and there wasn't a damn thing either he or you could do about it.'"

It is doubtful that Kennedy is such an accomplished actor that he could carry on the charade for months, even years. There is little doubt that the accident had a severe effect on him emotionally, a large amount of which is probably due to the public ordeal he went through. He has never gotten over it and was still overreacting nine years later. According to a *National Enquirer* note of October 24, 1978:

"Ted Kennedy stormed out of a Democratic fund-raising reception in the Capitol when a wise-guy Congressional candidate from California showed up wearing a name tag reading 'Jo Kopechne' — the name of the girl killed at Chappaquiddick. Ted shook the man's hand before noticing the name tag. Then spinning around in horror, the Senator bolted for his car and drove home alone."

This is hardly the sort of reaction one would expect from a ruthless, self-serving politician nine years after the fact.

Picture snapped by a tourist as Senator Ted Kennedy rushed off the ferry on his way to report the accident to the Edgartown police. (UPI July 19, 1969)

Attorneys for Senator Kennedy and others who attended the ill-fated cook-out leaving the Massachusetts Supreme Court. Edward B. Hanify (front left), and Robert G. Clark, Jr. (center); attorneys for Senator Kennedy; Daniel Daly (front right) and Paul J. Redmond (rear left), attorneys for five women and three men who attended the cook-out; Joseph P. Donahue (rear right) attorney for Joe Gargan and Paul Markham. (UPI September 12, 1969)

CHAPTER XXI

DID KENNEDY GET OFF EASY BECAUSE OF HIS INFLUENCE AND MONEY?

The people who believe he got off easy are not familiar with the case. If one goes to any lawyer, sheriff or judge and describes the accident without mentioning any names and asks what would happen to the driver who left the scene, yet reported the accident on his own in the morning, the answer would either be "nothing" or he would be cited for leaving the scene, and if there is no previous record he would certainly receive a suspended sentence, especially since he did eventually report the accident. His license would probably be suspended for a year and he would be put on probation, but that would be about it. Auto accidents are the number one cause of death among this nation's young people; if the courts spent as much time on every unwitnessed accident trying to prove negligence or manslaughter as they did on this one they wouldn't have time to do anything else. In this case, the driver even confessed to leaving the scene, so there was no contest.

If the accident had happened to Mr. Average Joe Citizen, Mr. Citizen probably would have been cited for leaving the scene. If he had pleaded guilty he would have received a suspended two month sentence and lost his driver's license for one year. The case wouldn't have been worthy of even honorable mention in anything but the local paper.

Unfortunately for Kennedy, he wasn't an average American citizen. Virtually the whole world took an interest in the case, especially the President of the United States, who had his own ax to grind. What happened? The same thing that would have happened to Mr. Citizen and more, much more. Kennedy was cited for leaving the scene of a fatal accident, pleaded guilty, received a two month suspended sentence and temporarily lost his driver's license. What followed never would have happened to Mr. Citizen. Jack Olsen quoted the Dukes County Special Prosecutor, Walter Steele, as saying,

"What's keeping this case alive, besides politics, is the public wants to know what the hell is a United States Senator doing on the Island of Chappaquiddick having a few pops and ending up on a lonely road with a blonde. Now, that's all very interesting, but it's not a criminal matter. The public's gonna keep on kidding itself for months and months, when in fact there's not a single goddamn reason to keep this case open."

When pressed about charging Kennedy with additional crimes, Police Chief Jim Arena explained, "In a driving case I have to have somebody who was a witness to the accident, who was a person who saw Senator Kennedy go off this Dike Bridge."

The case was kept open by a demanding public and an excited group of Republicans who at last had Kennedy where they wanted him and intended to keep him there. Wouldn't it be wonderful if they could get the leading opponent of the President locked up in the state pen. Even if they knew they couldn't do that, they could destroy his credibility with the voting public by continuing to ask questions and by keeping the incident in the headlines.

At the hearing held Friday, July 25, 1969, where Kennedy pleaded guilty to the charge of leaving the scene of an accident, the judge asked the probation officer, "Is there no record, Mrs. Tyra?" To which the probation officer replied, "None, your Honor, sir."

Immediately the cry of cover-up sounded. Why, it was common knowledge that Kennedy was a wild driver and had lots of traffic tickets. How could the court claim that he had no record? He must have paid them off.

Until July of 1969, Edward M. Kennedy had been cited for four different traffic violations in his lifetime. They are as follows:

March 1957 — speeding — fine $15.00

June 1958 — speeding — fine — $15.00
  plus reckless driving and racing — fine $35.00
December 1959 — failure to stop at a red light — fine $10.00

It should be noted that Ted Kennedy had gone an entire decade without a single traffic violation. He had received his last citation at the age of 27.

The reason the court disregarded the three tickets of a decade earlier is that in almost every state of the Union a driver is considered rehabilitated if he goes three years without a citation for a moving violation. There was nothing sinister about disregarding the earlier citations. Kennedy certainly didn't pay anyone off. The tickets are still on file in the archives of the Massachusetts Motor Vehicle Department. They were simply too old to be considered by the judge in rendering his decision.

Likewise there have been charges that Kennedy whisked away the party goers so that they could not be questioned by the local authorities. Kennedy spent several hours at the police station. In his written statement given to Police Chief Arena he said, "I recall walking back to where my friends were eating." Mr. Arena himself typed the statement. He knew Kennedy had been with other people on the island. Kennedy never asked the Sheriff not to question them. He was probably too concerned about what he was going to say in his statement to have thought about it. Gargan, Markham, Crimmins and Tretter were all at the police station at one time or another that day. The girls (who the sheriff also knew about because he talked to them on the phone to get the spelling of Miss Kopechne's name and also to tell Miss Keough her purse had been recovered from the car and was at the station) did not leave the island until late Saturday afternoon. The fact that no one besides Kennedy was questioned was not because they were not available. What were they supposed to do? Should all eleven grief-stricken people have invaded the local police station and demanded to tell all whether the local authorities wished to hear it or not? They were easily located at any time and were all at the inquest. They never tried to avoid questioning; they were simply not asked anything officially until the inquest.

Esther Newberg talked to reporters a few days after the accident but the others declined since some of Miss Newberg's statements were twisted and she had been hounded unmercifully by reporters wanting her to clarify things she had said. The false reporting was very unsettling. From the way Esther's statements had been handled it was obvious that some reporters were not interested in getting the story straight, but were looking for anything they could find that would make it appear that Kennedy was lying. This, of course, distressed his friends, and no one wanted to give the muckrakers anything else they could blow out of proportion.

As mentioned earlier, Kennedy was accused of body snatching when in reality he was only trying to help Mr. and Mrs. Kopechne retrieve their daughter's body. Apparently some people thought he should have just forgotten about her after he accidently caused her death, and let the bereaved parents worry about it. He might have been better off if he had, but then he probably would have been ridiculed for callousness. In any event, he had nothing to do with the District Attorney's decision not to require an autopsy. In view of the pain it has caused him, he, more than anyone, must wish a post-mortem had been done. There is no evidence at all to support the radical claim that Kennedy purposely prevented an autopsy. As a matter of fact, the shipping of the body on Sunday morning had been arranged for from the Kopechne's end, not by Dun Gifford, Kennedy's legislative aide.

Kennedy has also been accused of using his influence and money to block the exhumation of the body for an autopsy, when in fact he had absolutely nothing to do with that decision. District Attorney, Dinis, petitioned the State of Pennsylvania for the exhumation, which was vigorously opposed by the

Kopechnes. Joe and Gwen Kopechne are very devout Catholics and were advised to oppose the exhumation by two parish priests who reportedly told them, "Mary Jo is with God. She is at rest. Don't disturb her." Mrs. Kopechne became quite distraught over the issue. Even so, an in-depth hearing was held and every detail of the accident was gone over before the court decided that the chances of finding anything new was too remote to upset the Kopechnes any further.

Kennedy's political enemies made the most of the situation by publicly calling for the exhumation to see whether or not Miss Kopechne had been pregnant. The court refused to consider that allegation because such a finding would have no bearing on the case. Those who asked for the pregnancy determination knew full well that the court would not allow it, but it was a terrific opportunity to cause the public to question Kennedy's morals. When the exhumation was denied, the public largely assumed Kennedy had blocked it and many thought Mary Jo must have been pregnant after all. Ted Kennedy would have been much better off had the body been exhumed, for many of these cruel and preposterous charges would have been put to rest. As it turned out, it was he who caught the brunt of the public criticism, and again the charges of cover-up were heard.

Next, an inquest was called to decide if there were any grounds to further prosecute the Senator. Since it was the hottest story in the country the news media wanted to attend. Kennedy's enemies hoped to make a public spectacle of the inquest and have full press coverage as if it were an actual trial. Their strategy was to keep the case before the public and have every little tidbit that popped up which might cast suspicion on the Senator reported on a daily basis. Kennedy's lawyers fought an open inquest. The argument was: The inquest was being held to see if there was just cause to bring further charges against Senator Edward M. Kennedy for the death of Mary Jo Kopechne. If he was charged with an additional crime then he would have to stand trial. If the press were allowed to attend the inquest and if Kennedy was subsequently brought to trial, it would have been impossible to select a truly impartial jury anywhere in the United States, much less in the locale of the accident. The jury members would have been subjected to so much pre-trial publicity that they would have preconceived opinions about the guilt or innocence of the defendant and it would be impossible for them to be totally objective in judgment.

The right to a fair trial rests squarely upon the constitutional guarantee of "due process". B. E. Witkin in his Summary of California Law discusses both Federal and State Constitutional Law under Chapter XI in Paragraph 178 (b) Control of Publicity to Insure Fair Trial, and states:

> "If the exercise by the media of the right to attend and publicize a criminal trial is so abused as to prejudice the defendant's right to a fair trial, the court can and should impose appropriate restraints; and, in the absence of such restraints, improper publicity may be a denial of due process and grounds for reversal of a conviction."

Among other references, Witkin cites Estes v. Texas, 381 U.S. 532; and Sheppard v. Maxwell, 384 U.S. 333; both cases having been decided by the United States Supreme Court.

The press, who protested loudly and publicly over being barred from the inquest, would have protested even louder if Kennedy had been brought to trial, been found guilty and the decision reversed because they had abused their reporting privileges. Of course that didn't happen, because Kennedy was not guilty of additional crimes, but that was not a known fact at the time. Had he been indicted, and pre-trial publicity allowed, it would have been impossible for him to receive a fair trial anywhere in the United States. To prevent that from happening, the Massachusetts Supreme Court ruled that no one but the judge, the court staff, the prosecutor, the witness and the witness' lawyer were allowed in the court room during the questioning. Not even the other witnesses or their attorneys could enter, which was meant to insure that the witnesses would not be subject to peer pressure and, hopefully, would be completely truthful. They further ruled that as soon as it was determined either that (1) Kennedy was innocent of any additional crimes and no further charges would be made, or (2) he was indicted, brought to trial and a decision rendered, the complete court transcripts would be made public and the press as well as the rest of the world would have free access to them. Until such time, the transcripts would be impounded.

The decision displeased the press. They wanted to report the inquest now, while it was still a hot issue, not after the outcome was already known. Kennedy won the court battle, but he lost again in public opinion. The press had a field day reporting about the "top secret" inquest which they weren't allowed to attend because Kennedy had something to hide. The public was never adequately informed of the real reasons for the decision to bar the press. Even today very few news sources have told the public that the transcripts have been open to the public since June 1970. To this day, whenever Chappaquiddick is mentioned, they bring up the "top secret" inquest and imply that it was all part of a massive cover-up to keep the truth from the people, when, in fact, the presence of the press would have been an obstruction of justice.

In recent years, because of the impressive ability of news reporters to transmit information to vast numbers of people, press reporting of notable crimes has become a real problem to the courts in trying to guarantee a fair trial. In 1979, the Supreme Court of the United States, in Gannett vs. DePasquale, held that neither the public nor the press has a right to attend crucial pre-trial hearings. And the guarantee of a public trial itself, five Justices agreed, belongs not to the public but only to a criminal defendant. Justice Potter Stewart wrote:

"The Constitution nowhere mentions any right of access to a criminal trial on the part of the public! Its guarantee ... is personal to the accused ... We hold that members of the public have no constitutional right ... to attend criminal trials."

Even though there had already been two hearings to determine whether or not Kennedy was guilty of additional crimes, he had to face yet another hearing, this one by the grand jury. The Martha's Vineyard Grand Jury was called by its head, Leslie Leland, who was convinced that Kennedy had to be guilty of something else, and the two judges were letting him off scott-free. Where Leland's sympathies lay was made clear by what he told reporters:

"Everyone feels that a great injustice has been done to the democratic process, that there's been a whitewash, a cover-up, and that things have been swept under the rug. I just feel we have certain duties and responsibilities as jury members to fulfill. A great deal of time has passed since the girl died, and it's time the public found out what happened."

On December 24, 1979, the *Los Angeles Times* reported:

"Leland says Dinis, a Democrat who was up for reelection, equivocated and suggested that Leland, a non-lawyer, should take responsibility for the probe. Leland said recently that as a layman he was at first reluctant to take such a step alone but did so after the 1970 inquest into Miss Kopechne's death left what he considered important questions unanswered."

The assertion that Edmund Dinis wanted to stay out of Grand Jury probe for political reasons is absurd. Dinis petitioned the Luzerne County Court of Wilkes-Barre, Pennsylvania for permission to exhume the body of Mary Jo Kopechne, which resulted in a lengthy hearing and involved Dinis personally. As the Dukes County Prosecutor, he was the one who called for the four-day-long inquest, was in charge of the investigation in preparation for the inquest, and did the bulk of the questioning of the witnesses. To say that Edmund Dinis wanted to stay out of a grand jury investigation for political reasons

188

when he was already so deeply involved in the case is ludicrous. It is true that Dinis was not enthusiastic about another investigation, but this was probably due to the fact that he had been over the evidence so many times that he knew nothing new would be discovered.

Judging from Leland's 1970 statements, made at the time he was calling for a grand jury investigation, the jury foreman did not need encouragement from anyone to involve himself in the case. Leland petitioned to call a grand jury investigation, which was granted. This court action in itself was highly unusual for there had already been an inquest held into the same matter. However, it is just as well for Kennedy that the grand jury did convene, for now no one can say that every possibility was not followed up. Even so, there issued yet another cover-up charge, for in its quest to find grounds to indict Kennedy for manslaughter, the grand jury was denied access to the inquest transcripts. At the time the Massachusetts Supreme Court ordered the transcripts impounded, it had no idea that a grand jury would be called, as the inquest should have substituted for the grand jury investigation. Therefore, no provision had been made giving the grand jury access. Kennedy's political opponents pointed the finger directly at him and accused him of blocking justice by pulling strings at the highest levels to keep the revealing inquest transcripts out of the hands of those who would punish him for his "dastardly deeds", a charge which many people believed.

In actuality, District Attorney Dinis informed the grand jury of most of the contents of the transcripts. He said that he doubted that they would find anything in them to bring additional charges against Kennedy. He went into detail about how his investigation had been handled and what they had discovered and who they had talked to. He added that he thought they would not discover anything new. The grand jury was free to call its own witnesses.

Although no other members of the grand jury have expressed dissatisfaction with the case, Leslie Leland has recently been charging that the investigation was blocked. According to the 1979 *Los Angeles Times* report

"Leland said his own efforts to pursue the matter foundered when Suffolk County Superior Judge Wilfred J. Paquet (who presided over the grand jury investigation) gave such narrow instructions to the grand jury that the probe got nowhere. The judge, Leland said, ordered that no witnesses who had appeared at the earlier inquest could be subpoenaed by the grand jury unless they had 'new information', or unless members of the grand jury themselves had 'personal knowledge' of events surrounding the accident. Reached in his chambers in Boston, Paquet said, 'I've been asked questions about this for ten years, and I've been misquoted for ten years. I'm not going to give you any information.' "

No matter what Judge Paquet may or may not have said to its members, the fact remains that a grand jury has sweeping powers. If the members of the jury had been sufficiently aroused they could have conducted a very thorough investigation. There were scores of other witnesses they could have called, such as: Tony Bettencourt, who had informed Kennedy of the accident; Mrs. Francis Stewart, the clerk whom Kennedy visited with the morning after the accident; Foster Silva, a resident of Chappaquiddick who had observed the party and could provide information on the tides in Poucha Pond; Silvia Malm, the occupant of Dike House; Steven Ewing, the ferry operator to whom Kennedy had been so friendly; Carmen Salvador, the police woman who observed Kennedy at the police station; Patrolman Robert Brougier, who assisted in recovering the wrecked car and to whom Officer Look confided that it was the same vehicle he had seen at the intersection the night before; and many, many others.

By June of 1970 Jack Olsen's book, *The Bridge at Chappaquiddick,* had been published and was in circulation. Olsen had done a fine job of investigative reporting and the grand jury could have drawn on his work. Certainly they had access to the same people Olsen did — and Olsen had also been denied access to the inquest transcripts at that time. If they had wished, the grand jury could have found "new evidence" which would have made it necessary to call all of the witnesses who had testified at the inquest. That they did not do so indicates that after hearing from the county prosecutor, Edmund Dinis, and four new witnesses, the majority of the jurors were satisfied that justice had been served. It must have been obvious to most that they had been called together, not to insure that the laws be upheld, but to rake Kennedy over the coals again for something that had already been investigated very thoroughly, not once, but twice before. It was a waste of the taxpayers' money as well as the juror's personal time to go over it all again just to satisfy Kennedy's enemies who seemed bent on causing him continuous grief. On the second day of the grand jury investigation, June 7, 1970, they announced that, "The grand jury has no presentments to make." The case was closed — and Kennedy was immediately assailed with charges that he bought the grand jury too.

As one juror said, "Most of us felt Kennedy was morally responsible for the death of that girl." So did Ted Kennedy. He had already pleaded guilty as charged with having caused the accident and then leaving the scene. He has never tried to avoid responsibility. Instead of ducking the charge, he volunteered most of the evidence against himself. What his opponents who continue to charge that a cover-up occurred and that the case should be reopened expect to find is difficult to determine. It appears that all of the legal possibilities have been studied. There are still some unanswered questions but none that pertain to any crimes he could be charged with.

As soon as the grand jury decision was in, the court made the inquest transcripts public. Anyone can order a copy from the Dukes County District Court in Edgartown, Massachusetts, yet we still hear about the "secret inquest". There is nothing secret about it and there hasn't been for ten years.

When the dust finally settled after three different hearings under three different judges, Kennedy was still in the clear because no one had turned up any evidence of wrong doing on his part other than leaving the scene and perhaps driving negligently at 20 miles per hour. The failure to find incriminating evidence was not for lack of trying; the President of the United States saw to that.

Anyone who doubts the zeal with which President Nixon pursued Ted Kennedy has only to read what Nixon himself, his top advisers and other qualified close observers have to say about it to realize that Ted Kennedy was the subject of a smear campaign the equal of which had never been seen in this country and hopefully will never be witnessed again. That Kennedy managed to survive might be classified as another wonder of the world. The following are exerpts of some of the more enlightening material on the subject:

From *The Memoirs of Richard Nixon:*

"I would also have to keep an eye on my own political position. The victory over Humphrey had been far too close for comfort. If it had not been for the debacle of the Chicago convention and the burden of Johnson's unpopularity, Humphrey might have won. There was no reason to expect that the Democrats would be so obliging as to provide me with similar advantages in 1972. If they were able to unite around Teddy Kennedy or Muskie or even Humphrey again, they would be very hard to beat. Therefore **I decided that we must begin immediately keeping track of everything the leading Democrats did.** Information would be our first line of defense."

From *The Ends of Power* by H.R. Haldeman:

"In battle, Nixon always wanted 'to go for the jugular.' The one jugular that fascinated him even more than Larry O'Brian's was Teddy Kennedy's. And some of my own orders, which might later be characterized as 'seamy', re-volved around Kennedy. **I was to place a 24-hour surveillance on him.** I was to 'catch him in the sack with one of his babes.' "

From *Blind Ambition* by John Dean:

"I had to pay for the trip myself, and Jack [Caufield] had offered to help my expenses by letting me stay at the planned undercover apartment. It was then being used for a special Ehrlichman-approved assignment which re-quired a luxurious ambience, and Jack had de-scribed it as 'quite a pad.' The apartment was meant to serve as a boudior; Tony [Ulasewicz] had enlisted aquaintances of amorous reputa-tion in a mission to seduce there some of the women who had attended Kennedy's Chappa-quiddick party. **(The women would, accord-ing to the plan, volunteer some details of Kennedy's conduct in a moment of ten-derness, or under fear of extortion.)"**

From *Watergate* by Lewis Chester, Cal McCrystal, Stephen Aris and William Shawcross:

"Caufield and Ulasewicz dug and dug into the mud of Chappaquiddick but never, it appears, came up with anything more than that exposed in the public prints. Part of the equipment ac-quired for this enterprise was an 'office on 46th Street in New York furnished with a king-sized bed, velvet walls, and deep fur rugs where, it was apparently thought, indiscreet girl friends of Mary Jo Kopechne might be encouraged to talk."

From *The Great Cover-up: Nixon and the Scandal of Watergate* by Barry Sussman:

"Nixon and his aides had great fear of one other Democrat, Senator Edward M. Kennedy, whom they considered more than just an oppo-nent. He was an enemy. From 1969 on, **one of Howard Hunt's first White House projects was to find out whatever dirt he could on**

the Senator and other members of the Kenney clan."

From *Blind Ambition* by John Dean:
   "September 18, 1971 memo from Haldeman to Dean ...
   The most recent EMK [Edward M. Kennedy] report has been submitted. It contains nothing.
   The question is whether or not the subject of intelligence shouldn't receive a greater allocation of time and resources than it is receiving now."

From *The Watergate Hearings — Break-in and Cover-up,* official transcripts of the Watergate Hearings printed by the New York Times. Testimony by John W. Dean 3d, June 25, 1973:
   "The pre-re-election White House thrived on political gossip and political intelligence. I knew of the type of information they sought even before I joined the White House staff. During the summer of 1969, while I was working at the Justice Department, the then Deputy Attorney General, Richard Kleindienst, called me into his office and told me that the White House wanted some very important information. Mr. Kleindienst instructed me to call Mr. DeLoach, then deputy director of the F.B.I., and obtain from him **information regarding the foreign travels of Mary Jo Kopechne.**
   "It was not until I joined the White House staff that Caulfield was assigned to develop political intelligence on Senator Edward Kennedy. Mr. Caulfield told me that within some six hours of the accident at Chappaquiddick on July 18, 1969, he had a friend on the scene conducting a private investigation. Caulfield also informed me that his instructions were to continue surveillance of Senator Kennedy.
   "Caulfield told me that he thought that this was most unwise because it could uncover his activites in that **Senator Kennedy was bound to realize he was under surveillance**

and it could easily be misinterpreted as someone who was planning an attack on his life, and the police or F.B.I. might be called in to investigate. I agreed fully with Caulfield. After some initial resistance, I convinced Higby that it was a bad idea and the day-in, day-out surveillance concept was called off. Instead, Caulfield was to keep general overview of Senator Kennedy's activities and pursue specific investigations of activities that might be of interest.

"Political intelligence often came from unexpected sources. For example, during the spring of 1972, a top man at the Secret Service brought me information regarding Senator McGovern. I asked Mr. Colson if he were interested. He was very interested and had the information published.

"The persons on the White House staff who were most interested in political intelligence were Ehrlichman, Haldeman and Colson. Principally Colson and sometimes Haldeman.

"In addition to the extensive efforts to otain politically embarrassing information on Senator Kennedy, there were also frequent efforts to obtain politically embarrassing information on Mr. Lawrence O'Brien, the Democratic National Committee chairman, Senator Muskie and Senator McGovern."

Finally, the most revealing and disturbing of all is the transcript of the March 13, 1973 White House tape of a discussion between President Nixon and John Dean which begins with a conversation about the Watergate burglary: ("P" stands for President and "D" stands for John Dean.)

P: I mean put the story out, PR people here is the story, the true story of Watergate —

D: They would never believe it. The two things they are working on are Watergate —

P: Who is "they"?

D: The Press (inaudible), the intellectuals —

P: The Packwoods?

D: Right — they would never buy it as far as one White House involvement in Watergate, which I think there is just none [no explanation] for that incident which occurred at the Democratic National Headquarters.

P: I tell you this, it is the last gasp of our hardest opponents. They've just got to have something to squeal about it.

D: It is the only thing they have to squeal —

P: (Unintelligible) They are going to lie around and squeal. They are having a hard time now. They got the hell kicked out of them in the election ... they are trying to use this as the whole thing.

D: Well, that is why I keep coming back to this fellow Sullivan. It could change the picture. [Sullivan was attempting to "buy" his way back into the FBI by incriminating various Democrats of miscellaneous crimes similar to Watergate].

P: If he could get Kennedy into it, too, I would be a little bit more pleased.

D: Let me tell you something that lurks at the bottom of this whole thing. If, in going after Segretti, they [Kennedy's committee] go after Kalmbach's bank records, you will recall sometime back ... That right after Chappaquiddick somebody [Tony Ulasewicz] was put up there to start observing and within six hours he was there for every second of Chappaquiddick for a year, and for almost two years he worked for Jack Caulfield ... If they get to those bank records between the start of July of 1969 through June of 1971, they say what are these about? **Who is this fellow up in New York that you paid? There comes Chappaquiddick with a vengence** ... If they get to it — that is going to come out and this whole thing can turn around on that. If Kennedy knew the bear trap he was walking into —

P: How do we know — why don't we get it

[Chappaquiddick information] out anyway?

D: Well, we have sort of saved it.

P: Does he [Ulasewicz] have any records. Are they any good?

D: He is probably the most knowledgeable man in the country [On the Chappaquiddick accident]. I think he ran up against walls and they closed the records down. There are things he can't get, but he can ask all of the questions and get many of the answers as a 20 year detective, but we don't want to surface him right now. But if he is ever surfaced, this is what they will get.

P: **How will Kalmbach explain that he hired this guy to do the job on Chappaquiddick?** Out of what type of funds?

D: He had money left over from the pre-convention —

P: Are they going to investigate those funds too?

D: They are funds that are quite legal. There is nothing illegal about those funds. Regardless of what may happen, what may occur, they may stumble into this in going back to say 1971, in Kalmbach's bank records in connection with Segretti, as to how he paid Segretti.

P: Are they going to go back as far as Chappaquiddick?

D: **Well, this fellow worked in 1971 on this. He was up there. He has talked to everybody in that town. He is the one who has caused a lot of embarrassment for Kennedy already by saying he went up there as a newspaperman, by saying: "Why aren't you checking this? Why aren't you looking there?" Calling the press people's attention to things. Gosh, the guy did a masterful job.**

The Congressional committee invesitgating the Watergate break-in discovered that Democratic National Headquarters was by no means the first to have its phones tapped. Nixon's infamous "Plumbers" had also placed taps on the phones of the girls who had attended the Chappaquiddick party.

It is quite obvious that Mr. Average Joe Citizen would not have been subjected to this kind of attack launched against him by the President of the United States. Kennedy may have had a battery of lawyers, but he needed them.

A decade later the Chappaquiddick smear campaign is still being conducted by those who wish to block Edward Kennedy's presidential bid. While there have been many right-wing groups circulating propaganda against Ted Kennedy centering around the Chappaquiddick accident, the most damaging piece of information was an article published by the *Reader's Digest* in February of 1980. The article contains flagrant misrepresentations and many outright falsehoods, the most serious of which is the fabrication of "evidence" which purports to "prove" that Kennedy had been speeding at the time of the accident. If this were true, Kennedy could then be accused of negligent homicide, a felony, which would make Kennedy ineligible to hold federal office. As shown in this book, the *Reader's Digest* study is not accurate so the speeding charge is not true, however, the millions of voters who read the article had no way of knowing that.

This particular attack on Senator Kennedy was very successful because the *Reader's Digest* is highly regarded by its subscribers who number 18½ million. The circulation of the *Reader's Digest* is greater than that of the *New York Times*, the *Los Angeles Times, Time, Newsweek, U.S. News and World Report* and the *National Enquirer* combined. In addition, the magazine is found in waiting rooms across the United States and is therefore more widely read than even its massive distribution indicates.

There exists a very interesting connection between the *Reader's Digest* and the Nixon administration of the Watergate era. The Senior Counsellor for the *Reader's Digest* is none other than Melvin R. Laird.

From 1968 to 1972, Laird was a member of Nixon's cabinet as Secretary of Defense. He then served as Counsellor to the President until Nixon resigned. Obviously Melvin R. Laird was deeply involved with the White House staff and the Nixon administration during the time it was conducting its vigorous smear campaign against Ted Kennedy.

In his memoirs Richard Nixon made some intriguing comments about Laird:

"I saw Eisenhower again on October 17. By now the political situation was beginning to develop very quickly and he was out-spoken in analysing the various political personalities who might play a role in 1968.

"I told him of my high regard for Jerry Ford. He agreed but was afraid that Ford was not exciting enough. 'We need someone who can charge up the troops,' he said. He called Mel Laird 'the smartest of the lot, but he is too devious.' In December 1968, after I had selected Laird as Secretary of Defense, Eisenhower expressed the same doubts. After the two men had a meeting in January, however, Eisenhower told me he thought I had made a good choice. Flashing his famous grin, he said, 'Of course Laird is devious, but for anyone who has to run the Pentagon and get along with Congress that is a valuable asset.'"

Later in his memoirs Nixon commented,

"I once jokingly remarked that Laird did not have this problem because he would answer questions and state his views whether he was informed or not."

How deeply involved Melvin Laird was in the publication of the extremely biased and damaging *Reader's Digest* article is not known, however, his past associations with the Nixon-Watergate group and his current work for the *Reader's Digest* is certainly cause to wonder if the Nixon gang is still hard at work on Ted Kennedy.

Some people continue to talk about how Kennedy

influenced the witnesses and bought them off. If this were true, why then didn't he do a better job of influencing his own friends? Nance Lyons, who worked in the Senator's office, presented some of the most damaging testimony. About the only point all of the party goers could agree on that supported Kennedy was that he left the party between 11:15 and 11:30 p.m. This has raised questions because people at parties usually don't pay close attention to the time, and while they couldn't seem to agree on much else, all ten agreed on the time Kennedy departed. The interesting thing here is that the time is the only matter that could be refuted by outside witnesses and by other evidence. It certainly appears that if the party-goers were coached at all, it was solely on the departure time. Perhaps that was the only thing Kennedy was worried about.

Since the inquest and subsequent release of the testimony to the public, still more questions have been asked, and the public has demanded that Senator Kennedy answer them. William H. Honan brought the subject up with him one day in 1970.

"I turned the conversation to Chappaquiddick. Boyle had raised a number of questions about the veracity of his testimony at the inquest, I said, would he care to comment on any of these questions? 'I'm not going to do that,' Kennedy answered firmly. 'Look, every time I say something — for example, that I swam across the channel — fifteen people turn up who say they were in a boat at about that time and they didn't see me swimming. So then I have to explain that. How *can* I explain that? Everything just adds. It just adds. There doesn't seem to be any way to end it.'

"I mentioned that he had once told Mathew V. Storin of the *Boston Globe* that one day he would reveal the full story of Chappaquiddick, but he had considered it unwise to do so then because the **truth would not be believed** in what Kennedy regarded as an atmosphere of suspicion. 'I did have such a conversation,' he

200

acknowledged, 'but that was last summer, **before the inquest.** It's all in the transcript now. So I don't have anything more to say.' "

Now that he is running for president, Ted Kennedy is granting interviews on Chappaquidick. However, he has nothing new to say and merely repeats, almost word for word, his 1970 inquest testimony.

As newsmen face the front door of Dukes County Court House (L), Leslie H. Leland (bkgd. L), foreman of the grand jury is escorted from the side door at the lunch break in the first day of proceedings. (UPI April 6, 1969)

District Attorney Edmund S. Dinis was mobbed by newsmen as he emerged from Dukes County Court House and announced that the grand jury investigation into the death of Mary Jo Kopechne was finished and the case was closed. (UPI April 7, 1970)

Newsmen scramble from the courtroom at Suffolk Superior Court, Boston, Massachusetts, after receiving the newly released transcripts of the "secret" inquest into the death of Mary Jo Kopechne.

CHAPTER XXII
THE CHAPPAQUIDDICK DECISION

A decade has passed since that tragic night on Chappaquiddick Island, yet the incident rides like a wave in the minds of the American people. It comes and goes with Ted Kennedy. When Kennedy fades into the background the incident is forgotten, then, as each presidential election approaches, it rides the swell up with the Senator and crests along with his popularity. Kennedy is stuck with Chappaquiddick. Like a scar it is part of him and while he has tried to ignore it, it will never go away.

In 1978 the word "Chappaquiddick" was seldom heard, but as President Carter's popularity ebbed, Ted Kennedy's rose, and once again the little island off Martha's Vineyard is in the public's mind. Admirers and critics alike still puzzle over the incident. Kennedy has never deviated from his original story and has long since given up trying to convince the suspicious that he told the truth. Once, when pressed, he angrily replied, "Do you think that if I knew there was anything else that could come out of this I would not have given up my Senate seat? I know what happened there and I'm the only one who knows. There's nothing else that can be said about it."

Kennedy is certainly right about one thing — he is the only one who knows what happened. He is the only one who will ever know for sure whether or not he has been totally truthful. However, if the facts are any different from what he testified to in court, he can never say so. If he changed his story now he would be admitting that he supplied false information under oath.

It is possible that Kennedy has been completely truthful about Mary Jo's death and his ensuing actions. Life consists of inconsistencies. Actual events never turn out neatly like television detective stories. There are always loose ends, unexplained coincidences and unanswered questions left dangling. None of the theories presented thus far have made as much sense as has Kennedy's imperfect story.

However, today we know many things the theorists of the pre-Watergate era did not know. In the aftermath of Watergate, we find that Kennedy was subjected to White House "gestapo" tactics from the day Nixon moved into 1600 Pennsylvania Avenue. If we study the Nixon-Kennedy relationship, look at Kennedy's personal life and family considerations at that time, couple them with the thousands of pages of information gathered over the years about the Chappaquiddick accident, we begin to see that there might be a logical explanation for Kennedy's supposedly erratic behavior after all. The testimony of Officer Christopher Look holds the key to the door that lets in the light. Once it is opened, the answers to all of the questions are simple, so simple one wonders why it took ten years to figure it out.

There is little doubt that Richard Nixon knows most of what happened at Chappaquiddick. With the amount of time and effort his people devoted to the case, he could not have missed it. Nixon's problem was this his findings would not have harmed Kennedy at all, especially if he — Nixon — and other Republicans were the ones to reveal them. If *they* told the story, it would be believed, whereas a suspicious public would never accept it from Kennedy himself. Kennedy was certain that the White House investigators would not turn up damaging evidence when he said, "I would say those who tend to look for things in this case are going to be disappointed." Whatever was discovered by Nixon and company was dropped like a hot potato.

Kennedy also meant it when he told the *Boston Globe,* "I can live with myself. I feel the tragedy of the girl's death ... that's what I have to live with. But what I don't have to live with are the whispers and innuendoes and falsehoods because these have no basis in fact."

Far from being the suffering victim of a tragic accident, stumbling around in the dark, confused and frightened as he has portrayed himself, I believe Kennedy acted quickly and decisively in the face of disaster. His move was so desperate that even the political pros were oblivious to it. Kennedy's advisers must have been shocked to the core, but the plan was wild and unexpected enough to fool everyone. It worked. The fact that he is a serious Presidential contender testifies to the astuteness of the maneuver.

I believe what actually took place the night of July 18 and the morning of July 19, 1969 is as follows:

The party was exactly as Kennedy described it, a reunion of some of Bobby's campaign workers and close friends. Kennedy himself did not have an especially good time, for he had put in several hours of work in Washington before flying up to Martha's Vineyard to participate in a grueling six hour boat race. Not only was he tired, but his back was bothering him. The party was rather loud and Kennedy may have been boisterous. However, as the evening progressed those present did much reminiscing about Bobby, and Ted was probably feeling melancholic, for he had taken his brother's death very hard.

About 12:30 a.m. he was standing near the door by himself, obviously not enjoying the festivities. Mary Jo walked over and engaged him in conversation, mentioning that she was tired and sunburned and would like to go back to her motel. Since he had been thinking about leaving anyway, when Mary Jo asked for a ride he abruptly told her, "Well, I'm leaving immediately," and walked out the door. In her haste to catch a ride, Mary Jo forgot her purse as she rushed after him. She need not have hurried, for as it turned out Kennedy himself had forgotten his car keys and had to return to get them from his chauffeur, Jack Crimmins, who was not going back to Edgartown but was spending the night at the cottage. Ted told Jack that he was leaving and was giving Mary Jo a lift back to her motel because she was tired and not feeling well. He did not bother to make a grand announcement of his departure because it would have signaled everyone that the party was over, and he did not wish to break it up.

By the time he and Mary Jo arrived at the intersection, Mary Jo must have realized that she had forgotten her purse and that she did not have her motel key. From Officer Look's description of the actions of the vehicle he encountered it is easy to imagine Kennedy and Mary Jo discussing the missing purse and Ted deciding that they'd have to return for it.

As Kennedy pulled to the extreme right of the intersection to allow room for a U-turn and glanced to the left, Officer Look's headlights hit him square in the face and also lit up the interior of the car. The officer slowed nearly to a stop for he thought that the car was going to come on around the turn, and wanted to give him plenty of room in case he cut it too close. Instead, Kennedy wished to turn around, but the officer's stationwagon was making it impossible to maneuver a U-turn with the big Olds in the small area, so Kennedy pulled straight ahead onto Cemetery Road — intending to turn around by backing toward the ferry and then returning the way he had come. However, when he backed up and looked to his right, he discovered that a deputy sheriff in full uniform was walking toward his car as if he wanted a word with him.

Several things must have flashed through Ted Kennedy's mind when he first saw the police officer. He would have wondered why the officer was approaching his car and must have felt the chilling realization that it was a perfect set up for an assassination. As detailed in the last chapter of this book, there is reason to believe that a uniformed security guard played a part in Robert Kennedy's murder. Ted Kennedy must have been well aware of the "second gun" theory involving the guard, for Allard Lowenstein, one of Ted Kennedy's good friends, was a perpetuator of the idea. Under the circumstances Kennedy would have been highly suspicious of a lone police officer — especially one who got out of a private vehicle, in the middle of the night, on a lonely road and appeared to want him to stop. With his background, it would have been foolish indeed for Kennedy to invite a person likely to be carrying a gun to come within firing range.

At the same time, Kennedy was uncomfortably aware of the Nixon administration's vigorous smear campaign against him in preparation for the 1972 presidential campaign. Even if he was not fearful of a possible assassination attempt, he certainly did not wish to speak to a small town cop and give him something to tell his friends about if he could avoid it. It was the middle of the night and he was on an isolated island alone with a lovely young blonde that obviously was not his wife. None of that would have mattered except for the fact that Nixon had a team of muckrakers following Kennedy around looking for information like that to use against him. If the officer mentioned the incident later on in Edgartown, Nixon's boys would be sure to pick it up and presto — full coverage in several newspapers, as had happened to him before.

In view of this combination of facts, Kennedy must have wanted to avoid the encounter completely The officer was blocking his way back to the cottage, his headlights were already shining down Dyke Road, so he hurriedly drove off in that direction. However, after departing the intersection, Kennedy had serious misgivings about his actions. If, by some remote chance, the man was a hired killer, Kennedy had just trapped himself on a dead-end road. On the other hand, the man probably was a police officer and had some reason to stop him. For all Kennedy knew, his tail lights might not have been working properly. Be that as it may, it would have been obvious to the officer that the driver had purposely avoided him. Ted knew that, in all likelihood, the policeman would pursue him, and he was in worse trouble than he had been before because now the officer would certainly have something to tell his friends and the headlines would read, "Senator Kennedy runs away from a police officer to avoid being caught with a blonde in his car." Then too, Kennedy still had no assurance that the officer was not a hit man and it is doubtful he felt like taking the risk of finding out for sure.

Kennedy knew that Dyke Road dead-ended at the

beach and that there was absolutely no way he could avoid the officer unless he got out of the car and disappeared. In the unlikely event the man was an assassin, Mary Jo would be safer alone for no professional would bother her when he realized his quarry had escaped. More likely, the man would prove to be a genuine police officer and Mary Jo would have to come up with some explanation for his absence. Chances were good that the deputy sheriff would not be positive who he saw in the car, and as far as Ted knew, he had done nothing illegal. Although the policeman's suspicions would be aroused if he talked to Mary Jo and realized the other person had departed the scene, the officer would probably assume that the two of them were out for a fling and let it go at that. The main thing was not to be identified.

I believe that Ted Kennedy stepped out of his car at Maitoi Park and Mary Jo continued toward Dike Bridge alone and was the sole occupant of the vehicle when it fell off the bridge and sank into the water where it was invisible to anyone who looked for it. Kennedy could not have heard the splash for between Maitoi Park and Dike Bridge there is a quarter mile of woods that would have scattered the sound waves so that they would not carry far enough for Kennedy to have been aware of the crash.

When Mary Jo did not return, Kennedy assumed that she had gotten the car stuck in the sand as had happened the year before and is very easy to do on Chappaquiddick Island. He returned to the party looking for help to retrieve her from the beach. There was no point in his walking clear down to the beach because, with his bad back, even if he found her, he could not have done anything by himself to extract the car from the sand. Also, his back had been aggravated by his activities that day and had flared up making walking painful and he didn't want to do any more than absolutely necessary. Strolling down to the beach only to have to return to the cottage for help would have added nearly a mile to an already unpleasant exertion.

When he returned to the cottage, Kennedy did not

bother to go to the fire station or ask Ray LaRosa for help because he had no idea of the seriousness of Mary Jo's disappearance at that time. Instead he apparently explained to LaRosa that his car was stuck in the sand and Mary Jo was waiting for him to return with help.

Kennedy, Markham and Gargan drove down Dyke Road and out to the beach but could not locate Mary Jo or the Senator's car. Even if they had used a flashlight to look over the side of the bridge they could not have seen the car, for the submerged headlights would certainly have shorted out by then. It was very dark and the water was deep enough to have made the car difficult to see even in the daylight. At that time I do not think they would have even considered the idea that she might have driven off the bridge. The thought is so unpleasant that they would have tended to avoid thinking about it, especially if they glanced into the water but could see no sign of the car. That area of Chappaquiddick Island is forested and brushy. They may have decided that she drove off into the woods somewhere in hopes of avoiding the officer and the car got stuck. Since the car was black it would be difficult to find in the dark and since Mary Jo was tired, perhaps they thought that instead of walking all the way back to the cottage, she went to sleep in the vehicle. Obviously that is not what happened but it is not difficult to picture them imagining it that way as they tried to figure out where she might be.

Kennedy was tired, and his back hurt. He did not feel like driving around all night and wanted to go back to his motel to sleep. He, Markham and Gargan finally went to the ferry landing and tried to locate a boat they could use, but all were padlocked to the dock. Kennedy did not want to call the ferry operator for several reasons. Everytime he went to Martha's Vineyard, the locals kept track of him and gossiped about his actions. It would not go over well if he got the ferry operator out of bed in the middle of the night to carry him across for one dollar. Second, and most important, he did not wish to be identified with the party because it had gotten a little loud, and he had learned from Gargan and Markham about Officer Look's encounter with LaRosa and the two Lyons sisters on Schoolhouse Road, where Nancy Lyons — his own employee — had obnoxiously told a deputy sheriff, "Shove off Buddy. We aren't pickups." Finally, he did not want it known that he had not left the group until two o'clock in the morning.

According to Kennedy, ". . . [A]s I looked over that distance between the ferry slip and the other side, it seemed to me an inconsequential swim." From where Kennedy and his friends were standing that night they could not have seen that the tide was running swiftly out in the channel beyond the breakwater formed by the ferry landing. Ted Kennedy is an excellent swimmer and Gargan and Markham knew this. Since he had not been in an accident and was not acting out of the ordinary, no one thought much about it when Kennedy decided to swim the channel. Such action wasn't at all surprising for him. However, I do feel that the swim proved very difficult for when interviewed he appears much more comfortable with that aspect of the incident than any other part of the story and seems to dwell on it. I think he does so because it is absolutely true and is therefore easy for him to talk about.

Upon returning to his room exhausted, Kennedy went to bed and tried to sleep, but his back was aching and there was a very loud party next door. His Irish temper was up, so he got dressed and stormed out of his room with the intention of reporting the noise to the manager. He was on his way to the office when he bumped into Russell Peachey, the manager of the Shiretown Inn, where Kennedy was staying. Ted was not sure who Peachey was, but the manager asked if he could help and Kennedy told him that the loud noise from the party had awakened him and he'd like to know what time it was. Peachey told him it was 2:25 a.m. Kennedy did not specifically ask the manager to do something about the noise, for by then he must have realized that it was coming from

210

the inn next door. However, Peachey very definitely got the impression that Kennedy was disturbed by it, and he called the Colonial Inn, which took care of the problem. Ted went back to bed and was finally able to sleep.

By the time Gargan and Markham arrived back at the cottage about 2:15 a.m. they had decided that for some reason Mary Jo had simply taken Kennedy's car and returned by herself to the motel. Perhaps they thought Kennedy had done something to make her angry enough to leave him standing out there all night, and when he gave up waiting and returned to the cottage for help, she drove down to the ferry and back to her motel. Joe Gargan, in fact, told the other party goers that Mary Jo had taken Kennedy's car and returned by herself to the Katama Shores Motel.

Their friends showed little interest in what Gargan and Markham had been doing. Upon discovering they were stranded, most of them had bedded down in the most comfortable spots they could find, on the couch, on the floor and in the beds. Those who were still awake were irritated that they had missed the ferry and couldn't get back to their motel, and Gargan caught the brunt of their wrath. He half-heartedly tried to explain that they had been looking for boats to get them across but that there weren't any. Gargan and Markham were exhausted, so shortly after their return everyone was asleep, completely oblivious to the fact that Mary Jo Kopechne was submerged in nine feet of water under Dike Bridge — in Ted Kennedy's car.

However, Paul Markham may have thought of the possibility that Mary Jo might have drowned. He had preemptied the living room sofa and was attempting to sleep with his leg elevated because it was throbbing and keeping him awake. He had injured it in a fall in the boat earlier that day. He may have lain there and thought very carefully about the road and where Mary Jo might be. At any rate, Paul Markham (according to his own testimony) got up in the middle of the night and went out to the car —

211

perhaps with the intention of going down to Dike Bridge — but the keys were in Joe Gargan's pocket and Gargan was sound asleep on the floor. Markham forgot the idea but I would guess that at first light he got Gargan up, and the two of them went back to Dike Bridge.

If they did check out the bridge in the early morning light, they probably could not have seen the car in the water, for it wasn't until after 8:00 a.m. that the tide was low enough for two fishermen directly above the submerged vehicle to notice it and report the accident. However, Markham and Gargan would have seen the gouge in the rub rail that was left by the car going off of the structure, and this discovery of course would have alarmed them.

Around 8:00 a.m. Gargan, Markham, Charlie Tretter, Crickett Keough and Suzie Tannanbaum returned to Edgartown. Gargan and Markham went straight to Kennedy with their fears while Charlie Tretter, I believe, went to the Katama Shores Motel to see if Mary Jo was there. Mary Jo had not been there so Tretter quickly returned to the Shiretown Inn where he informed Kennedy and company of that fact.

Backtracking a little now, Kennedy arose about 7:30 a.m., fully expecting to be participating in the race. He went for a walk, but it is unclear where — perhaps to check on his boat — it certainly wasn't to the police station. While he was wandering around, he bumped into fellow sailing contestants, Ross Richards and Stanley Moore. The three of them returned to the motel and sat around enjoying the early morning sun, happily discussing the impending race and various problems Moore's crew was having with their housing arrangements. Kennedy offered his suggestions for solving the problem — he obviously wasn't at all worried about Mary Jo's mysterious disappearance the night before.

Around 8:15 a.m. Joe Gargan and Paul Markham puffed onto the scene. From their damp clothes it appeared they had been running around in the fog; they were rumpled, unshaven and generally disturbed and asked to see Kennedy in private. I believe that they told the Senator that they had been unable to locate Mary Jo and that there was a fresh gouge in the bridge as if something had gone off of the structure. The three of them were extremely worried at this point and waited anxiously in Kennedy's room for Charlie's return, hoping that Mary Jo had made it safely back to the Katama Shores.

At approximately 8:30 a.m. Tretter arrived with the alarming news that Mary Jo was not at the Katama Shores, her bed had not been slept in, nobody had seen her, and Kennedy's car was not in the parking lot. At this point there may have been some discussion about what they should do if she had gone off the bridge. Even though by now they must have been thinking seriously of that possibility, it would still be hard to believe, and they were probably telling themselves that there had to be another explanation — they were getting worked up over nothing and she was no doubt asleep in the car some place. Nevertheless, by this time Kennedy was sufficiently worried to attempt to contact his most trusted legal adviser, Burke Marshall — just in case. He went down to the office to make the call, discovered he had no change and had to borrow a dime from the clerk, Mrs. Francis Stewart. Still not really believing anything so terrible could have happened, he also asked to have a couple of newspapers delivered to his room later for he was fully expecting this thing to be cleared up shortly and that he'd still be around to read them. He placed the call but could not reach Marshall. He then attempted to obtain one of Marshall's phone numbers through Steve Smith but again was unsuccessful. When he returned the dime, he thanked the clerk and briefly discussed the previous day's race saying, "I'm not sure how I did, Mrs. Stewart. I think I came in sixth or seventh."

Kennedy returned to his room where he, Markham and Gargan tried to decide what to do next. I think they came to the conclusion that they should go back and take another look under Dike Bridge. They could stop at the ferry landing on the way and Kennedy could make another attempt to reach Burke Marshall. This is exactly what they did; however, Marshall was still not in. As they discussed whether to go down to the bridge or wait a few minutes and try Marshall again, Tony Bettencourt walked up to Kennedy and asked, "Are you Mr. Kennedy?" To which Kennedy replied, "Yes." Then Bettencourt said, "Senator, they just took a dead girl out of your car. Do you want a ride up to the bridge?"

It doesn't take much imagination to see how that must have hit Ted Kennedy, who after a stunned silence finally managed to reply, "No, I'm going over to town."

But Kennedy did not go immediately over to town. He, Markham and Gargan were desperately trying to decide what to do and were still attempting to locate Burke Marshall. The ferry operator observed, "They appeared to be just milling around waiting for something or someone." Kennedy did manage to contact his administrative assistant, David Burke, in Arlington, Virginia. He outlined what had happened and told Dave to go to his Senate office and man the phones. He also told his assistant to locate Burke Marshall and to tell the attorney he needed to talk to him. Kennedy might have asked Dave to have Marshall call him back at the Chappaquiddick phone if he located the attorney soon ... for whatever reason, they remained near the pay phone for a time while trying to decide what to do next.

Kennedy had to be quite shaken at this point ... a friend was dead and she was dead because of his actions, for he was the one who had put her behind the wheel and sent her down the road in an aggitated and slightly intoxicated state to her death. Then, when he couldn't find her, instead of calling for additional help to try to locate her, he had simply gone back to his motel and gone to bed, taking it for granted that she was all right. He had gone to sleep while she was trapped in his car in nine feet of water! It would be logical to assume that even though Ted Kennedy had not actually been the

214

driver of the vehicle, he blamed himself for the accident just as much as if he had been.

But that wasn't the half of it — the detour he had made at the intersection in order to avoid the deputy led to the accident and that officer would probably identify him as the driver of the car he saw take off toward the bridge at the approximate time of the accident. Kennedy had to work from the assumption that he would be positively identified, because the officer's headlights had hit him right in the face and they had been looking directly at each other from less than thirty feet apart. It was also common knowledge that he was spending the weekend in Edgartown, and in addition, the first thing any police officer does when he stops a car is to get its license number. Couple these probabilities with the fact that it was indeed his car which went off of the bridge, and it would be apparent to all that he had been behind the wheel when the accident occurred.

What was he going to say — that he got caught with a blonde in his car and ran away from a police officer, but that he did not drive off of the bridge because he got out and hid in the bushes like a common fugitive? That confession would be damaging enough, but what was worse was that it was hard to believe.

What would follow was that the officer would make his report and Kennedy would make his. Then the grand jury would review it and decide whether there was just cause to believe that Kennedy had been guilty of criminal conduct in the case ... and there would be cause. If he claimed to have gotten out of the vehicle and knew nothing about the accident that night, he would be pleading innocent to all charges. On the basis of Officer Look's testimony, the grand jury would have to conclude that there was reason to doubt Kennedy's claim of having gotten out of the vehicle and therefore would have to call for an in depth investigation culminating with a public trial by jury. Thus, the grand jury would have to indict him for something, and those charges could range from leaving the scene of a fatal accident to negligent driving and manslaughter. Worse yet, as far as Kennedy knew, there was absolutely no proof that he had gotten out of the vehicle to back up his word that he did so. He also knew that a prosecutor would ask the jury whether or not Senator Kennedy had something to gain by hiding the fact that he had caused a fatal accident and then left the scene. The answer to that question was obvious — any politician would have plenty to gain by saying he had gotten out of the car if in fact he had not and was guilty as charged.

If he denied being the driver, there was no doubt that Kennedy would be indicted by the grand jury and brought to trial. The jurors would be selected randomly from Edgartown where many were hard-boiled conservatives, who did not like the Kennedys as Ted well knew from the publicity he frequently received in the local papers following his visits . . . so there were likely to be some people on the jury who were already hostile toward him. Furthermore, the jury would be under an incredible amount of pressure for the trial would be the most publicized in the history of the United States. A great deal of the information disseminated to the public would be written from the standpoint of sensation rather than reporting the facts relevant to the findings of the jury. The jury was going to be criticized no matter what its findings were, but if he was acquitted there would be accusations that Kennedy had bought the jury. The jury members would be quick to recognize that fact and thus would tend to be very hard on him. The fact that his name was Edward Moore Kennedy instead of Edward Moore was going to make it much more likely that he would be found guilty. If not, the trial would almost certainly result in a hung jury, which would be just as damaging to his career as if he were found guilty. As a matter of fact, any politician who is indicted for manslaughter might as well pack up and go home — no matter what the verdict.

Even if the jury unanimously came to the conclusion that he was innocent, it would not alter the fact that a deputy sheriff would have testified that he saw Kennedy driving rapidly toward the bridge with a girl in his car and that car was fished out of Poucha Pond, and the girl was dead. The public would naturally assume that he had driven off the bridge and left the scene of the accident whether or not he was convicted of a crime. If the jury let him off, to many people he would be a killer who had lied, bought the jury, hired the best lawyers, and got off scott-free. He would be finished politically. Even being a Kennedy could not save him. Public opinion would convict him and sentence him, and with Nixon and friends directing publicity he didn't stand a chance.

Could he win if he lost? If he were convicted of, say manslaughter, what would happen? That would be worse yet. He would be an adjudicated liar. He would be so evil, in fact, that even the best attorneys in the country could not get him off. With all of the reporting that would go with the trial, along with a guilty verdict, he would be labeled as a rogue who seduced a girl, then, in a drunken stupor, drove off a bridge and left her to drown in the car. Nobody needed to tell Ted Kennedy the consequences of a guilty finding.

The Senator definitely did not want to face a public trial. Not only would he be finished politically no matter what the verdict, but also the stress it would put on his family and himself would be unbearable. His father was very ill, and since he was bedridden he watched television constantly. There would be no way that the frail Joe Kennedy could stand another severe — and in this case prolonged — emotional blow. A public trial would kill his father.

Ted's wife, Joan, would not be able to take the strain. She already had a drinking problem with which she could not seem to cope, and such a trial would aggravate the situation. In addition, Joan was two months pregnant and had suffered two miscarriages in the past. She had a delicate hormone balance and was under doctor's orders not to exert herself in any way or she could lose the baby; the emotional pressures of a public trial would most certainly trigger another tragedy. Sadly, those fears were well-founded for a few weeks later Joan did miscarry.

What about his children? They would be ridiculed by their classmates if their father had to stand trial. The accusations about his moral conduct which were going to grow out of this, especially in view of the smear campaign which had been in full swing against him for months, were going to be vicious and hard to handle — it would be even worse if his past drinking habits and conduct were testified to in a court of law and duly reported by the press.

Surely Ted Kennedy wanted to avoid a public trial at any cost. He recognized the fact that there was only one way to do that and that was to plead guilty to a crime he did not commit. He chose to plead guilty to leaving the scene of the accident and not to a more serious crime such as negligent driving, which could result in a manslaughter charge, in hopes that the court would be satisfied with the lesser charge. In order to plead guilty to a crime and get it over with, he had to admit that he had been the driver of the car and had been involved in the accident when in reality he had not. However, I am certain that Ted Kennedy felt at that time, and has continued to feel, that Mary Jo's death was entirely his fault. Whether he had driven her to her death personally or put her behind the wheel of his car, it was his poor judgment which resulted in her death. Therefore, I doubt that Kennedy thought it was a horrendous lie when he said he drove the car off the bridge ... he might as well have ... Mary Jo was dead because of his actions.

The political ramifications of his decision are also interesting. Long ago, the Kennedys discovered that they are much better off accepting the full blame for their actions rather than attempting to justify them. For instance, after the Bay of Pigs disaster, Jack Kennedy took the blame for the fiasco declaring, "I am the responsible officer of the government." Heads rolled in private, but publically he declared it to be his fault. Robert Kennedy did the same in 1967

concerning Vietnam. Although he had not been involved in the vast majority of the Vietnam decisions
either under the Kennedy or Johnson administra-
tions, most people assumed that he had been. So
when Robert Kennedy came out against Vietnam he
started by declaring, "If fault is to be found there is
enough to go around including myself." And last but
not least, Ted Kennedy himself, with the helpful
guidance of JFK, applied the same tactics to his
Harvard cheating episode which had occurred when
he was a naive 18-year old freshman, but which was
brought up in the 1962 campaign. The published
reports were not completely accurate and made it
appear that Ted had hired somebody to take the test
for him when in actuality they had done it on a dare.
Rather than attempt to explain his way out of the
story, Ted admitted to the whole thing saying,
"What I did was wrong. I have regretted it ever
since. The unhappiness I caused my family and
friends, even though eleven years ago, has been a
bitter experience for me, but it has also been a
valuable lesson." The full confession completely took
the wind out of his opponents' sails for they could
not add to what he had said, and the issue was dead.

The episode was indeed "a valuable lesson" for I
believe Ted Kennedy used the same tactic with the
Chappaquiddick accident. He told the public exactly
what they wanted to hear. He told them in the worst
possible way he could think of and still hopefully
stay out of jail. He admitted to driving the car. He
declared that the accident was all his fault, and he
said that he was guilty of leaving the scene of the
accident. By taking the entire blame, Ted Kennedy
knew no other accusations would grow out of Officer
Look's testimony. Being in the middle of another
tragedy, he gained a great deal of public sympathy,
especially after all that he and his family have been
through, and today a great many people are irritated
by the critics who continually attack Ted Kennedy
over his behavior at Chappaquiddick. "After all,"
they say, "he admitted it, didn't he? What else do
you want him to do? Why don't you just leave the

poor man alone?"

Ted Kennedy made the most important decision of his career in the fifteen or twenty minutes he was standing around the ferry house waiting for a call from Burke Marshall which never came, and I think he made it by himself, against the advice of Paul Markham, who had just retired from his position of Attorney General for the state of Massachusetts.

The ferry operator, Richard Hewitt, had also been informed of the accident by Tony Bettencourt. After watching Kennedy, Markham and Gargan for a period of time and seeing that they weren't going anywhere, Hewitt wasn't sure they had been told of the accident so he went over to inform them. Kennedy saw him coming and purposely walked off because he didn't want to talk to anyone at that time. Hewitt asked Paul Markham if they knew about the accident, to which Paul Markham replied, "Yes, we just heard about it." — Which I believe is the truth.

By this time Kennedy realized that the longer he waited, the more trouble he was going to be in. He had made his decision and nothing Burke Marshall had to say was going to change it, so he suddenly told Markham and Gargan what he was going to do and sprinted for the ferry. Markham was right behind him, obviously horrified by the idea. All the way across the channel Markham tried to talk him out of it, but to no avail and when they reached the other side Kennedy jumped off and hurried to the police station, deliberately leaving the out-of-shape and slightly lame Markham hopelessly behind.

When Kennedy arrived at the police station, he was quite shaken and acting somewhat confused. He asked the policewoman, Carmen Salvatore, if the police chief was in; receiving a "no" he said that he wished to speak to him and would wait. Kennedy then asked if he could use the phone and she let him use the police chief's office. Apparently the first person Kennedy called was his wife, Joan, who was staying at their Squaw Island home. He told her that there had been a bad accident in which Mary Jo Kopechne had been killed and that she and the children should stay home in order to avoid reporters. He then called his mother and left a message for her not to attend the book sale at St. Francis Xavier Church where she had been planning to autograph books about her dead sons.

The police chief called in with the intention of putting out a bulletin to locate Senator Kennedy, for by that time he had determined it was the Senator's car under Dike Bridge, and to his surprise learned that Kennedy was already at the police station. Arena spoke to him on the phone and later testified:

> I would have to say it would have been after 9 o'clock, but I don't really know how much time elapsed. At any rate, when I called her she said, "He is here."
>
> She meant the Senator and he wanted to talk to me so he got on the phone and I said words to the effect that I am sorry. I have some bad news, your car was in an accident over here and the young lady is dead. He said, "I know."
>
> I said, Can you tell me was there anybody else in the car?
>
> He said, "yes."
>
> I said, Are they in the water?
>
> He said, "No."
>
> I said, Can I talk to you?
>
> He said, "Yes."
>
> I said, Would you like to talk to me?
>
> He said, "I prefer for you to come over here."

After speaking to Police Chief Arena, Kennedy decided that he had better break the sad news to Mr. and Mrs. Kopechne before they heard it on the radio or TV. From what the observant policewoman told Jack Olsen and from what Mrs. Kopechne remembers of the distressing call, the conversation went as follows.

Mrs. Kopechne answered the phone and Kennedy said, "Hello, is this Mrs. Kopechne?"

To which she replied, "Yes."

"This is Senator Kennedy." He seemed to choke up and had difficulty getting his next words out but managed to continue, "I'm afraid that I have some very sad news to tell you. Mary Jo's been in an accident."

Mrs. Kopechne quickly asked, "Was she killed?"

And Kennedy shakily replied, "Yes, she was."

That was the end of the conversation for Mrs.

Kopechne became hysterical, dropping the phone and running out of her house crying. A neighbor had to slap her before she became coherent again.

In the meantime, Kennedy was left holding the receiver, listening to the upsetting background sounds. Carmen Salvatore observed that he looked very upset as he replaced the receiver on the hook and slumped dejectedly into the chair.

After a few minutes Kennedy started making phone calls again. According to Jack Olsen, the policewoman overheard snatches of his conversation which went, "He's out sailing? When do you expect him? I see ... You say he just left the office? Well, where was he headed? ... When will he be back? ..." At this time Kennedy contacted Dun Gifford and asked him to come to Edgartown to take care of Mary Jo's body. He asked William vanden Heuval to go up to the Kopechnes and help them make the arrangements from that end and to try to keep reporters away from the bereaved parents. He also contacted his press secretary, Dick Drayne. Although he didn't give him many details, he told Drayne to be prepared for the worst day of his life.

Police Chief Arena arrived to discover that Kennedy had taken command of his office. He testified:

> I walked into the station and in my office in the station was Paul Markham on my right and Senator Kennedy on the telephone.
>
> The Senator hung up the phone, came over, said hello, shook my hand, and I think I said something to the effect, I am sorry about what happened.
>
> He said, "Yes, I know, I was the driver," so I don't think I said anything there for a minute.
>
> He said, "What would you like for me to do, we must do what is right or we will both be criticized for it."
>
> I said, "The first thing we will have to do is have a statement from you about what happened."
>
> He asked me if it would be all right if he wrote it.
>
> I said, "Yes, it would be." ... At this time, even at this early time the reporters were beginning to crop up in the station and I said, "If you would like to have a little privacy to write this statement, I will let you in the Selectmen's office." I took him in the Selectmen's office down the hall.

It took Kennedy quite a while to compose the statement which he dictated to Markham. He appeared periodically, pacing the hall, and spoke to Carmen Salvatore a couple of times about the accident and the gathering crowd in front of the police station. Ted Kennedy was in a tight spot, because he did not know as much about the accident as the police did. What he said in his original statement clearly shows this. His description of the accident is "The car went off the side of the bridge ... The car turned over and sank into the water and landed with the roof resting on the bottom." About all Kennedy knew at this point was that his car was upside down under Dike Bridge. From his description it appears that he thought it had sailed off of the structure and landed on its wheels, then turned over ... which of course, is not what happened. "Turned over and sank" is a poor description of what the car actually did. In addition, Kennedy said, "I attempted to open the door and the window of the car but have no recollection of how I got out of the car." He obviously did not know if the car door had been found open or the window down, so he hedged. Those scanty items are all that are contained in the statement because that is all Kennedy knew at the time ... which obviously wasn't much.

Kennedy gave his statement to Arena, who typed it while Ted filled out some motor vehicle forms which also asked for a description of the accident as well as the speed at which it occurred. After conferring with Markham, Kennedy decided that Mary Jo must have been going about twenty miles per hour and included that speed in the report but other than that, his story was almost identical to the statement given Arena. The supervisor of the Motor Vehicle Department, George Kennedy, was not satisfied with the sketchy report and when he questioned the Senator about it Kennedy grew snappish. According to the supervisor's testimony, "He said, 'No comment.' I asked him this: I would like to know about something. He said, 'I have no comment.' " The reason Kennedy had no comment is that he didn't know anything else about the accident and did not want to answer any questions which would expose that fact.

About this time Joe Gargan and Jack Crimmins appeared at the police station and had a conference with Kennedy, who apparently instructed Gargan to clean up the cottage (which had already been done) and to pay all of their bills in full, even for things they would not be using, in order to keep everybody happy.

Arena made arrangements for Bob Carroll to fly Kennedy and Markham to Hyannis. Upon departing the police station Kennedy had another discussion with Police Chief Arena concerning the handling of the case. He told Arena to release the statement to the waiting reporters. Arena was surprised because it was not a common practice for the police to release such statements to the public. However, Kennedy felt that they had to give the reporters something because the press was going to publish a story and Kennedy wanted to make sure it was the one he wanted told. Before Ted left, however, Markham asked Arena to hold up the statement until Kennedy's lawyer, Burke Marshall, had a chance to read it, but as it worked out Kennedy was a long time catching up with Marshall, and Arena was under a great deal of pressure from the press so he released it before Kennedy called back. The action was apparently acceptable to the Senator, for when informed that it had been prematurely released, Markham said that was fine.

Ted Kennedy had gone through an exceedingly emotional ordeal that morning, but even though shaken by events, he had remained in complete control, giving orders to everyone — including the police chief. This is hardly the kind of action one would expect from an injured man who had run away from an accident in a state of shock, confusion and panic. Instead he remained on top of the situation — cool and rational, guiding events the way he wanted them to go.

However, once in the car being chauffeured to the Edgartown Airport, he began to think about what had occurred. At this time, he let down and became quite distraught. According to the testimony of George Kennedy, the Motor Vehicle Supervisor who drove the Senator and Markham to the airport, Ted Kennedy was distressed and sat slumped in the front seat muttering over and over, "Oh, my God! What has happened? What has happened?"

If we examine the consequences of Ted Kennedy's confession at the Edgartown Police Station, we see that as politically astute as the move might have been, Kennedy did not have time to carefully consider all of the angles, and he made one error which has caused him a great deal of difficulty. He apparently manipulated the time. I believe that Kennedy did not wish to volunteer that he was the driver of the vehicle the deputy saw in the intersection, for in doing so he would have to admit that he ran away from a police officer. However, it was also true that Kennedy suspected that the officer might be able to positively identify him so he tried to wriggle around the problem by moving the time up about an hour, which would look much better to the public. If it did turn out that the officer was sure it was he in the intersection at 12:45 a.m. then all Kennedy would have to do was to say he really hadn't been paying much attention to the time since he was socializing — and had only been guessing. Most people would be willing to accept that explanation. Unfortunately, the officer could not positively identify him so Kennedy did not concede the time right away and his friends backed him up on it. As the days passed Officer Look began talking more about it and people started double checking tides, but by then Kennedy had locked himself in on the time and was stuck with it.

He also made a serious error when he said that he accidently took the wrong turn. He probably thought the explanation was plausible for he really hadn't paid much attention to the layout of the intersection. Unfortunately, it was quite obvious that he did not make a wrong turn. He attempted to drop the idea, but since he had put it in his original statement he couldn't take it back without admitting to having supplied misinformation to the police, so he decided to ride it out.

At the time he reported the accident at the police station Kennedy must have been hoping that the whole incident would blow over quickly ... which of course was only wishful thinking. Had he had more time to think about it, he probably would have realized that he wasn't going to get out of the accusation of having turned down the road purposely to avoid the police officer. If he had admitted it from the start he might have gotten away with the confession. Then again, if he had had more time to think about it he might have gotten cold feet and chickened out altogether, which would have been the end of his career, since he would have had to stand trial.

If we accept the premise that Ted Kennedy did alter the facts in that he was not the driver of the vehicle at the time of the accident but admitted that he was, we must also ask ourselves exactly what he did which was wrong. Some will argue that Ted Kennedy technically committed perjury by making inaccurate statements under oath. However, in the narrow sense, the law differentiates between perjury, which is lying under oath in regard to a *material* statement (a statement which has a bearing on the outcome), as compared to false swearing, which is lying under oath on a matter which will not alter the findings of the court.

The reason perjury is considered a serious crime is that it is usually done either to injure someone else or to protect oneself or another person from being punished for a crime against society. In Kennedy's case he did neither. The only person he injured was himself, and rather than attempting to protect himself he did just the opposite by convicting himself of a crime he did not commit. Not only that, but his testimony did not have a bearing on the outcome of the case because it was already foreordained by his original admission in the accident report of having been the driver, that he would be found guilty of leaving the scene of the accident. Nothing he said that day under oath changed the outcome of that decision.

In the event a witness had appeared or other evidence was discovered which proved that Kennedy had lied under oath and had not been involved in the accident at all after having provided the court with an elaborate fabrication of an event which never took place, the court would have had an interesting decision to make. Under the circumstances any court would have found that Kennedy made an "admission against his own interest" (some might even call it a confession under mental duress) and convicted himself thereon. Since he did not obstruct justice and harmed no one other than himself it is highly unlikely that the court would have found him guilty of anything other than stupidity which, of course, is not a criminal offense and Kennedy probably would have been laughed clear out of the court. However, since there was simply no evidence to support a claim by Kennedy that he had stepped out of the car and was not involved in the accident, the situation he found himself in was certainly no laughing matter as far as Ted Kennedy was concerned.

Kennedy has staunchly stated again and again that the accident was entirely his fault and that he is the one who walked off and left Mary Jo to die in his car. Whether or not he was actually aware of the accident, the fact remains that in view of the final outcome, he simply did not try as hard as he should have to locate her. The failure was a gigantic mistake on his part. In my opinion, Ted Kennedy was indirectly responsible for Mary Jo's death because he put her behind the wheel of his car. However, Kennedy himself has gone further by accusing himself of directly causing her death when he claimed that he personally drove her off the bridge . . . so what it boils down to is that Kennedy has always felt responsible for having caused the accident and for his failure to summon help and has therefore reported his basic guilt truthfully. His statements have been questionable only in regard to the relatively unimportant circumstances surrounding the accident.

Once those details and his subsequent behavior became known, instead of further incriminating him of wrong doing, Kennedy's actions, while not the best, become much more acceptable than his own story makes them appear.

Some people believe that Kennedy was intoxicated and was therefore guilty of drunk driving; the same group also subscribes to the idea that he was planning to seduce the girl. Other than what has been covered in this book, there is very little that can be said which will prove or disprove those ideas. However, I tend to believe that he is innocent of those charges. Add drunkenness to all of the other obstacles confronting a person swimming the channel that night at that time, and the sharks far out to sea would probably have been presented a Senatorial feast. Had he been drunk there would not now be anything to write about. Also, in the past when charged with similar misdeeds he has either shrugged or laughed it off but in this instance it was very important to him to be believed, and not just by the public. He apparently spent a good deal of time trying to convince his Senate collegues of his innocence in that respect. According to Burton Hersh, who interviewed many of the congressmen who work with Kennedy,

> "No fornication; not drunk; Kennedy would
> *swear* to it, raise his right hand without realizing it like a witness in the box, over and over,
> to individuals who mattered."

Hersh is not the only one who reports having seen Ted Kennedy doing this. In my opinion, had he indeed been drunk and fornicating, rather than continually bring the subject up he would have been trying to duck it and wishing it would just go away. In the past Kennedy has overindulged on occasion and admits it, he has possibly been involved in some minor immoral conduct, although in view of the vigorous smear campaign which has been conducted against him these accusations may or may not be true. After all, it might have been "smear fear" that sent him down the road in the first place. But ironically this time he was in all likelihood behaving properly — yet it was this instance which ruined his moral standing with a large segment of the public.

As far as avoiding the police officer at the intersection was concerned, while in retrospect he should not have done so, there was nothing illegal about it, for he had done nothing wrong and the officer did not signal him to stop. To the contrary, given the fact that Kennedy had reason to believe there could be an attempt made on his life, it would have been foolish for him to stop for a man dressed as a police officer who got out of a private car on a lonely road in the middle of the night and walked toward him.

Be that as it may, Kennedy himself is not pleased with the actions he took that night. In an interview with Tom Jarriel, aired on November 2, 1979, Kennedy became irritated with Jarriel's accusatory tone and in frustration declared, "Look, I wish I'd done many other things that evening. And as you bring these matters on up I wish I'd done many, many other things that particular evening and I've relived this a thousand different times and wish that I had taken other kinds of action. I wish I had."

I am sure he was completely honest in that statement for whether you believe his tale or my theory, one thing is certain — he feels completely responsible for Mary Jo's death and has said so repeatedly ... "It will remain a personal tragedy for me. I've accepted full responsibility for it. There isn't a day of my life that goes by in which I don't feel a sense of anguish and a sense of loss about it."

He has also stated, and I believe truthfully, "I've been impacted by a number of tragedies in my life. The loss of life of members of my family, those were circumstances of which I really didn't have control. I felt a sense of regret, a sense of sadness and a sense of loss but this was a circumstance in which I did have a responsibility. In that sense it was quite different from others of life's experiences and so I'm a very different person than prior to that tragedy. My own inner views and attitudes of life and of people and faith in God — I'm a different person and I know that."

CHAPTER XXIII
THE LEGAL CONSIDERATIONS

There are those who believe that Ted Kennedy was not the driver of the car when it left Dike Bridge, but that he made a serious mistake by not reporting the incident accurately in the first place. However, a figure prominent in the political world leads a life completely different from that of the average citizen, and in situations of potential scandal must think and act defensively. It would have been better for almost anyone to have admitted to detouring around a police officer and having stepped out of the car rather than to confess to having been the driver in a fatal accident which was not reported until ten hours later. Except in rare instances, the matter would have been settled between the defendant, his attorney and a court of law. However, in Kennedy's case, the matter was between him, his lawyers, a court of law, a worried District Attorney, a vengeful President, an excited press, a public clamoring for information, and a nervous jury.

The vast majority of people never have a serious confrontation with the law and go through life naively believing that honesty is always the best policy, although most are not above bending the truth when in their own best interests. One of the functions of a court of law is to separate the truth from the lies; unfortunately a judge or jury has no crystal ball and must make value judgments based, in large part, on guesswork and the image the defendant projects in the court room.

Most of us are aware of instances where the court guessed wrong. The press often reports cases of persons being convicted and sentenced for serious crimes, who were later proved to be innocent after having been incarcerated — sometimes for years. Those who have served on a jury can attest to the frustration felt in making their decision, and the worry that they could guess wrong and allow a criminal to be released to prey on the public again, or sentence an innocent person to prison. Those who have experienced the inner turmoil of making such a decision will not soon forget it.

Edward M. Kennedy is a lawyer trained in arguing court cases and very good at it, as he proved when he won the Moot Court competition with John Tunney at the University of Virginia Law School. Robert F. Kennedy, too, was a lawyer and served as minority counsel during the McCarthy hearings, chief counsel to the Senate Rackets Committee, and Attorney General of the United States. The Kennedys have always been a legally oriented family, and from an early age Ted Kennedy knew what to expect from a court of law — and the abuses which occur in our legal system.

On a 1979 segment of *60 Minutes,* Attorney Roy Cohn declared:

"I would do *anything* that is legally permissible to do to get my client to win. Yes I would. That's my job. There isn't anything I would not do because I believe there's only one answer in an adversary profession like law and that is winning."

Roy Cohn's attitude is characteristic of many attorneys who have received recognition because of their "winning ways." However, Cohn's philosophy did not endear him to the Kennedys during his infamous Communist witch hunts for the McCarthy Committee. Robert Kennedy, who also served on the McCarthy Committee, did not approve of his colleague's methods and wrote:

"With two exceptions no real research was ever done. Most of the investigations were instituted on the basis of some preconceived notion by the chief counsel or his staff members and not on the basis of any information that had been developed. Cohn and Schine claimed they knew from the onset what was wrong; and they were not going to allow the facts to interfere. Therefore no real spade work that might have destroyed some of their pet theories was ever undertaken. I thought Senator McCarthy made a mistake in allowing the Committee to operate in such a fashion, told him so and resigned."

In his book *The Enemy Within* Robert Kennedy pointed out how legal proceedings can be used for political purposes.

"I am not claiming that when I questioned a witness I always had positive proof on the subject matter of the interrogation. In many instances, where a gangster was concerned, the information came from police files and could not be positively verified. These people not only wouldn't talk to us, they wouldn't and haven't talked to anyone. However, if I had some information to support the question, I believed that I was justified in asking it.

"But this is where abuses creep in.

"For instance, a witness from the Midwest was pleading the Fifth Amendment on every question when suddenly Senator Curtis asked him what his relationship was with the Governor of Iowa. I knew this was an unfair question at the time, for we had no information that the man even knew the Governor of Iowa or had had any dealings with him. The witness, of course, did not have to plead the Fifth Amendment on that question, but since he was pleading it regularly, once more made no difference to him. In any case, he exercised his privilege and refused to answer on grounds of self-incrimination. And in Iowa, as I had expected, the story was 'Gangster Takes Fifth Amendment on Ties with Governor.' I immediately put out a statement that we had absolutely no information about any relationship between the Governor and the witness. But the damage had been done. It was low politics and a perversion of the use of the Congressional investigating committee."

Although Ted Kennedy, who serves on the Senate Judiciary Committee, has been more involved in congressional hearings than in criminal court proceedings, the same unethical tactics are used in both places. Through his work on the committee, Ted was keenly aware of misuses which can occur in court proceedings — no one had to tell him about the political consequences of having to stand public trial. The prospect of Senator Kennedy facing a jury titillated every Republican in the country — President Nixon in particular. Kennedy was well aware of the kind of activity he could expect from the Nixon Administration, and his fears were realized. The President's plant, Tony Ulasewicz, posing as a reporter at Kennedy's July hearing, "did a masterful job" of inserting questions into the dialogue among reporters — questions which might never have been raised otherwise. Imagine what Tony could have done with an open inquest, or better yet, a public trial.

Presidential "investigators" like Tony Ulasewicz could do severe damage to Ted Kennedy, but the prosecutor could completely destroy him if he so desired. For instance, even though the prosecutor would have known from the testimony of Officer Look that the woman in the vehicle he met at the intersection was alive, and from the testimony of several doctors that Mary Jo lived for a few minutes after the accident, he still could have asked Kennedy, "Was Mary Jo Kopechne already dead when you ran away from the officer at the intersection?" It does not take much insight to see how the press would report such a startling question. The possibilities would be limited only by the prosecutor's imagination, and the Prosecutor of the Southern District who would be in charge of any proceedings against Senator Kennedy, was District Attorney Edmund Dinis — a long-time Kennedy antagonist.

Edmund Dinis was formerly a Democratic State Representative from New Bedford, later a State Senator, and finally Southern District District Attorney. Animosity had existed for years between the Kennedys and the Dinises, going back to 1914 when Ted's grandfather, John (Honey Fitz) Fitzgerald, the incumbent Mayor of Boston, was defeated by James Michael Curley, a friend of the Dinis family. "Honey

Fitz" was constantly at odds with James Curley, considered him a crook and pointedly described himself as "the last honest mayor of Boston." The antagonism that existed between the Kennedy and Curley camps can hardly be overstated. Representative Jack Kennedy delivered a dreadful punch to the ailing Mayor Curley, for which the Kennedys were never forgiven by Curley's friends. Kenny O'Donnell described the incident,

"Kennedy's refusal to sign the petition for Curley's pardon, when it was handed to him on the floor of the House, was a startling display of political courage in 1947. [Curley supporters were more inclined to view it as political get-evenness.] Curley, then doing time in the Federal penitentiary at Danbury, Connecticut, for wartime construction-contract frauds, was such a popular figure in Boston that he continued in office as mayor while serving his prison sentence. He had made a dramatic appeal, appearing in court in a wheelchair, pleading that he was suffering from nine ailments, including an 'impending cerebral hemorrhage' and wearing a collar too large for his neck, but the judge refused to suspend his sentence. Curley was regarded as a martyred hero in Kennedy's Congressional district where he had served as the previous representative and where, as his followers loudly recalled, his retirement from the House seat had made Kennedy's election possible. Furthermore, Kennedy was the only Massachusetts Democrat in Congress who declined to sign his predecessor's pardon petition, which had the endorsement not only of McCormack, who controlled Federal patronage in the state, but also the backing of the Democratic National Committee and the blessing of President Truman himself. Despite this pressure, Kennedy held back his signature because he doubted that the imprisoned mayor was as ill as he claimed to be, a suspicion that later appeared to be justified. When Curley was finally released after five months in the penitentiary, he made a sudden recovery, returned immediately to his office at City Hall, and announced to crowds of jubilant well-wishers that he was feeling better than he had felt in the past ten years."

Although Ted Kennedy and Edmund Dinis had been on opposite sides of the Massachusetts Democratic fence, there had been no personal conflicts until 1962 when Edmund Dinis supported Eddie McCormack in his bid for the Senate seat vacated by Jack Kennedy and being pursued by Ted Kennedy. McCormack's vicious attack on Ted Kennedy during a televised debate did not endear McCormack's avid supporters who had encouraged the onslaught, to Ted — who succeeded in winning the election.

In 1968 Edmund Dinis won the Democratic nomination for Congressman from the Tenth District, and his fellow Democrat from the state, Senator Ted Kennedy, refused to back his election bid — preferring to stand on the sidelines and calmly watch Republican Margaret Hecker defeat Dinis for the seat he coveted. Dinis complained loudly that Kennedy had snubbed him because he (Dinis) had supported McCormack in 1962. However, such was not the case, according to Burton Hersh:

"There was a large, richly paneled office in the Dinis Building in New Bedford out of which he had openly conducted, throughout his public career, a *most* lucrative insurance and law practice ... The fact was that the forever watchful Senator [Kennedy] had been — behind closed Committee room doors — warned away even from such a gesture as permitting himself to be trapped and photographed in company with Dinis because — Republican Attorney General Elliott Richardson had tipped the Kennedy managers off — an investigation in depth was pending into Dinis' alleged practice of soliciting insurance business beneath his Office of the District Attorney letterhead."

Regardless of the reason for Ted Kennedy's refusal to help Edmund Dinis (only a few months prior to the Chappaquiddick accident), Dinis attributed his loss in large measure to Kennedy and appeared to be bitter about it. Kennedy was clearly worried about the treatment he could expect from the disgruntled D.A. This concern was apparent in the exchange between Kennedy's lawyer Edward Hanify and Chief Justice Wilkins of the Massachusetts Supreme Court where Hanify was asking for a closing of the inquest into the death of Mary Jo Kopechne;

CHIEF JUSTICE WILKINS: Before you make your point, I was going to ask: Do you claim that the inquest is unconstitutional anyway, no matter how it is conducted?

MR. HANIFY: No, your Honor. I claim it is possible for the honorable Court to infuse the inquest with constitutional vitality and relieve it from the present infirmity. And those basic infirmities, I believe, are curable by appropriate directives.

CHIEF JUSTICE WILKINS: Do you mean it is always accusatory, no matter how it is conducted?

MR. HANIFY: I think, your Honor, that it has always the potentiality of being an accusatory proceeding. In other words, it may start to be accusatory because the district attorney, who required it, intends it to be such. **It may commence to be investigatory, and after five minutes of evidence it may be accusatory."**

As nervous as Ted Kennedy must have been knowing that Edmund Dinis would be his prosecutor, Dinis had to have been even more worried about Kennedy being the defendant he was prosecuting. No matter what he did, the D.A.'s political asperations were in serious trouble. If Dinis came down hard on Kennedy and it appeared to Massachusetts Kennedy supporters that Dinis had unfairly caused their beloved Senator's demise, the D.A. would never get another Democratic nomination in Massachusetts. On the other hand, if he was perceived as letting Kennedy off easy because he was a fellow Democrat, Dinis' ethics would be questioned and he would be finished.

In the first few days following the accident Edmund Dinis was clearly casting about looking for a way out of his dilemma. In the end the District Attorney dissatisfied everyone, for after a nervously slow start he pursued the case vigorously. In being slow to begin, Dinis antagonized the anti-Kennedy observers and in coming on very strong later, he angered the pro-Kennedy group. The unhappy Dinis looked back and complained, "The papers — everybody that said I was after Kennedy — they were reading my mind. When somebody reads my mind it gets my ass."

Dinis was defeated for reelection in November of 1970 and bitterly remarked:

"She died and I got defeated. The press! They take you for a Nantucket Sleighride. You know what that is. Once they put the harpoon into you you've had it. You go where it makes you go, even to the bottom. And that is where I went. You're perhaps a little wiser but much, much sadder."

CHAPTER XXIV
"IN OUR FAMILY
IT DOESN'T PAY
TO PLAN TOO FAR AHEAD"
— Ted Kennedy, 1969

With the approach of the 1980 election, attention is again focused on Chappaquiddick — but this time the focus is taken out of context. At the time the accident occurred Robert Kennedy had been dead barely a year. Jacqueline had suddenly married Onassis and left the United States and Ted Kennedy had refused the 1968 Presidential nomination. There had been scattered reports that the Kennedys were not coping well. There was Ted Kennedy's surprise plea to spare Sirhan Sirhan's life when the accused assassin was sentenced to death. RFK's assassination and news interviews by Rose and Joan Kennedy made people aware that the family feared for Ted's safety. It was also well known that Joe Kennedy Sr. was dangerously ill and perhaps dying; indeed, when Bobby was killed it was rumored that his father had died from the shock.

The public was aware of the fact that there was much turmoil within the Kennedy family. Chappaquiddick was viewed in the context of personal tragedy. Americans may not have believed the Senator's tale, but most felt sympathy for him and his family. Today that feeling of sympathy is gone, faded by time and replaced by feelings of anger and distrust.

Ironically, we are in a better position today to understand the emotion and physical stress Ted Kennedy endured for many months before the accident. Few have cared to look. Yet, if they did, they would discover many of the answers concerning Senator Kennedy's behavior at Chappaquiddick and

* The extraordinary nature of the material presented in this chapter makes documentation necessary. Footnotes appear on page 286.

Joan Kennedy's difficulties in coping with her life.

In order to understand Ted Kennedy in 1969, one must go back six years to the assassination of President Kennedy in 1963. Although both Robert and Ted Kennedy publically supported the Warren Commission's conclusion that Lee Harvey Oswald had acted alone, privately they did not believe it. Robert Kennedy discussed his brother's murder with President Johnson shortly after it happened and told the new President that he suspected organized crime was behind the shooting.[1] Both agreed at the time that the public must be convinced that Oswald was the lone assassin because false leads had been laid which pointed to pro-Castro Communists, and if Castro was perceived by the public as being behind the murder, we could quickly find ourselves in WWIII with the Soviet Union which had pledged to defend Castro from U.S. "aggression". Therefore, the Warren Commission was provided only the information it needed to come to the "proper" conclusion. RFK and his Justice Department associates had no intention of letting Jack Kennedy's murder go unsolved, but they knew it would be a tough case to crack. Much of the information made public for the first time in July of 1979 by the House Assassinations Committee, was known to Robert Kennedy at the time of the JFK assassination, and he learned most of the rest before he was murdered.

On the day JFK was killed Robert Kennedy mournfully confided to Ed Guthman, "I thought they'd get one of us, but Jack, after all he'd been through, never worried about it ... I thought it would be me."[2] Robert Kennedy had good reason to expect to be killed. In one of the first interviews he gave as Attorney General, Bob had stated unequivocally, "I'd like to be remembered as the guy who broke the Mafia."[3] Then, with Jack Kennedy's wholehearted approval and support, he set about doing it. While on the Senate Rackets Committee, Jack once declared, "We have only one rule around here. If they're crooks, we don't wound 'em, we kill 'em."[4] He meant it — they pursued organized crime with a passion and made some extremely dangerous enemies. Three of the more notable were Jimmy Hoffa, Carlos Marcello and Jack Ruby's friend, Santos Trafficante.

The vehemence with which Jimmy Hoffa hated the Kennedys cannot be exaggerated. RFK wrote:

> "When Hoffa can't buy what he wants, his weapons become fear and intimidation. The day before the first public hearing into his affairs by the Rackets Committee ... I went to the Teamsters building in Washington for a final interview with him. He glared across his desk ... for a long moment, and then said: 'Someday, somewhere, I'm going to get you.'"[5]

The House Assassinations Committee reported that on September 29, 1962, Teamster official Edward Grady Partin told the Justice Department that Jimmy Hoffa was planning to murder Robert Kennedy. Being a top Baton Rogue Teamster official, Partin had often worked closely with Jimmy Hoffa. Although he didn't like the man, he was forced to deal with him because of the power Hoffa held over the Union. Hoffa knew Partin (1) was under indictment by Walter Sheridan (a special assistant to Robert Kennedy) on a 26-count charge involving alleged embezzlement of union funds and making false entries in the books of Baton Rouge Teamster Local 5, (2) was a gun fancier, and (3) had access to explosives. As Partin put it, "Hoffa always just assumed that since I was from Louisiana I was in Marcello's hip pocket."[6] (The Marcello to whom Partin referred was Hoffa's syndicate friend, Carlos Marcello, the Louisiana Mafia boss). For these reasons, Partin was brought in on the plot to rid the Teamsters of their tormentor, Robert Kennedy. Partin's job was to obtain plastic explosives. "Something has to be done about that little SOB Bobby Kennedy," Hoffa had fumed to Partin and others present that day, "He'll be an easy target, always driving around Washington in that convertible with that big black dog. All we need is some plastic explosives tossed in with him, and that will finish him off."[7]

In the event they were not successful in blowing up the car, Hoffa had an alternate plan to firebomb Hickory Hill, Robert Kennedy's Virginia estate. Hoffa had it all figured out and told Partin that even if Kennedy managed to survive the explosion, "he and all his damn kids" would be incinerated, "the place will burn after it blows up."[8] Hoffa was going to have Frank Chavez do the job. (Chavez, the leader of Puerto Rico Teamsters Local 901, had been charged with a firebombing murder once before but had not been convicted.)[9] If both of the explosive methods failed, Hoffa planned to shoot Bobby the next time he was riding in a convertible in the South where racial fanatics would be blamed. One way or another, "Somebody needs to bump that son-of-a-bitch off! Bobby Kennedy (has) got to go!" Hoffa had heatedly declared.[10]

Partin told the Justice Department officials that he didn't want any part of murder, that he had kids of his own and couldn't live with himself if any of RFK's children were killed. Since Partin was a known associate of Jimmy Hoffa, the officers were at first skeptical of his story, but Partin volunteered to take a lie detector test, which he passed with flying colors.[11] What convinced them beyond any doubt that Partin was being completely truthful, was that Partin recorded a call he made to Jimmy Hoffa in which he informed the Teamster boss that he had located the plastic explosive and could get it to him. Hoffa was obviously pleased and seemed to know exactly what it was to be used for.[12]

Partin cheerfully volunteered reams of information on the activities of Jimmy Hoffa and his friends and revealed that Hoffa was working with Santos Trafficante and Carlos Marcello, running guns to Cuba for both sides.[13]

Robert Kennedy was not limiting his attack on hoodlums and organized crime to Jimmy Hoffa and Carlos Marcello. He went into the office of the Attorney General with a "hit list" of forty syndicate members, which he expanded to 2300 members whom he was determined to prosecute.[14] In 1961 Attorney General Kennedy authorized the installation of listening devices in the favorite hang-outs of mob members, which picked up fascinating and sometimes frightening conversations.[15]

In May of 1962 a New York Mafia member noted that; "Bob Kennedy won't stop today until he puts us all in jail all over the country. Until the commission meets and puts its foot down, things will be at a standstill."[16] Commission member Magaddino bitterly cursed the Attorney General, commenting that the Justice Department was increasing its knowledge of the syndicate's inner workings. "They know everything under the sun. They know who's back of it they know there is a commission. We got to watch right now — and stay as quiet as possible."[17]

By October of 1963 Mafia insiders were becoming paranoid about the Kennedys, and in response to one member's heated suggestion that President Kennedy "should drop dead" Magaddino exploded, "They should kill the whole family, the mother and father too. When he talks he talks like a mad dog, he says, 'My brother the Attorney General!' "[18]

After JFK was assassinated, the hidden microphones picked up such interesting comments as the November 25, 1963 remark by Sam Giancana, the Chicago Mafia boss, that Oswald "was a marksman who knew how to shoot."[19] On November 29, 1963 Magaddino cautioned his associates not to joke openly about the President's murder saying, "You can be sure that the police spies will be watching carefully to see what we think and say about this."[20] Several weeks later during a discussion between Angelo Bruno of Philadelphia and his lieutenants, one participant remarked, "It is too bad his brother Bobby was not in that car too."[21]

Although the electronic surveillance was highly successful in most cases, two of the Attorney General's prime targets, Carlos Marcello and Santos Trafficante, managed to avoid them. The House Assassinations Committee found that "The Bureau did make two attempts to effect such surveillance during the early 1960's but both attempts were unsuccessful. Marcello's sophisticated security system and a close-knit organizational structure may have been a factor in preventing such surveillance."[22] One FBI agent who had attempted to plant listening bugs in Marcello's organization agreed, "That was our biggest gap ... With Marcello, you've got the one big exception in our work back then. There was just no way of penetrating that area. He was too smart."[23]

Not only was Marcello smart when it came to security, but he was also careful with his cover. To many, including some law enforcement people, Marcello appeared to be a legitimate businessman. His cover was hard to penetrate. Even so, RFK was determined to get rid of the Louisiana Costa Nostra boss and personally expedited deportation proceedings against him.

The Justice Department charged that Carlos Marcello had gained illegal entry into the United States. In April of 1961 government agents swooped down upon the unsuspecting Marcello as he walked along the street, handcuffed him, loaded him on a private plane and flew him to Guatemala, dumping him off unceremoniously in the country he claimed as his birthplace. Carlos Marcello was enraged and seethed that he had been illegally "kidnapped" by government agents working for the Attorney General.[24]

Marcello slipped back into the United States in 1962 and was immediately indicted again for illegal entry. This time Marcello had a lawyer and was prepared. He fought the deportation proceedings and appeared before a Louisiana court to answer the charge on November 22, 1963, the morning of the day Jack Kennedy was killed.[25] Some have wondered if it was a coincidence that Marcello was in a court of law; it certainly provided the perfect alibi to both him and his friend, David Ferrie, who was later indicted for conspiracy in the murder of John F.

Kennedy, by Louisiana District Attorney Jim Garrison.

In September of 1962, convinced that he had been targeted for mob execution, a soldier in the Vito Genovese family, Joseph Valachi, "accidentally" killed a fellow inmate whom he thought was a hit man sent to finish him off as he served time in Atlanta Prison. Targeted for death by the Mafia and convicted of murder by the state, Valachi, turned state's evidence. By the end of the month the former Mafia henchman was "singing tunes that were music to Robert Kennedy's ears."[26] RFK called Joseph Valachi's revelations the biggest single intelligence breakthrough yet in combatting organized crime and racketeering in the United States.[27]

When word reached Marcello that Valachi was talking, he called a meeting of his top henchmen at his Churchill Farms estate outside of New Orleans. The angry Marcello shouted an old Sicillian death oath against the Kennedy brothers, "Livarsi na petra di la scarapa!"[28] which means "take the stone out of my shoe." He elaborated on his plans to those present, "Don't worry about little Bobby son-of-a-bitch. He's going to be taken care of!" When asked how, he told them that they had to "take care of Bobby Kennedy by killing his brother . . . you don't cut off the tail, you cut off the head." Marcello added that they were going to "use a nut to do the job."[29]

One of the men in attendance passed the word to the FBI but instead of following it up, Hoover and other senior FBI officials initiated action to "discredit" the informant. According to the House Assassination Report, an internal FBI memo read that the informant must be discredited "In order that the Carlos Marcello incident would be deleted from the book."[30]

The House Assassinations Committee discovered that Carlos Marcello wasn't the only one who had decided that President Kennedy must go. The same month that Marcello revealed his plans to his men, Santos Trafficante, the Florida boss and very good friend of Marcello, was talking to Jose Aleman, a Cuban exile financier who was a respected FBI informant, about his hatred for the President and his brother — on whose prosecution list Trafficante was near the top. "Have you seen how his brother is hitting Hoffa, a man who is a worker, who is not a millionaire, a friend of the blue collar?" Trafficante asked Aleman. "He doesn't know that this kind of encounter is very delicate. Mark my words, this man Kennedy is in trouble, and he will get what is coming to him."[31]

Aleman, who was talking to the Cosa Nostra boss about a $1.5 million Central States Pension Fund loan which Hoffa had personally cleared for Trafficante, responded that President Kennedy would probably be elected for a second term.[32]

"No, Jose," Trafficante told him firmly, "He is going to be hit."[33]

In the last six months of the Eisenhower administration, the number of indictments against racketeers was twenty-four, but in 1962 under Robert Kennedy the total for the first six months was 171. Actual convictions were up 400 per cent.[34] Robert Kennedy was hitting organized crime and hitting it hard. If he had been able to keep it up another five years he probably would have broken the Mafia.

Ralph Salerano, former supervisor of detectives in New York and expert on organized crime, summed up the meaning of President Kennedy's death in terms of the syndicate when he said:

"There is no solid evidence yet that Carlos Marcello, Santos Trafficante, Jimmy Hoffa or any other criminal or criminal associate had been involved in the conspiracy to kill President Kennedy. Regardless of whether they knew or not, they should have built the largest statue in the world to Lee Harvey Oswald. No one man has done as much damage to this country's war on the underworld as he did. Because the bullet that killed John Kennedy killed Robert Kennedy's dream to destroy the organized crime society."[35]

There was little doubt that even if Oswald had acted alone, he had only beaten the others to the punch. It was obvious from several foiled murder plots that there were certain groups out to kill the President. From the moment Bob was informed that his brother had been shot, he had suspected the syndicate was behind it. He and President Johnson had discussed what Robbert Kennedy knew about such plots immediately after the assassination and RFK arranged for the appointment of Charles Shaffer, a Justice Department attorney, to the Warren Commission staff with specific orders to check out the possibility of Teamster-Mafia involvement, Jimmy Hoffa in particular. RFK also had any and all information concerning underworld connections forwarded directly to him.[36]

One of the first connections that turned up was the fact that Oswald's assassin, Jack Ruby, was from Chicago where he had gone by the name of Jack Rubenstein and had been a Teamster official who ran around with members of the old Al Capone gang. In 1947 when Ruby first moved to Dallas, the Chicago Mafia attempted to bribe members of the Dallas Police Department, but Sheriff Guthrie did not go for it and told the Kefauver Committee, the first congressional committee to investigate organized crime, that Ruby had been frequently mentioned in discussions with Chicago underworld representatives. In 1960 Jack Ruby himself had appeared before the Kefauver Committee, for they had learned from other witnesses that Ruby was "a syndicate lieutenant who had been sent to Dallas to serve as liaison for Chicago mobsters." Ruby was known as "the payoff man for the Dallas Police Department."[37]

In 1959, shortly after Castro took over Cuba, Santos Trafficante, the Mafia boss in charge of Cuban operations who thought himself friendly with Castro, found himself residing in a Cuban jail, his cassinos taken over by the Cuban government. Jailed with him was Frank Cammarata, a former Detroit racketeer deported after his release from a Michigan state penitentiary. While Cammarata was serving time, Jimmy Hoffa had implored the governor of Michigan to pardon him, but to no avail.[38]

Although Trafficante was imprisoned, his loyal employee, Lewis McWillie, remained free in Havana and working for his boss' release. McWillie had moved to Havana from Dallas, Texas. His good friend Jack Ruby visited McWillie frequently — with McWillie picking up the tab.[39] There has been speculation that Ruby was a mob carrier who transported money and possibly narcotics from Cuba to the United States for the syndicate. A barmaid in Ruby's Carousel Club, Nancy Perrin Rich, testified shortly before her own violent death in the mid-sixties, that she and her husband were offered a gun running job and that Ruby was the "bagman".[40]

After Trafficante's arrest, Jack Ruby again went to see McWillie and this time he had with him $25,000.00 in donations from friends of Trafficante who had gambling interests in Las Vegas. Ruby met with gun runner, Robert McKeown, who had been Castro's chief supplier and through him made an offer to Castro of the money in exchange for the release of three prisoners.[41] Ruby and McWillie then went to Trescornia Prison in Cuba where they visited Trafficante. Not long afterward Santos Trafficante was released and returned to the United States where he became boss of the Florida area.[42]

Through study of Jack Ruby's long distance phone call records for 1963, the Justice Department was able to solidly link Ruby with the Teamsters and organized crime elements. During the summer of 1963, Ruby called his old friend, Leonard Patrick, in Ruby's home town of Chicago. At the time Patrick was lying low, for he had been implicated by Chicago law enforcement in the murder of black alderman and political protege of Mayor Richard Daley, Benjamin F. Lewis. Patrick got off for lack of evidence, as he had in 1947 when he and David Yaras, another good friend of Jack Ruby, had been indicted for the murder of James M. Ragen, underworld Chicago racing boss. There had been four witnesses to the Ragen murder but two were murdered and the surviving two suddenly lost all interest in testifying against Patrick and Yaras. Immediately after their release, the police captain who had insisted on bringing the charges was murdered. About the same time that Patrick and Yaras were under indictment, Ruby himself was under suspicion of being an accomplice in the shooting of Leo Cooke, the head of the Chicago Waste Handlers Union of which Ruby was an organizer. Ruby's colleague, John Martin, was the person who had done the actual shooting and later got off on self-defense. The most significant result of Cooke's death was that Ruby's friend, Paul (Red) Dorfman, then became head of the Union.[43]

On October 26, 1963 Ruby called a Chicago number, SH-3-6865, which belonged to Irwin S. Weiner, a veteran member of Jimmy Hoffa's closest circle of underworld advisors and a major bondsman for the Union. Weiner admitted that he and Ruby were close friends. On October 30, 1963 Ruby called a New Orleans number, CH-2-5431, and spoke to Nofio Pecora, a key member of the Carlos Marcello organization. On November 8, 1963 Ruby called Murray W. (Dusty) Miller, who was the head of the powerful Southern Conference of Teamsters who was also one of Hoffa's deputies and a key Teamster official in Union operations in Dallas as well as in New Orleans. On November 7, 1963 Barney Baker, one of Hoffa's top aides, called Ruby from Chicago. When questioned, Baker said that he was merely returning Ruby's call to him about labor problems. On November 20, 1963 David Yaras' close friend from Chicago, Paul Roland Jones, visited Ruby in Dallas. On November 21, 1963 Barney Baker, Hoffa's aide, called Yaras, the go-between for Trafficante and Marcello.[44] That same day Jack Ruby and Jim Branden both visited the offices of Hunt Oil which was owned by the fanatically anti-Kennedy Texas billionaire, H. L. Hunt.[45] (It is noteworthy that George de

Mohrenschildt, Lee Harvey Oswald's best friend, was deeply involved in the Texas oil group, even having been married to Winifred Sharples, the daughter of an oil millionaire.)[46] Braden had just changed his name from Eugene Hale Branding, and had recently divorced his wife who was the widow of a Chicago Teamster official. Branden had been arrested thirty times and had served several prison sentences. He was arrested again on November 22, 1963, minutes after President Kennedy was shot, as he tried to leave the vicinity of Dealey Plaza, but he was not held because, since he had changed his name, his record appeared clean.[47]

On November 20, 1963, after meeting with Paul Jones, Jack Ruby went to the Cabana Motel where he met some friends, one of whom had a girl friend who had been in contact with David Ferrie of New Orleans — a close associate of Carlos Marcello. Ferrie had also been renting an office suite in New Orleans in the same building and on the same floor as was another of the men at the meeting with Ruby that evening.[48]

Links were discovered between Jack Ruby and Lee Harvy Oswald. Ruby and Oswald both lived in the Oak Cliff section of Dallas, had post office boxes at the terminal annex and knew some of the same people. Most disturbing was the fact that Earlene Roberts was Oswald's landlady, and her sister Bertha Cheek, had visited Ruby at his nightclub on November 18, 1963.[49] Thomas "Hand" Killam, whose wife worked for Ruby and whose best friend roomed in the same house with Oswald, was found dead in Pensacola, Florida on March 17, 1964. He must have been very clumsy for he appeared to have slit his own throat by falling through a plate glass window. The same month, Bill Chester who had told several persons he knew that Ruby and Oswald knew each other, died suddenly of an apparent heart attack.[50] The violent death rate of those who had worked with Jack Ruby or knew anything about him has been astronomical, especially in the first few years after the assassination of President Kennedy.

Other friends of Jack Ruby were of particular interest. One was Joseph Civello, the Marcello associate who allegedly headed organized crime activities in Dallas.[51] Ruby was also friendly with a New Orleans nightclub figure, Harold Tannenbaum, with whom he was considering going into partnership, which is the reason he gave for his frequent trips to New Orleans.[52] Also in contact with Ruby was Frank Chavez, the Puerto Rican Teamster who Jimmy Hoffa had selected to be the one to carry out the firebombing of Robert Kennedy's home.[53]

The evidence which has pulled all of the loose ends together is the finding released by the House Assassinations Committee that Lee Harvey Oswald was involved with New Orleans organized crime elements. Oswald's aunt and uncle, Lillian and Charles "Dutz" Murret lived in New Orleans. Oswald had been exceptionally close to "Dutz" who had acted as his serrogate father when Oswald's own father walked out. In April of 1963, immediately after he shot at General Edwin A. Walker in Dallas, Oswald moved back to New Orleans and stayed with the Murrets. It was Murret who arranged bail for Oswald after his arrest in August of 1963 for fighting with anti-Castro radical Carlos Bringuier. At that time Murret was accompanied to the police station by two friends, one of whom happened to be Nofio Pecora, the Marcello deputy who received the October 30, 1963 phone call from Jack Ruby. It turned out that "Dutz" Murret was well known in New Orleans as a minor underworld gambling figure. In 1963 "Dutz" had an especially good job ... **he was a personal aide or driver for none other than Carlos Marcello himself.** Oswald had been impressed with his uncle's connections and frequently bragged to his wife, Marina, about them. Oswald's mother, Marguerite, was acquainted with several men associated with lieutenants in the Marcello organization.[54]

The information thus far presented is a small portion of what the Justice Department and the House Assassination Committee know about the circumstances surrounding the assassination of

President Kennedy. Before his death Robert Kennedy had to have been aware of most of it, therefore one can assume that Ted Kennedy was also privy to the information. This probably explains why Ted Kennedy was so opposed to Robert Kennedy's 1968 presidential bid — which cost his life.

The pressures under which the Kennedy family was living after President Kennedy was assassinated quickly became apparent to watchful observers. Shortly after Jack Kennedy was killed, while Robert Kennedy was still Attorney General, the Kennedys had a frightening experience which was related by Joe Kennedy's nurse, Rita Dallas, in her book *The Kennedy Case*. Mrs. Dallas surprised a man walking into the Senior Kennedy home who claimed to be a television repairman. She pretended to accept his explanation for being in the house but quickly summoned the security guard who caught the intruder upstairs with the fuse box open. The man was whisked away by secret service agents dispatched by the Attorney General. Later, as she left for home the curious Mrs. Dallas asked one of the high-ranking guards about the intruder. "I received a brief answer, 'He has connections in Dallas.'" Startled, Mrs. Dallas asked how he knew and the guard replied, "I've already said too much, but you were involved, so I'll stick my neck out and tell you that he let something slip."

The incident was not reported by the press and Mrs. Dallas could offer no further information on the break-in but the incident affected everyone. "There was, however, an apparent dread in everyone, a jumpy nervousness. A feeling of apprehension and unrest," said Mrs. Dallas. Even the indominatable Rose Kennedy was affected as is shown by this encounter with Mrs. Dallas:

"A few days after the intruder, Mrs. Kennedy called me to her room and said, 'Nurse, I want to ask a favor of you.'

"Of course, Mrs. Kennedy."

"Well" — she hesitated — "I don't want you to think I'm afraid or even worried about anything. It's nothing like that. But I'm wondering if you will stand at the window and watch me when I go for my swims. I don't want to change my habits, and I do enjoy the ocean. But if I should disappear, they'd wonder, you know, so if you'd just watch when I'm out, I'll feel safer ... for their sakes. Now mind you, I'm not worried. It's just ... well ...' "[55]

When Robert Kennedy made the decision to run for President in 1968 he wasn't under any illusions as to his life expectancy, especially if it appeared he might win. Contrary to popular belief, the Kennedy family was not happy with his decision. Ted opposed the idea from the start, Joe Kennedy Sr. was terribly upset by his son's decision and Jackie pleaded with Arthur Schlesinger to try to talk her brother-in-law out of it. She told Schlesinger, "Do you know what I think will happen to Bobby? The same thing that happened to Jack ... There is so much hatred in this country, and more people hate Bobby than hated Jack ... I've told Bobby this, but he isn't fatalistic, like me."[56]

The reasons why Robert Kennedy chose to run are many, and entwined with the Vietnam War. Michael Novak, a college professor who helped with the campaign, summed up Bob very well when he told audiences:

"You people just won't understand Robert Kennedy unless you understand that he doesn't know if he's going to live tomorrow. And therefore, he's got to do it today. If you think he's ruthless, you're crazy! He's a man who feels anything but ruthless. He feels positively trapped and he's just got to act because he can't care about the consequences."[57]

After RFK was dead Novak sadly observed. "He didn't really know if he could win the thing. He just knew that he, Robert Kennedy, had to do it now ... if it killed him. And I think he meant that both literally and emotionally. It just had to be done."[58]

RFK knew he was a prime target for every type of potential killer from the Communist fanatic to organized crime — especially organized crime. As a public figure he was exposed to the people and he refused to shrink from the danger. He would quote Emerson, "Always do what you are afraid to do," and plunge ahead. Pierre Salinger complained to Roman Gary when the French novelist told him that he thought Bob would be killed, "I live with that fear. We do what we can, and that isn't much. He runs around like quicksilver."[59]

RFK fatalistically shrugged off the danger saying, "I play Russian roulette everytime I get up in the morning. But I just don't care. If they want you, they can get you."[60]

In Lansing, Michigan, the police notified Kennedy's head body guard, Bill Barry, that a man with a rifle was seen entering the building across the street from the Senator's hotel. Fred Dutton discreetly entered Bob's room and began to close the shades. RFK knew what was going on and immediately stopped him, "I don't want that! Don't ever do that. I'm not going to start ducking or running."[61]

Because of the report, Barry had the Senator's car taken to the basement so he could avoid the front of the building. When ushered to the garage, Robert Kennedy was furious. "Don't ever do this again! Don't ever change whatever we're doing until you talk to me, and I don't ever want to change it because I'm not afraid of anybody. If things happen, they're going to happen."[62]

With that he drove to the front of the hotel where he got out and visited as he had planned to do before. As they drove away he muttered to no one in particular, "You know if I'm ever elected President, I'm never going to ride in one of those goddamn (bubble top) cars."[63]

Barry worried, "I get mixed up with the crowds and I can't see and I get tired."[64] Walter Sheridan who worked with Barry on security said, "And we knew, that really there wasn't anything you could do about it because he was uncontrollable, and if you tried to protect him he'd get mad as hell."[65]

Ethel was beginning to feel the stress too, as was

virtually everyone else. RFK wouldn't let his body guards carry guns; he didn't want them to shoot into a crowd and accidently kill an innocent bystander. Everyone who accompanied Bob was prepared to jump between him and danger, but when there was a threat they realized how helpless they really were. On June 3, 1968, in San Francisco, Robert Kennedy and Ethel were standing in the back seat of a convertible on a ride through Chinatown. Suddenly fire crackers went off. Everyone froze except Ethel who crumpled into a corner of the car, curling up into a little ball, shaking and sobbing into her hands — afraid to look back at Bob who remained standing, refusing to duck.

Some thought Robert Kennedy was foolhardy for not being more cautious, but Barry didn't think so, "He just didn't want to live in fear. So I think he was making a personal judgment of his own, based on his own life force."[66] And when RFK finally was shot it was in a place no one expected, a place he probably would have been shot regardless of how careful he had been.

Several full time correspondents accompanied Robert Kennedy on his travels, flashing every detail back to their anxiously waiting publications. John Lindsay of *Newsweek* started out as a professional observer and found himself emotionally involved in the melodrama being acted out on the 1968 campaign trail. Lindsay later recalled:

"They had a birthday party on board the flight for him, and they put up balloons all over the place, and Ethel took charge of the whole thing: and somebody in the party, one of the television guys, inadvertently burst one of the balloons, and Bob jumped instinctively. He knew ... he knew ... that this kind of thing could happen. It's a dreadful thing to live with, but the Kennedys have always lived with it ... this is the thing that's always fascinating. This kind of fear would shatter me. I'd become paranoid about it. But these people don't do that."[67]

When Robert Kennedy was killed, the family was

devastated — but not surprised. They had all prayed it would not happen but everyone had been more or less expecting it while hoping against hope that it would not come to pass. They loaded Bobby's body on the jet Vice President Humphrey provided, and it was on that flight home that Ted Kennedy, overwrought with grief and lack of sleep, let some of his feelings show to reporters. Over and over he declared, "I'm going to show them! I'm going to show them what they've done, what Bobby meant to this country, what they lost."[68] He angrily stalked down the aisle causing an observer to remark, "Watch out for Teddy, he looks like he's going to hit someone."

Ted settled down with NBC correspondent Sander Vanocur and spoke to him of the nightriders in our society who make public service a nightmare. Turner and Christian in their book *The Assassination of Robert F. Kennedy* report:

> "When the plane carrying his [RFK's] body back to New York landed at Kennedy International Airport, NBC television correspondent Sander Vanocur, who had covered the RFK campaign, came down the ramp to face his own network's cameras. Forcing back tears, he reported that during the flight Edward Kennedy had remonstrated bitterly about the 'faceless men' who had been charged with the slayings of his brothers and Dr. Martin Luther King, Jr. First Lee Harvey Oswald, then James Earl Ray, and now Sirhan Sirhan. Always faceless men with no apparent motive. 'There has to be more to it,' Ted Kennedy had told Vanocur."[69]

When Robert Kennedy was shot the assailant was immediately apprehended. It was an open and shut case — so everyone thought. However, there have been many very unsettling developments in the case which point uncomfortably in the direction of organized crime. William W. Turner, an ex-FBI agent who worked on the investigation of the assassination of President Kennedy and was not satisfied with the

Warren Commission report, and John G. Christian, an ex-ABC newsman, worked together for several years carefully investigating the RFK assassination. They compiled their findings into a disturbing book, *The Assassination of Robert F. Kennedy,* hoping that their groundwork will lead to the re-opening of the case. In light of the recent House Assassinations Committee's findings and connections uncovered between the murders of JFK and RFK, such a re-opening would seem to be in order.

Over the years one of the most persistent and determined investigators into RFK's murder has been Ted Kennedy's good friend, Allard Lowenstein. Lowenstein agreed with Ted's assessment that "There has to be more to it," and set out to prove the "second gun theory." He met with a certain amount of success for much of the evidence points directly to conspiracy. According to Turner and Christian, there is even serious question as to whether Sirhan Sirhan could have fired the shots which killed Robert Kennedy. Sirhan never got closer than two or three feet, and RFK was facing his assailant, yet the shot which killed him was fired from within an inch of his head — from behind. Several people saw the security guard, Thane Cesar, standing behind Bob with his pistol out, and Don Schulman, a CBS News employee who was standing behind RFK when he was shot gave a tape recorded interview to radio reporter, Jeff Grant, immediately after the shooting in which he said that he actually saw the security guard shoot Bobby.[70] That could explain why RFK turned around and grabbed Cesar by the neck tie, falling on top of him. Surprisingly the fatal wound to the head did not knock RFK unconscious ... although dazed at first, Robert Kennedy did not lose consciousness for several minutes.

There have been several instances of important witnesses connected with the case being shot at. In August of 1971 William W. Harper, a veteran criminalist, was chased as he left his home, and heard something strike his car. After managing to elude his pursuers, Harper went to the home of Raymond Pinker, another prominent criminalist. According to Turner and Christian:

"They examined the dent in the rear bumper and agreed that it had been caused by a slug from a high-powered gun — possibly a .45 or a .357 Magnum ... The attempt on Harper's life came within days of the sniper attack on John Chris Weatherly in Chino. As in the case of Weatherly, the timing was too exquisite to ignore: Harper was scheduled to testify the next day before a grand jury investigating the handling of firearms evidence in the RFK case. Harper had set in motion the train of events leading to the grand jury probe by fathering in 1970, what has become known as the 'second gun' theory."[71]

Over the years more and more evidence has been uncovered which points not only to conspiracy, but perhaps in the same direction as The House Assassination Committee findings in President Kennedy's death. One of Sirhan Sirhan's best friends, Ivan Valladares Garcia, was a citizen of Guatemala, the country to which RFK exiled Carlos Marcello for a year. Sirhan Sirhan also associated with people around the Hollywood Park race track and Granja Vista del Rio Ranch near Corona, who had syndicate connections.[72] But the key seems to rest in an evangelist preacher, Jerry "The Walking Bible" Owen, who has been solidly linked to Sirhan Sirhan. Owen himself appeared at the Los Angeles Police Station to say that he had given Sirhan Sirhan a ride to the Ambassador Hotel and was involved in a horse trade with him, but Turner and Christian have turned up a great deal of evidence which points to a much more involved relationship between Sirhan Sirhan and Jerry Owen. They have successfully linked Jerry Owen, through his brother Richard Owen, to Edward E. Glenn who is a close friend of Jim Braden ... the same Jim Braden who visited Hunt Oil the same day Jack Ruby did (the day before JFK was assassinated), the same Jim Braden who hailed from Chicago and was connected with the Teamsters, the same Jim Braden who was picked up by Dallas police in Dealey Plaza immediately after President Kennedy was shot.[73]

Unlike the JFK assassination, the accused assassin is still alive and residing safe and sound in a California prison. The fact that Sirhan Sirhan is still alive can be attributed in large part to the fact that when the California courts sentenced Sirhan Sirhan to death, Senator Edward M. Kennedy wrote a letter to State Attorney General Evelle Younger pleading for leniency and asking that Sirhan Sirhan be spared. The letter was published in most of the major California newspapers and was probably a heavy factor in the decision to stay the death penalty.

If there was a conspiracy in the murder of Robert Kennedy, could Jimmy Hoffa have been one of the conspirators? At the time RFK was murdered, Hoffa was residing in the Lewisburg Pennsylvania Federal Penitentiary where Robert Kennedy had put him. However, a fellow inmate overheard Hoffa telling his cronies, two weeks prior to the assassination, that there was "a contract out to kill Bob Kennedy".[74] When interrogated by the FBI, Hoffa refused to discuss the matter and his friends denied that he ever told them about any such contract. A Mafia contract was a very real possibility, for according to Turner and Christian:

> "An FBI document [was] released, disclosing that a wealthy Southern California rancher who had ties to the ultra-right Minutemen and detested RFK because of his support of Cesar Chavez, reportedly pledged $2,000.00 toward a $500,-000.00 to $750,000.00 Mafia contract to kill the senator 'in the event it appeared he could receive the Democratic nomination' for President."[75]

Bobby was killed immediately after winning the key California primary . . . but to insiders, the nomination was still far from his. As grief stricken Larry O'Brien kept sobbing on RFK's funeral train to Arlington cemetery, "Why did they do that, why did they have to *do* that? Couldn't they see? Couldn't they see? He didn't have a chance!"[76]

The death of his third brother marked the beginning of a personal nightmare for Ted Kennedy. Joan once commented that she didn't see how her husband had managed to stay sane that summer. Ted not only had to cope with his own grief and that of a distraught family, but he also had to face some harsh realities concerning his own mortality.

On June 17, 1968 an El Paso man was idly leafing through a yellow legal pad which had been left at a soft-drink stand in Juarez, Mexico, just across the Rio Grande. There was an entry dated June 4 which said:

> "I will have to try to erase completely from my memory — before the world learns about me — that I was in on the plot to kill Robert F. Kennedy. That crazy Arab has a tremendous hate for all the Kennedys ... easy enough to get him to take some of the money and do the job. The whole world knows it was a grand plot but, unfortunately, they do not know the whole truth. I never knew who organized the assassination but that's not important. I know the world will never know all about it. I'll probably die soon in some part of Mexico."[77]

The El Paso man had contacted the Mexican police who immediately descended upon the soft drink stand where they learned that the woman behind the counter had purchased the pad from a Mexican youth, Crispan Curiel Gonzalez, who was completely broke. An all out manhunt was launched and the Juarez police quickly apprehended Gonzalez, who proved to be rather talkative, and told the police.

> **"You wait and see, the next will be Edward Kennedy. All they have to do is wait — wait — wait for the best time.** They told me the Kennedys wanted to be dictators of the United States."[78]

He refused, or perhaps could not, identify "they", but he claimed to have been a friend of Sirhan's and had

260

visited with him in a Santa Monica library a few days before RFK was killed. The U.S. Border Patrol had picked up Gonzalez as an illegal alien and was in the process of deporting him when Robert Kennedy was shot.

The Juarez police contacted the American authorities and Juarez Deputy Police Chief, Jose Regufio Ruvalcava, issued a statement to the press,

"There were so many factors connecting Curiel with Los Angeles that when we arrested him we decided he should be investigated thoroughly. We checked with your FBI and a spokesman there told us definitely that Curiel knew Sirhan — was a friend of his. There is no doubt that Curiel knew Sirhan — They had met a number of times at the Santa Monica library and elsewhere and had usually discussed politics."[79]

FBI agent, Roger LaJeunesse, confirmed that there was a definite link between Gonzalez and Sirhan.

Ruvalcava talked at length with Gonzalez and concluded that he was a very sophisticated young man, intelligent and not at all unbalanced. He talked about forming a political party "to replace the socialistic structure of Mexico."

Due to the international problems of the case, U.S. detectives had not fully investigated the Gonzalez connection when, on July 4, Gonzalez was found dead. He was hanging in his Mexican jail cell from a noose fashioned from strips torn from the mattress cover ... an apparent suicide. The boy's father, Crispin Curiel Gonzalez Sr., was convinced that his son had been murdered. He made a statement on July 6, 1968:

"In the last letter we had from him, he hinted at a promise of big money for him — but it was very dangerous."[80]

The authorities had done what they could to follow up on the death. Robert Kaiser, a journalist working with the LAPD and acting as a defense investigator for Sirhan, asked his subject about it.

"I produced a picture of Crispin Curiel Gonzalez from a newspaper clipping, telling of his ar-

rest in Juarez, Mexico. 'Ever see this kid before?'
I asked.

" 'No,' said Sirhan, 'Who is he?' I told him
he was a young man who had been picked up
in Mexico with some puzzling notes on his person that indicated he'd known Sirhan and
known Sirhan planned to kill Kennedy. 'Where
is he now?' asked Sirhan.

"I said he was dead. 'He was found hanging
from his cell bars one morning.' A brief look
of dismay passed across Sirhan's face. Why? . . .

"I learned why a week later when Sirhan im-
plied he knew Gonzalez."

" 'That kid didn't have to die,' said Sirhan.
'He didn't do anything.'

" 'Who would have wanted to get him out of
the way?' I asked.

"Sirhan paused reflectively for a moment,
then smiled. Then he changed the subject."[81]

Since the FBI was privy to the Gonzalez case, in
all likelihood Ted Kennedy was informed of it as he
was of most of the serious threats against him. It
is one thing to suspect that you might be a target
if you ever decide to run for President, but it is quite
another to have someone associated with your
brother's murderer say that you will be next, and
then have the informant discovered dead under suspicious circumstances. How can anyone doubt that Ted
Kennedy had good reason to be suspicious of Officer
Look that night on Chappaquiddick Island and to
have avoided him at all costs? To have done otherwise would have been foolhardy.

Ted Kennedy had other concerns besides possibly
being targeted for assassination. The first and foremost was trying to pull together the distraught family. A Kennedy aide described the turmoil:

"Jackie was very bitter after Bobby's death.
She became quite hysterical at one point and
said, 'I hate this country. I despise America, and
I don't want my children to live here anymore.
If they are killing Kennedys, my kids are the
number one targets. I have the two main tar-

gets. I want to get out of this country and away from it all!' She was terrorized, but then the whole family was for a while. Teddy spent at least two hours on the phone every night talking to his nieces and nephews, assuring them that he was not going to be shot. He told them that he would be there alive and well for them in the morning. Each one of those twenty-seven kids was traumatized by Bobby's assassination and each of them needed good psychiatric counseling. They had severe emotional problems. It was a terrible experience for everyone. No one knew exactly how to cope with it. Some of us rented a boat after the funeral and went out on the water and got very drunk and cried a lot."[82]

Robert Kennedy's older children were the most unsettled at this time. Ted managed to talk Joe III into finishing school at Milton Academy when the boy wanted to quit, but was less successful in dealing with the long string of emotional problems some of RFK's other children have suffered.

An example of the early difficulties Ted was having with them was the August party Ethel's children held two months after their father was killed. Ethel allowed her children to invite about twenty-five friends over and gave them the pool house and area to use. One eighteen-year-old participant later told Lester David:

"It was a wild kind of night. We were all down by the swimming pool. The Kennedy kids were there, all but the very little ones. I remember very distinctly getting the feeling from the way they were acting that a kind of recklessness had taken hold.

"They began throwing pool furniture in the swimming pool tossing in tables and chairs, breaking soda bottles and tossing the ash trays around. It was a raucous scene of kids getting up on tables and yelling and lots of noise, with the jukebox playing. A few of the other kids were doing it too, but it was mostly the Kennedy kids, all but Kathleen.

"I got the feeling very definitely that it was a kind of reaction on the part of the older Kennedy kids, a kind of letting loose."[83]

Even as late as 1979 Ted Kennedy was still concerned about his nieces and nephews. When speaking of the possibility of running for president and the dangers involved he said:

"The idea of death doesn't bother me. I love life. I've had a full life. I don't mind about my own children. I think they're all right now. It's the others, my brother's children: I'm sort of an anchor in their lives."[84]

Rita Dallas, Joe Sr.'s nurse, described Ted's attempts to cope with the Kennedy children:

"I remember seeing him sitting on the steps of the porch watching the children at play: Bobby's, the President's, his own. From the pain in his eyes, I could tell he knew there was no way for him to replace their losses. He tried valiantly but it was too much. He would exhaust himself on weekends taking all the children out in the sailboat even though to do it meant hours of 'taking turns.' "[85]

The usually buoyant Rose Kennedy conceded to an interviewer:

"Everything has been so demoralized this summer, there used to be my husband, my sons, to help with things. Now, Sargent [Shriver] is abroad and Teddy must carry most of the load, with Steve Smith. He [Teddy] makes a great effort to help Ethel, to see his father frequently because he knows my husband misses Bobby so."[86]

Joe Kennedy Sr. had suffered a stroke in 1962 and Ted had spent a great deal of time with his aging father, especially after his own near fatal plane crash in 1964 and subsequent rehabilitation through which he had gained a new understanding of what it was like to be incapacitated. In 1968, however, Ted became especially attentive to Joe. Rita Dallas observed:

"Mr. Kennedy was not doing well at all after Bobby died, and that fall there was speculation that he would not be able to make the trip to Palm Beach. At times he was very, very poor. He was not as yet in a terminal condition, but he was visibly going downhill. Teddy seeing this and keenly aware of it, grew more and more concerned and apprehensive."[87]

Ethel was also a cause of concern. Outsiders marveled that she was able to carry on so magnificently — entertaining, encouraging games, going to dedications, and anything else she could think of to keep busy. But insiders worried that Ethel was purposely exhausting herself so she didn't have to think about what had happened and could sleep at night ... which would have been fine except that she was pregnant. Nurse Dallas shared everyone's apprehension and wrote:

"As the time drew near for her to have her child, the atmosphere around the compound was filled with anxiety. Ethel did not seem to be able to let up, and everyone felt the chilling threat of yet another tragedy. They desperately wanted her to have Bobby's last baby very much, and I remember the look on Teddy's face the day she fell on the tennis court.

" 'She can't lose the baby,' he said, 'She can't".[88]

Her doctor ordered the uncooperative Ethel to bed, and that December Rory Elizabeth Kennedy was born while Ted Kennedy, weaving unsteadily on his feet, held Ethel's hand during the Cesarean delivery. He had nearly fainted when the operation started. A doctor noticed and ordered a nurse to "watch him!" but Ted quickly recovered and began offering "helpful" suggestions until told to keep quiet.[89]

During the traumatic summer of 1968, Ted leaned heavily on his wife. Joan's biographer Lester David wrote,

"At Cape Cod, where he remained for two and a half months that summer, he broke down a number of times after despair had replaced rage. 'I realized that summer,' Joan told me, 'that Ted needed *me*! . . . Nobody is as close to a man as his wife, and this was something I had not really understood or felt until that time. It was the very beginning of a new closeness between us, a closeness that came from the knowledge that Ted needed a loyal wife and a loyal friend.' "[90]

While Ted Kennedy is congenial by nature, he is a loner when it comes to deep personal feelings. A close friend once commented, "When Ted wants to consult with someone he trusts completely he gets in a room alone, and locks the door, and talks to himself."[91] Apparently Ted had something important to take up with himself, for in July of 1968 he simply disappeared in his boat for two weeks. When he finally returned he had the look of a grizzled seaman — or perhaps an unkept hippie — and was sporting an orangish-red beard of two week's growth. Thinking nothing of his appearance he simply walked into his parents' home to say hello. Later he happily reminisced:

"Dad rose up in his chair, his eyes wide, pointing a finger at me. I didn't know what was wrong — the old sweater I was wearing, or something. I went over to kiss him, and he held up his hand and put it on my chin. It wasn't much of a beard, a couple of weeks or so. But I hadn't had a haircut the whole time. My mother threatened to shave off the beard herself right there, but I did it. We all had a good laugh afterward, and, seeing my father laugh like that at last, my mother said, 'I wish we could do this every day.' "[92]

In the weeks that followed Bobby's death, Ted Kennedy's Senate office was run by his competent staff who contacted Kennedy by phone when something important came up, but the absentee Senator took little interest in what was happening on Capitol Hill. In late July Ted drove all the way from Hyannis Port to Washington, D.C. to sign some important papers, and perhaps try to return to work. However, when he arrived and parked his car he could not seem to get out of it and sat there for several minutes staring at the Old Senate Office Building. Then he simply turned around and went home admitting, "I just couldn't go in and face them all."[93]

Although Ted had lost his enthusiasm for politics, the people had not lost their enthusiasm for him and a cry went up to draft Ted Kennedy for President in 1968. Bill vanden Heuval related Ted's reaction to the draft campaign:

"We had lunch in New York a couple of weeks after Bobby's funeral, and I mentioned that it seemed to me that it wouldn't be too long before things settled down and a lot of people started thinking, and there was going to be pressure on Ted to make himself available for the Democratic ticket. He seemed surprised at that, very surprised at that. Then, as events worked out, Teddy and I were sailing on the *Mira* — not really many weeks afterwards. Perhaps it was August? Early August? We were at anchor for the night, I remember it was off Maine, terribly foggy, and we were signaled somehow that there was a very important call for Teddy, he had to get to a telephone. So we untied the dinghy and rowed ourselves ashore. There was this little pay phone in a booth among the rocks, and Ted used that. It turned out to be Mayor Daley — they wanted Ted on the ticket. The implication was that the brokers had decided that Hubert wasn't going to win all by himself, that with Ted on either the bottom or the top of the ticket they probably could — they didn't make that awfully clear, I gathered — and what was his thinking?

"Ted was quiet, he kept very much to himself whenever I saw him. He kept asking — mostly to himself, aloud at times, 'What was it all about?' It was not the fatalism of Bob; it was a much larger fatalism. He kept wondering, was it worth all this? He has a great desire to live, takes a great joy out of life. And he had begun to realize the danger, the fear, that he was going to be next."[94]

Not only had Ted Kennedy realized the fear that he would be next, but so had the family and many of his close friends. Archbishop Philip Hannan, of New Orleans, who had conducted the graveside services at Bob's funeral, tried to deflect the national clamor for Ted to run for president by telling reporters that the family reaction was that Ted should get out of politics. Another family friend publicly stated, "Teddy is so distraught that he is in no condition to make a decision about a place on the ticket. But I have come to the opinion that Teddy might be in physical danger if he ran. I do not want to see him get out of politics but I am deeply concerned about what might happen this year."[95] And Ted himself issued a simple plea, "Please, don't."

But the call to draft Ted Kennedy would not be stilled and close family friend Lem Billings worried:

"None of his family or anyone of his close friends wants him to be President. Nobody who cares a damn about Teddy wants it for him. It's a dangerous job, more so for Teddy than anybody else because there are damned crazy fools in this country. We don't know where they are and they're very hard to avoid."[96]

Harry Bennett, Joan's father revealed his daughter's fears:

"Nobody wants him to run, nobody in the family on either side. They're all scared to death. Over and over, Joan keeps saying she hopes he does not run. Can you blame her? But they all know, and Joan knows it too and this is what terrifies her, that he's got to do what he feels he must. But they all pray he doesn't."[97]

The week before the Democratic convention Ted Kennedy appeared in the public limelight for the first time since Robert Kennedy's death. He delivered an impressive speech in Worchester, Massachusetts in which he dealt in depth with the volatile issues of Vietnam and civil rights. It was a speech which sent thrills through the draft Kennedy ranks for it had the ring of a serious candidate:

"There is no safety in hiding. Not for me; not for any of us here today; and not for our children, who will inherit the world we made for them ... Like my brothers before me, I pick up a fallen standard. Sustained by the memory of our priceless years together, I shall try to carry forward that special commitment — to justice, to excellence and to courage — that distinguished their lives."[98]

According to Lester David, upon hearing those words, Ethel, who had been listening to Ted's speech on the radio at Hickory Mill "collapsed into sobs, her face in her hands. She wept convulsively for many minutes."[99]

Kenedy's speech caused an up-roar at the Democratic National Convention a week later because many read it to mean that Ted Kennedy was an available candidate, which may have been what he intended them to think. Kennedy wanted the Democrats to adopt a peace plank on the Vietnam war and he hoped that by threatening to make himself available he might get the "hawks" to compromise their position. Ted later explained, "I didn't call it [the draft effort] off as strongly until Tuesday, because those who were involved in the minority plank felt that my being involved might help their position."[100]

The ploy did not work and Humphrey refused to compromise the war issue, but a surprising thing happened ... Ted Kennedy was drafted. Ted had not even gone to the convention, but remained at Cape Cod while his brother-in-law, Steve Smith represented the Kennedy interests. Kennedy later told *Look's* Warren Rogers:

"I was here, with just two people, my sisters Jean and Pat. The three of us talked among ourselves, and on the phone with Steve, and more and more, I felt confirmed in my original decision not to accept a draft. You can't imagine what pressure there was. We sat here, the three of us, with those phone calls coming in from Steve, and we made decisions as they were required."[101]

Steve Smith finally called to tell Ted he had the delegates for the nomination on the first ballot, "We had it" Steve told Rogers, "There was no question but that the Senator could have had the nomination. All he had to say was yes." Ted dragged his feet and later explained to Rogers:

"Basically, I just didn't have the feeling at that time for politics and campaigning and, beyond that, I was too vulnerable. After all, how could I conscientiously combat allegations by Nixon — and we had to anticipate he would make them — that I was too young, that I had no record in public life strong enough to recommend me for the high office of President, that perhaps I was trying to trade on my brothers' names. I could not expose the Democratic party to that kind of vulnerability. I would rather do what I have always tried to do: to perform to the best of my ability, and then, if that performance is considered to be of a caliber qualifying for greater responsibility, to submit my record to the people."[102]

They had lost the peace plank and the only way to save it was for Ted to take the unwanted nomination. While Kennedy stewed over his dilemma at home, the explosive 1968 convention boiled over. Anti-war demonstrators were thrown into paddy wagons and hauled off to jail and fist fights erupted on the convention floor. Newsman, Dan Rather, received a punch in the stomach from a security guard while attempting to make a televised report. Pierre Salinger phoned Kennedy, giving him the ultimatum. They had to bring this convention to a close, his support was waning, "You must either fish or cut bait", Sallinger told the absentee contender. Ted threw in his cards, called the anxious Hubert Humphrey and told him, "I have been listening, but I am not a candidate." Then Kennedy declared to all that he did not want the nomination, pointing out "This was Bobby's year."[103]

Reflecting on his difficult choice Ted said:

"On the one hand here would appear to be, if it were able to be worked out, the opportunity to carry out in the most effective way possible the things Bobby had lived and died for ... On the other side was the complete real loss of spirit in terms of willingness to run, I just didn't have the stomach for that, I didn't feel I was personally equipped for the race, I thought it was much too great a burden to place on my family at that time. People would be considering the candidacy for entirely the wrong reasons ... Was there ever a time I ever *seriously* thought of making the race? No."[104]

Ted campaigned to some extent for Hubert Humphrey, and returned to his Senate duties. He tried to attract as little attention as possible but after Humphrey's defeat speculation never ceased that Kennedy would be the nominee in 1972. Mike Mansfield's evaluation was, "It's preordained. With Ted, I'm afraid it's not a question of choice, but a matter of destiny."[105]

The man of destiny did not seem overjoyed by the prospect. One friend noted of Ted, "He was so raw; there was no need for banter, it was all understood. He would go through the necessary performances and then a lot of times it would be — goddamn it, it's me now, it's me for the bullet, it's me for the brass ring."[106] On several occasions he lamented to close friends, "I know I'm going to get my ass shot off — and I don't *want* to get my ass shot off."[107]

The Washington Post noted that "immediately following the assassination of his brothers ... he would sit in his office and jump at the raucous buzz of quorum calls. Aides and friends resorted to macabre jokes such as, 'If it comes, Ted, it's not going to sound like a quorum call,' to kid him out of his edginess."[108]

But his aides felt it too and Gerry Doherty confided to Lester David:

"I hope to God he and Joan will just go some-where and live long, happy lives, that he won't try to be President. Because if he does ... When I tell him this, he just shruggs and says, 'What will be, will be. What God ordains will happen.' He tells me that if he must fulfill a challenge he will."[109]

Ted may have tried to brush off the dangers but he began keeping a well worn copy of Shakespeare's *The Tragedy of Julius Caesar* on his desk and frequently read this underlined passage:

Cowards die many times before their
    deaths;
The valiant never taste of death but once.
Of all the wonders that I yet have heard,
It seems to me most strange that men
    should fear;
Seeing that death, a necessary end,
Will come when it will come.[110]

Although he went through the motions, Ted's heart was not in his work. He wanted to carry on the things his brothers had started but he could not seem to generate the enthusiasm. In December of 1968, while on a skiing trip to Sun Valley, Ted suddenly decided that he wanted to become majority Whip of the Senate. To do so he must unseat the incumbant Whip, Senator Russell Long, by convincing his colleagues to vote for him instead. Ted called his administrative assistant David Burke who tried to talk him out of going for such a "nothing" job, but Ted would not be dissuaded and Burke conceded to Theo Lippmen that he was:

"delighted ... flabbergasted and delighted. After Bob's death, he had been a different per-son. There was a lot of wind out of him. He was very slow in coming back. It ended when he ran for Whip. That fight was a delight, not because of the Whip's job but because the other period was ending. He was spunky and wanted

272

to do something — even if it wasn't a good thing to do. It wasn't a good thing to do because he wasn't built for that job, hustling around and taking care of everybody's little problems, or sitting on the floor endlessly minding the store. But it was still worth doing, because of what it was bringing back."[111]

Ted won the Whip job which set off a whole new round of speculation as to why he did it. To the Republicans, it appeared that Kennedy was attempting to set himself up as a party leader to be in a good position for the presidential nomination in 1972. One Republican Senator was moved to remark, "No matter how good a President Nixon makes, Ted will be a formidable opponent. I don't say he necessarily can beat Nixon — but Nixon will know he's been in a fight."[112]

But Ted was not looking for a fight and did not view the Whip job as a stepping stone to the White House. To the contrary, he seemed to be looking for someplace to hide and he mistakenly thought the trivial job which kept him involved on the Senate floor for hours on end would take him out of the limelight. When quizzed on what possible attraction the endless busy work of counting noses for votes and bargaining for the Majority Leader could have he would reply, "I just thought it an opportunity to learn more about the range of issues that was coming up, to become more of a generalist rather than a specialist."[113] But in an interview with *Life Magazine,* in a rare moment of personal candor, he admitted, "I felt that coming back to the Senate, coming into this year, I had to become involved and active and busy. It was important for me to do that ... in very personal terms ..."[114] In other words, Ted Kennedy was finding it difficult to resume his Senate duties and to force himself back into the grind. He hoped that by taking a job which required him to be present and do little things he did not have to think a great deal about, he might be able to ease himself back into his work.

Unfortunately, Kennedy's plan backfired for instead of quietly allowing him to slip back into his Senatorial role, it drew attention to him, especially from the ever watchful Richard Nixon. When asked in 1969 why Nixon was always so worried about what Ted Kennedy was doing, Ted replied that he thought it had to do with Nixon's own insecurities, "Quite frankly . . . he's uneasy with me." But Kennedy made it plain that he was not interested in the Presidency. "You know there are so many things that are so much more *important* than that," he told a *Life* reporter, then wishfully added, "I love to sail into one of those Maine harbors where nobody knows you . . . couldn't care less. It's the only way I can get off by myself."[115]

Shortly after winning the Whip job, Kennedy was interviewed by William H. Honan who, like everyone else, was trying to figure out the "real" reason for Kennedy's assault on Russell Long and why he was persisting in public life. "I asked Kennedy what he had accomplished in the Senate and what he thought could be done there," Honan wrote, "He started talking about Bobby's achievements and Bobby's expectations. Once when he mentioned his brother, he choked and looked away from me. When he returned his gaze, his eyes were filled with tears. Bobby had been dead six months."[116]

People were morbidly fascinated by the "last of the Kennedy brothers" and wondered why he continued to pursue a public career. It was dangerous for him and he could certainly afford to quit any time he wanted to. In March of 1969 when asked why he didn't retire he replied:

"Why should I quit? What would I do? I don't know, maybe sometime I would like to do other things. There is so much to be learned about music, art, literature, and so many places to be seen, but my work in the Senate and in politics won't permit it. I would like to sail more.

"But it seems to me, if you have the ability and the training for public service, and the opportunity, it would be a sin not to pursue it. I don't have any feelings of guilt, any of that

conscience bit about noblesse oblige because I
happen to be born with money. It's just that
there is so much wrong in the world, so many
people suffering needlessly, and, if I think I can
help, it seems to me I must try.

"And there is a challenge in politics. You say
to yourself, 'I wonder if I can do it,' and then,
later, you might say, 'I think I can do it,' and
you try and you succeed, and it's a wonderful
thing. I used to like the people, the rough-and-
tumble of politics, but all that changed after
... after ... 1963."[117]

Ted was trying to cope with his new role as liberal
leader without bringing the presidential nomination
upon himself again. Not long before the Chappaquiddick accident he mused:

"I ask myself 'What can I *do*?' I can stand
up and speak out ... and get credit for that.
But is there something else I can do that will
really *help* ... that will get something *done*
about it. Last week, a couple of weeks ago ...
no one maybe knows it ... but I went over to
see Kissinger. We talked for a long time and
I told him how I felt ... you know, the death
rates up, the battles are escalating. Then Nixon
made the speech. I don't know, but maybe I
helped ... maybe without making a lot of noise
you can get thing thing working .."[118]

In 1969 Joan Kennedy was asked if she agreed with
Ted's statement that there is no safety in hiding, to
which she replied, "Yes, you can't go on living like
that. I believe it and Ted lives it."[119]

Although Joan may have agreed with her husband
in principle, she lamented, "Why must it be my husband? Why must he be the man to carry these terrible problems of the world on his shoulders? "Joan
was clearly not enjoying the turn their lives had
taken and bitterly asked, "What is that 'monolith of
Kennedy power' now? Just Teddy and me. All the
others are either dead or old."[120] She worried to a
Ladies Home Journal reporter,

"Patrick is too little to ask questions, and

Kara isn't the type to ask them — although I know they're inside her head. Teddy is the one who asks. He wants to know why all these things happen to Uncle Jack and Uncle Bobby, and will they happen to Daddy too? What do you tell an eight-year-old when he asks you why that man shot his uncle? I tell him he was just a bad man who didn't know Uncle Bobby, that there is something wrong with a man who would shoot somebody he doesn't even know. Teddy accepts my answers, but he is quite aware of the risks involved, as aware as a child his age can be ...

"Frankly, I worry all the time about whether Ted will be shot like Jack and Bobby. I try not to but I can't help myself. Ted trys to keep things from me — serious threats against his life, that kind of news — but I know what's going on. Ted doesn't want me to worry. But I do. And I know he worries about it, too. Ted is a brave man, but he is only human. You want to hear something awful? A few months ago we were in a plane and a child exploded a balloon right behind us. It sounded just like a gun shot. Ted jumped so. What a terrible thing! A balloon pops and my husband thinks he's being shot. I could read his mind — and I could have cried for him ... What's the answer? I don't know. You can't hide. Well you can, I suppose, but Ted won't. Quit politics? No. Public service means too much to Ted; it's what he has chosen for himself, and I don't think he can be frightened off. This is such a painful subject with us that we can't even discuss it. But we both know it's there ..."

"I never wanted Ted to be President. Never! I still don't want him to be. I don't think Ted has ever wanted to be President either. Of course, I won't discourage him if he wants to run. A man's work is his life. I believe that. I want Ted to be happy in his work and thus in his life. He has said he will not run in 1972, and it's foolish to speculate beyond that . . . And all this you hear about the Kennedy family pressuring Ted to run for President . . . What family! What's left of the Kennedys besides Ted, only women and children! You don't seriously think *we* want Ted to be President, do you? To have the one Kennedy man left risk having happen to him what happened to his brothers? You think all those children — Ethel's, mine — would be better off? No, we don't want him to run for President. We want him. We need him. Ted knows the Kennedys are not pushing him toward it. He is quite aware of how we feel."[121]

As time went on, instead of pulling themselves out of their uneasy state, both Ted and Joan seemed to have greater difficulty coping with their problems. Ted became louder, more boisterous, driving too fast, appearing at more parties and raising hell in general, causing one relative to comment that his attitude seemed to have become "Eat, drink and be merry for tomorrow we die."

On the other hand, Joan, consumed by a justifiable fear, withdrew. She shocked a magazine editor who was interviewing her in her home during a picture taking session with Otto Stupakoff, by suddenly bursting into tears and crying, "We're naked here! Naked!" Looking fearfully around she continued, "Here we are with the children. There's a maid. Nobody else. You saw when you came in how close we are to the main road. My God! Someone can come up across that bridge, make that turn, come here. There's no name on the mailbox but that doesn't hide us. The cab drivers know where we live. Every newspaper has printed where we live. I'm scared something will happen to him." The distraught Joan sobbed, "There may be a person out there trying to make a clean sweep of the Kennedy brothers. Whatever has been written about that is true. My husband knows it and I know it."

Joan was obviously terrified and sat with her arms

wrapped around herself, weeping. The worried and concerned editor tried to comfort her saying, "Joan, perhaps you're exaggerating, perhaps it isn't really the way you think. I'm sure the country is more mature than that ..."

It proved to be the wrong thing to say for Joan burst out, "Exaggerate? Exaggerate? How can you say that? Let's get in my car and I'll drive you down the road just over a mile to Hickory Hill where Ethel lives. Let's go in there and you can look at a house filled with eleven children without a father, and then tell me if I exaggerate the dangers of being a Senator Kennedy!"[122]

Ted was painfully aware of the effect his remaining in public life was having on his wife and more than once sighed that she wasn't made for the pressures that went with his life, and sadly concluded that Joan should have married a banker. He once blurted out to an AP reporter traveling with him on a long plane ride, "Do you know what it's like to have your wife frightened all the time?" The startled reporter failed to come up with an adequate reply and Kennedy boldly added, "I'm not afraid to die," then reflected, "I'm too young to die."[123]

The pressure was clearly beginning to affect Ted. He drank more and spoke more often of being killed — little comments like "I'll get it someday I suppose." One of his admiring aides made the mistake of calculating all of the presidential elections Ted would still be young enough to enter and had gone through only 1972 and 1976 when Kennedy interrupted, declaring "Forget about 1980 because by that time I'll probably be dead."

The nervous aide hesitantly asked, "You mean ..."

"Shot?" Kennedy cut him off ... then shrugged, "Maybe, or more likely an airplane or an automobile."[124]

Some commented that the way Kennedy had been acting lately, he was trying to drive all of his admirers away from him — and perhaps they were not far from wrong. Ted recklessly plunged ahead with his exaggerated lifestyle and suddenly rejuvinated Senate activities, boldly declaring, "All I want, if someone's going to blow my head off, I just want one swing at him first. I don't want to get it from behind."[125]

Kennedy was working hard at being a good senator. He took his Whip duties seriously and chaired endless committee hearings. He began to remind people of his aggressive brother Bob ... which only fueled speculation about 1972. Senator Ed Muskie told Steward Alsop in March of 1969, "Teddy's got it locked up. There's the money, and the mystique, and Teddy's an able, charming guy too. When everybody begins saying this early it's going to be Teddy, why, it's going to be Teddy — almost sure to be."[126]

Since no matter what he did he could not avoid attention Ted decided to put the attention to use publicizing a worthy cause. Robert Kennedy had planned to take a Senate subcommittee to Alaska to study the Eskimo's problems first hand. He had been especially concerned with the plight of the American Indians — the citizens who suffered the most and were heard of the least; an embarrassment America did not want to talk about. However, Robert had been forced to cancel his trip in order to attend the funeral of Dr. Martin Luther King, Jr. and did not live long enough to reschedule the trip. After RFK's death, Ted succeeded to the chairmanship of the Senate Subcommittee in Indian Education. To fulfill his brother's promise, Ted organized an investigative trip for April of 1969 and was accompanied by Senators Walter "Fritz" Mondale, William Saxbe, Theodore Stephens, Henry Bellmon and George Murphy.

The press was invited along, first because they wanted to go — anything Ted did was big news — and second because Ted hoped the publicity would bring the plight of the Eskimo home to all Americans so that there would be public support for the funds necessary to improve the situation. With the Vietnam war draining funds it was almost impossible to get congressional approval for such programs unless the public demanded action. Unfortunately, instead of zeroing in on the downtrodden Indians, the press corps focused undivided attention on Kennedy and ignored the other Senators to the point of even ordering "Fritz" out of the way so they could get a good shot of the Massachusetts Senator.

With the other Senators in tow, Ted charged across Alaska, searching out the ills of Eskimo society. At one village he was disgusted to find that the villagers had to haul water two miles because their well was contaminated and they could not afford a purifier. What made the situation intolerable was that the village school had a perfectly good well but the residents were not allowed to use it because it was under the jurisdiction of the Bureau of Indian Affairs and that agency had not OK'd its use for the village people. It didn't look like they intended to either.

The state of education was deplorable. None of the teachers spoke the Eskimo language so the children had to use English, which made learning extremely difficult for them. They were behind before they even started. The textbooks were completely inadequate; having been designed for use in the lower forty-eight states, they depicted such common objects as cows, horses, firemen and fruit trees which were completely unknown to the Eskimo children and not at all relevant to their lives. They not only had to deal with a foreign language, but also a foreign culture. No wonder few finished school. They were beaten before they began and many ended up committing suicide or drinking themselves to death at an early age.

Throughout the trip George Murphy of California kept his own camera rolling and had a grand time ribbing and being ribbed by the other Senators. He and Ted hit it off well and Ted kidded him about always looking so fresh and clean while the rest of them became bedraggled. George claimed he knew how to live right, being one of the beautiful people from Hollywood. He danced a soft shoe to demonstrate his ability and he and Ted sang a duet of "Hollywood" to entertain the rest of the entourage. But the next day George phoned the leader of the expedition in his room at the Anchorage Westward Motel and in no uncertain terms informed Ted that he had

had it with all of Kennedy's grandstanding. He and two other Republican Senators, Saxby and Bellmon, were going home. Ted was caught completely by surprise and was deeply stung. All he said was, "Well, I hope you got some good pictures, George."[127]

Kennedy and the few remaining senators continued their mission while the trailing reporters tried to figure out what had happened. One had been told by a Murphy aide that George was tired of Kennedy's one man show. Another said that someone in Washington had gotten hold of a subcommittee memo which showed that from the beginning the trip had been a publicity stunt for Kennedy — it *was* a publicity stunt but Kennedy had intended it to be publicity for Eskimos. However, the discovery of greatest interest was the report that some very high ranking Republicans put the squeeze on Murphy and others and told them to get the hell out of the "roadshow."[128] It was getting too much publicity and they did not like to see Kennedy building up his public image any more than it already was. The desertion left a bad impression of the whole trip. As designed, it caused the public to question Kennedy's motives.

Mondale was furious and released a strong statement to the press.

"I deeply regret that the Eskimos' desperate need to be seen and heard should raise doubt as to the intent of our efforts. I suppose the reason is to discount recommendations we will probably make to relieve conditions we have seen destroying these decent people. The conditions are tragic enough that one would think they could at least be spared being made a political football."[129]

The Republican desertion and the subsequent ruination of his investigative trip had an obvious effect on Ted Kennedy, who reacted first by joking about it; when one reporter called out, "I told you to see that Murphy got his box lunch on time,"[130] Kennedy promptly wrote Murphy's name on several of the prepared lunches they took with them on the C-130 which shuttled them between villages. Kennedy became rambuncious and teased *Life's* Sylvia Wright, pointing to the darkened sky and shouting, "Look, Look, Look, Sylvia, Sylvia, Sylvia. Stars! Stars! First one to find the northern lights gets a beer!"[131] ... And — Kennedy was nipping at the bottle. Holding up a silver flask he carefully announced to *Life* writer Brock Bower who was attempting to interview him, "First time I've used it — Bobby's."[132]

As he had more to drink Ted Kennedy loosened up and began talking about his family, his father, his lost brothers — comparing himself to them. Soon he was insisting to the overwhelmed reporters, "They're going to shoot my ass off the way they shot Bobby's!"[133] When someone would disagree he'd become adamant and repeat over and over that it was going to happen, it was just a matter of time.

The trip ended with Kennedy becoming quite drunk, jovially whacking people over the head with a pillow and weaving up and down the aisle shouting "E-s-s-kimo Power! E-s-s-kimo Power!" One of his aides tried to explain to a concerned reporter that Ted had been under terrific pressure and that he just had to blow off some steam, "I figure we lose sixty voters every time this happens, but it's worth it."[134]

The Alaskan encounter was an eye-opener for newsmen. Burton Hersh reports:

"Ted Kennedy had never been particularly guarded during his less discrete moments but there had been about this performance on that long plane ride home an intensity of desperation, of abandon, that bothered everyone there: limited-distribution memos circulated, especially inside the editorial offices of the magazines. The most celebrated of these became the one John Lindsay of *Newsweek's* Washington office pulled together. Lindsay ... had seen enough of Edward Kennedy over the winter to pick up constant signals of deep-seated emotional disruption: a tendency to stop in mid-sentence, shift moods inexplicably, break into unexpected tears, turn up boisterous with a few early "pops" at public events. Kennedy, Lindsay concluded was slipping out of control, careening toward some unavoidable crack-up."[135]

The other amateur psychologists aboard the flight agreed with Lindsay and Sylvia Wright sent a memo to her editors saying, "He's living by his gut: something bad is going to happen."[136]

Throughout the nation alert newsmen were expectantly watching Ted Kennedy, waiting for something to happen — perhaps a nervous break-down. They weren't sure what it would be, but they knew he could not go on the way he had been. When Ted's car went off of Dike Bridge the watchful reporters congratulated themselves on their preceptiveness. They *knew* something like this was going to happen. To them it was obvious that Kennedy had been blowing off steam again, and for some reason — only God knew, but they could guess — he had sped down Dyke road and off the bridge. Faced with the prospect of reporting a fatal accident, he had finally cracked and run away.

It was the preconceived notion that Ted Kennedy was ready for a nervous break-down that made it so easy for informed observers to accept his version of the accident. Kennedy confirmed their own suspicions when he admitted, "All kinds of scrambled thoughts, all of them confused, some of them irrational, many of them which I cannot recall, and some of which I would not have seriously entertained under normal circumstances, went through my mind during this period ... I was overcome, I'm frank to say, by a jumble of emotions: grief, fear, doubt, exhaustion, panic, confusion and shock."[137]

It is true that given the personal battle of nerves Kennedy had been waging for a year, such a reaction might have been expected. However, it certainly does not account for Joe Gargan's and Paul Markham's actions the night of the accident. Surely if Ted Kennedy had come unglued and finally fell apart emotionally, Gargan and Markham would have noticed it. They certainly would not have allowed him to swim the channel and spend the night alone ... and they certainly would have reported the accident. Ted Kennedy's irrational behavior was no excuse for their own. If Kennedy had suffered an emotional collapse it seems highly unlikely that he would be in such good control the following day when he finally did report the accident.

While Ted's shaky nerves might not explain his failure to report the accident promptly, it certainly explains why he would avoid a person he thought was likely to be carrying a gun — even to the point of leaving his vehicle. It is also reasonable to assume that Kennedy was not up to the added pressure of a public trial ... and neither was his wife nor any other member of the family. At that point Kennedy may have preferred the idea of hiding away in some jail to the ordeal of standing trial ... after all, the accident was his fault. He probably took the attitude, "The hell with it. Why fight it? I'm going to confess and get the whole thing over with."

Given the circumstances of his life in July of 1969 and knowing that his family would have welcomed his retirement from public service, it is highly unlikely that Ted Kennedy's foremost goal was protecting his career. Today's critics who accuse him of masterminding a massive cover-up to save his precious career at the expense of Mary Jo Kopechne's life, should take a closer look at that career and lifestyle they say Senator Kennedy was guarding at any cost. The rewards hardly seem worth the price.

After Chappaquiddick both Ted and Joan underwent dramatic personality changes. Ted calmed down considerably. At first he was severely depressed and shaken but over the years he has come out of it and settled down to become a serious, steady and competent senator. Today's observers have concluded that the tragic accident had a sobering affect on his wild, playboy disposition and say that it made Ted Kennedy grow up. They seem to take it for granted that the way Kennedy behaved between 1968 and 1969 was typical for him, but this premise is simply not true. While Kennedy had always been happy-go-lucky and ready to enjoy himself, the reckless, wild abandon which characterised him shortly before the accident was hardly his nature prior to Robert Kennedy's death.

One of Joan Kennedy's close friends observed:
"The woman [Joan] was under incredible pressure, pressure that you and I cannot possibly conceive. She was cracking under the strain. She was seeing two psychiatrists, one on a Tuesday, one on a Wednesday. She wanted to confirm one's analysis with the other's, one's dialogue with the other's. This went on for a year. Then she began pulling out. I think what really pulled her out, what really turned her around, was Chappaquiddick. Before Chappaquiddick, she was only an adornment, but afterward she was the only ally Ted Kennedy had. He needed her desperately, and she knew it, and she rose to the occasion."[138]

Like many people, Joan's friend was blaming most of Joan's troubles on Ted and his lifestyle. At that time few people could even imagine the very real dangers Ted Kennedy faced and that Ted and Joan were living each day wondering if today was the day he was not going to come home. Thanks to the revelations of the House Assassinations Committee and other persistent investigators, we now know that Ted Kennedy had been a living target for certain syndicate members who did not want him in the White House where he could harm them. The Kennedys had been living with the knowledge that it is much easier and safer to bump off a Senator than a President, or even a presidential candidate.

The Chappaquiddick accident had a major impact on Ted Kennedy's career. It took him out of the running — at least in the forseeable future — for President of the United States. Upon returning to the Senate after the accident, Kennedy declared that he would NEVER be a candidate for President — and this time he was believed — and he knew he was believed by everyone. This had to have taken a great deal of pressure off of him.

In 1972 and again in 1976 Ted Kennedy adamantly declared that he was not available for the nomination under any circumstances. Then in 1978 the House Assassinations Committee confronted Carlos Marcello and Santos Trafficante with the evidence that had been accumulated implicating them in the murder of President John F. Kennedy. Although both denied that they had been involved, government lawyers made it clear that they expect to get a conviction if their investigation is funded for another year. More important, the world was informed that organized crime elements had an interest in keeping Kennedys out of the White House.

Within months of Marcello's and Trafficante's appearance before the House Assassinations Committee, Ted Kennedy declared his candidacy for President of the United States ... was it a coincidence? Or was there a connection?

Ted Sorenson's words, spoken as he mourned another Kennedy in June of 1968, ring as true today:

"There is no curse upon the Kennedys. They have more than their share of ill-fate because they had more than their share of the courage and the conviction required to dare and to try and to tempt fate. They believed with Sir Francis Bacon that there is no comparison between that which is lost by not succeeding and that which is lost by not trying."[139]

CHAPTER FOOTNOTES
1. *The Final Assassinations Report: Report of The Select Committee on Assassinations U.S. House of Representatives,* 206
2. *Robert Kennedy and His Times,* 636
3. *The Kennedy Government*
4. *Triumphs and Tragedies*
5. *The Enemy Within*
6. *The Final Assassinations Report,* 217
7. *Look,* May 15, 1964 and *The Final Assassinations Report,* 218

8. *The Hoffa Wars*, 148
9. Ibid, 150
10. *The Final Assassinations Report*, 218
11. Ibid, 218
12. *The Hoffa Wars*, 149
13. Ibid, 107
14. Ibid, 169
15. *The Final Assassinations Report*, 212
16. Ibid, 201
17. Ibid, 201
18. Ibid, 202
19. Ibid, 204
20. Ibid, 204
21. Ibid, 204
22. Ibid, 212
23. Ibid, 212
24. Ibid, 208
25. Ibid, 172, 174
26. *The Hoffa Wars*, 138
27. *The Final Assassinations Report*, 25
28. *The Hoffa Wars*, 130 and *The Final Assassinations Report*, 211
29. *The National Enquirer*, July, 10, 79
30. *The Final Assassinations Report*, 211
31. Ibid, 214 and *The Hoffa Wars*, 139
32. *The Final Assassinations Report*, 217
33. Ibid, 217
34. *The Hoffa Wars*, 169
35. Ibid, 170
36. *The Final Assassinations Report*, 207
37. *The Final Assassinations Report*, 181
38 *The Hoffa Wars*, 126
39. *The Final Assassinations Report*, 183
40. *The Assassination Chain*, 327
41. *The Final Assassinations Report*, 185-186
42. Ibid, 186-187
43. Ibid, 179, 182, 188, 189 and *The Hoffa Wars*, 154-157
44. *The Final Assassinations Report*, 188
45. *The Hoffa Wars*, 159
46. *Legend, the Secret World of Lee Harvey Oswald*, 181
47. *The Hoffa Wars*, 159-160
48. Ibid, 159
49. *The Final Assassinations Report*, 179
50. *The Assassination Chain*, 288
51. *The Hoffa Wars*, 159
52. *The Final Assassinations Report*, 189
53. Ibid, 220
54. Ibid, 168, 169, 209
55. *The Kennedy Case*, 268
56. *Robert Kennedy and His Times*, 895
57. *American Journey,*
58. Ibid
59. *Robert Kennedy and His Times.*
60. *Newsweek* June 17, 1968
61. *American Journey*
62. *Robert Kennedy and His Times*, 942
63. Ibid, 942
64. *Newsweek* June, 17, 1968, 22
65. *Robert Kennedy and His Times*, 942
66. Ibid, 942

67. *American Journey,*
68. *The Education of Edward Kennedy,* 331
69. *The Assassination of Robert F. Kennedy,* XV
70. Ibid, 161
71. Ibid, 158
72. *RFK Must Die.*
73. *The Assassination of Robert F. Kennedy,* 142
74. *RFK Must Die*
75. *The Assassination of Robert F. Kennedy,* 320
76. *The Education of Edward Kennedy,* 329
77. *The Assassination of Robert F. Kennedy,* 90
78. Ibid, 90
79. Ibid, 91
80. Ibid, 91
81. *RFK Must Die,* 23
82. *Jackie Oh,* 271
83. *Ethel, The Story of Mrs. Robert F. Kennedy*
84. *The New York Times Magazine,* June 24, 1979
85. *The Kennedy Case,* 322
86. *Look, November 26, 1968*
87. *The Kennedy Case,* 332
88. Ibid, 325
89. *Look* November 26, 1968
90. *Joan, The Reluctant Kennedy*
91. *The Education of Edward Kennedy,* 354
92. *Look* March 4, 1969
93. *Ted Kennedy: Triumphs and Tragedies,* 223
94. *The Education of Edward Kennedy,* 338
95. *U.S. News and World Report,* June 24, 1968
96. *Joan, The Reluctant Kennedy*
97. Ibid
98. *Ted Kennedy: Profile of a Survivor,* 133
99. *Ethel, The Story of Mrs. Robert F. Kennedy.*
100. *The Education of Edward Kennedy,* 350
101. *Look,* March 4, 1969
102. Ibid
103. *The Education of Edward Kennedy,* 352
104. Ibid, 351
105. *Edward Kennedy and the Camelot Legacy*
106. *The New York Times Magazine,* June 24, 1979.
107. *The Education of Edward Kennedy.*
108. *The Best of Post*
109. *Ted Kennedy: Triumphs and Tragedies,* 337
110. Ibid, 336
111. *Senator Ted Kennedy, The Career Behind the Image*
112. *Edward Kennedy and the Camelot Legacy*
113. *Senator Ted Kennedy*
114. *Life* August 1, 1969
115. Ibid
116. *Ted Kennedy: Profile of a Survivor,* 141
117. *Look,* March 4, 1969
118. Ibid
119. *Ladies Home Journal,* July, 1970
120. *Good Housekeeping September* 1969
121. *Ladies Home Journal,* July, 1970
122. *Joan, The Reluctant Kennedy*
123. *The Education of Edward Kennedy,* 382
124. Ibid, 256
125. *The New York Times Magazine* June 24, 1979

126. *The Education of Edward Kennedy*, 365
127. *The Bridge at Chappaquiddick*, 59
128. Ibid, 59
129. Ibid, 59
130. *The Education of Edward Kennedy*, 379
131. Ibid, 379
132. Ibid, 379
133. Ibid, 379
134. Ibid, 379
135. Ibid, 380
136. *The New York Times Magazine*, June 24, 1979
137. *The Exhumation Hearing Transcripts.*
138. *Joan, The Reluctant Kennedy*
139. *An Honorable Profession*

CONCLUSION

In 1969 Ted Kennedy pled guilty to the charge of "leaving the scene of an accident". Whether or not the plea accurately represents what took place only Senator Kennedy will ever know. However, all attentive observers know that by pleading guilty he was able to avoid a court trial. Yet, by entering the 1980 Presidential race Ted Kennedy subjected himself to an even harsher and more prolonged public trial than the one he had previously avoided. This time the jury is made up of millions of American voters who sit in judgment of him as they are deluged by televised and written accounts uncontrolled by a court of law. There are thousands of unethical prosecutors handling this case, whose ultimate goal is not to decide the guilt or innocence of the defendant, but is to win an election.

The prosecutors can say almost anything they wish in regard to Kennedy's behavior at Chappaquiddick because he is a public figure and has little or no protection from libel and slander. One of the most treasured rights in our free society is the right to say what we wish about the men who run our government, without fear of retribution. Unfortunately, there are those who abuse this right by twisting the facts and telling lies in the effort to remove from office those politicians who do not share their political views.

The only real defense an elected person has against malicious attacks lies in the ability of the American people to see the schemes for what they are. Never before in the history of our nation has there been a smear campaign of the magnitude and duration of the one which has been conducted against Senator Kennedy since 1968 when Robert Kennedy was assassinated, and Ted became the predominent Democrat in the country. It is a tribute to the perceptiveness of the American people that Ted Kennedy has been able to remain in public life, much less run for the Presidency. However, the gossip and innuendoes caught up with him. As the 1980 campaign intensified so did the smear campaign, and even though many found Ted Kennedy an attractive and well-qualified candidate, the underhanded tactics had their affect.

Noting his dismal slip in the polls and more frequent voicing of doubts among voters in regard to Chappaquiddick, on January 29, 1980 Kennedy issued a plea to the people of New England, "I know there are people who will never believe me, no matter what I say. I do ask you to judge me by the basic American standards of fairness, not on the basis of gossip and speculation."

In writing this book the author has made a sincere effort to present the facts fairly, but it is up to you, the reader, to decide how you are going to judge Ted Kennedy in the case of "Chappaquiddick versus Kennedy".

In reviewing the evidence one must come back to Joe Gargan's key question:

"What happened, Ted? Were you driving the car or was Mary Jo driving the car. Who was driving the car?"

If you believe that Ted Kennedy was the driver of the car then the only story that makes any sense at all is the one he tells. You simply have to accept the fact that the accident shook him up sufficiently that he panicked and failed to report it. Kennedy himself concedes his story is terrible and on November 4, 1979 he admitted on a televised interview with Roger Mudd, "I found the conduct and behavior almost — sort of — beyond belief myself — but I think that that's the way it was ... The behavior was inexplicable but that happens to be the way it *was*. I find ... questions in my own soul as well."

On the other hand, if you believe that Ted Kennedy was not the driver of that car and was not even aware of the accident until the following morning, you have to accept the fact that he really isn't guilty of any wrong doing at all. Instead, he got caught in the middle of the most terrible set of circumstances imaginable, yet he was able to extricate

291

himself. However the deception has finally caught up with him for, unlike most other accomplished politicians, Kennedy is a terrible liar. When confronted with questions about Chappaquiddick he seems to withdraw and when he finally manages to think of an answer he can't look either the reporter or the camera in the eye and repeats an obviously rehearsed answer, thus confirming the public's suspicions that he is not being truthful. If he were as deceitful and callous as his critics charge he would be much more convincing when speaking about the accident.

Whether you are for or against Ted Kennedy, whether you think he has been straightforward with the American people or not, you must admit that Edward Moore Kennedy is an exceptional individual to have stood up to the public ordeal he has been through which must have taken a tremendous amount of will power and fortitude over the decade. It cannot help but be a humiliating and emotional experience every time he goes through an interview and is confronted with those difficult questions over and over again. How much easier it would have been for him to have dropped out of public life altogether rather than to live with the constant accusations and innuendoes that have followed him everywhere and which have never been allowed to fade into the past. And, finally, imagine how much nerve it must take for him to run for President and stump the country always wondering if there is an assassin waiting out there intending to make sure Ted Kennedy will never make it to the White House. He fits Jack Kennedy's description of his brother Robert, "He either shows a lot of guts or no sense at all depending on how you look at it."

APPENDIX
LEGAL ANALYSIS

A Legal Consultant was furnished a manuscript copy of this book along with the transcripts of the Court of Inquest and the Exhumation Proceedings in Pennsylvania where Mary Jo is buried, and an analysis of the entire matter was requested. The response was a letter which has been reproduced here in full:

Dear Larryann Willis:

The material you furnished has been studied and my views are set forth in this letter. The material is being returned to you under separate cover.

This analysis, as far as possible, attempts to avoid the use of legal terminology which tends to complicate matters for some who are unfamiliar with the language of the bar.

For simplification of this digest, the analysis has been divided into two parts. *Part I* has some general application to both Parts, but is predicated upon the fact that the accused was in fact the driver of the involved vehicle at the time of the bridge disaster. *Part II* is primarily based upon the assumption that the accused was not driving the vehicle at the critical moment of impact.

PART I

The only official accusation lodged against Senator Kennedy as a result of the accident was a charge commonly referred to as "leaving the scene of an accident". To the charge, Kennedy pleaded "guilty", which was consistent with the accident report he filed in which he admitted driving the vehicle at the critical time. His admission and plea assured his conviction without a trial since he offered no defense whatsoever. The prosecutor presented to the court only enough evidence and testimony from witnesses to establish the elements of the offense charged, and that someone was criminally responsible. Kennedy's plea of "guilty" relieved the prosecution from proving that he was the responsible person. The participation of Kennedy's attorneys was limited solely to the degree of punishment to be imposed, which the court finally set as a short suspended sentence and a temporary suspension of his driver's license.

By that judgment, the Commonwealth of Massachusetts had extracted its pound-of-flesh, and prosecution on that charge had come to an end, never to be legally tried again, In legal parlance, the accused had been once placed in jeopardy and under the American system cannot be retried for the same offense. This did not mean that Kennedy was immune from prosecution for any other offense which would require proof of some or all of the facts and circumstances common to it and the prior conviction, provided that one of the offenses was not necessarily included in the other.

The former conviction offered no immunity to a possible charge of homicide by means of an unlawful act such as driving under the influence of alcohol, or criminal negligence. The Commonwealth continued to press for an indictment based on an unlawful act. After the inquest was concluded and before the results were published, the Commonwealth scheduled a special meeting of the Grand Jury to look into all aspects of the case. The Grand Jury found no evidence of intoxication and no commission of an unlawful act resulting in homicide.

At the conclusion of the grand jury investigation, the results of the inquest were released. The inquest produced no evidence of intoxication. That Kennedy was not charged with driving under the influence of alcohol was entirely consistent with the findings of the Grand Jury and Court of Inquest.

A Court of Inquest is not a court which determines guilt or innocence; its aim is to determine the cause of death where it appears that death may have been the result of violence or some other unlawful act, and its findings should include all factors which contributed to the death.

Unfortunately, Kennedy's earlier conviction of the minor offense seems to have had the practical effect of focusing the inquest upon him as if he were solely responsible for Mary Jo's death. Before announcing its findings the court explained its belief that Dike Bridge constitutes a traffic hazard, particularly so at night, and must be approached with extreme caution, then added that if Kennedy knew of this hazard, his operation of the vehicle constituted "criminal conduct". The judge tied Kennedy to the knowledge of the hazard when he stated that he believed it probable that Kennedy knew of the hazard, and assigned as one reason that Kennedy had been driven over Chappaquiddick Road three times the day before. That observation is irrational in the face of the physical fact that the road never gets nearer to the bridge than seven-tenths of a mile. As a more rational reason, the judge stated that Kennedy had been driven over the bridge twice, but he failed to make it clear that twice meant only once each way, and that the crossings as a passenger were both made in the daylight when hazards appear much less hazardous than they do in the dark of night. Although the statement made by the judge referred to "criminal conduct", his findings did not. In part, the findings said, "I therefore, find there is probable cause to believe that Edward M. Kennedy operated his motor vehicle 'negligently' ... and that such operation appears to have contributed to the death of Mary Jo Kopechne."

The judge was extremely unkind when he used the term "criminal conduct" which is broad enough to cover all sorts of intentional crimes, and served to incite the media and others to use the grossness of their imaginations which in turn excited the public in general to illusory thoughts and feelings unwarranted by the true import of what the judge had found.

In the findings the judge found the "probability of 'negligent' operation". He did not even label it "criminal negligence". It is difficult to understand why a learned judge would be so negligent as to use in his explanation a legal term so much broader than the specific finding.

In order to find that Kennedy was negligent, the court explained that the bridge and the approach were extremely hazardous, particularly so at night, and that Kennedy was aware of the hazard and drove into it.

The puzzling point is that the Court of Inquest is commissioned to make a determination of the cause or causes of death and the contributing factors, yet the court used the hazard to bolster its finding against Kennedy but made no official finding against the governmental agency responsible for the safety conditions of public roads and bridge structures. Dike Bridge and the approach were utterly devoid of any protective devices, lights, reflectors, signs or other warnings of the impending danger. In spite of these defects the court failed to make a finding on unsafe maintenance and made no mention of responsibility therefore. Although the agency would not have had to stand trial for negligent homicide, Senator Kennedy would have been more fairly treated by such a finding. The court could have made it clear that the county's passive negligent maintenance created the hazard without which the accident would not have occurred and that if Kennedy was not aware of the hazard, his driving could not be greater than simple negligence and clearly would not be criminal negligence.

At the bar, simple negligence is generally understood to mean "failure to use due (ordinary) care". Criminal negligence or negligent homicide is of a much more serious degree of carelessness. In automobile cases it is "the operation of a motor vehicle in reckless disregard for the safety of others, and thereby causing the death of another."

This is not a case where the driver drove into a crowd in utter disregard for the safety of others. Instead, in this case it appears that the decedent and the driver were in the same vehicle and subject to the same perils. How could Kennedy have been driving in reckless disregard for the safety of Mary Jo and not have been driving in reckless disregard for his own safety? A driver bent upon suicide or one extremely drunk could be consciously or subconsciously in reckless disregard for his own safety as well as the safety of others. However, no evidence whatsoever has been produced to indicate that either condition existed in this case.

There were no signs anywhere along Dyke Road giving warning of or the slightest indication of the existence of Dike Bridge. Senator Kennedy was chauffeured on his only previous trip to and over the bridge, then back. He ordinarily was chauffeured and was unaccustomed to noticing road signs or the absence of them. He didn't even know the bridge existed when he made the initial trip to Poucha Pond. How unusual it would be for a person as a passenger to be impressed with the absence of signs warning of a bridge he did not know existed. The trip was in broad daylight so when the bridge came into view it is highly unlikely that the absence of lighting or reflectors would have attracted attention. He must have noted that the bridge was narrow and without elevated guard rails but in the light of day that would not have appeared to create any great hazard. On the return trip, also in broad daylight, Kennedy was chauffeured over the bridge and back along Dyke Road in the opposite direction. The fatal trip was made in darkness except for the head-lights of the Olds. Kennedy did not know that he would not encounter bridge warnings. All prudent drivers, especially at night, rely heavily on posted warnings which caution of dangers, narrow bridges, animal crossings, curves, wet and icy conditions and others too numerous to mention. Knowing the bridge was somewhere down the road, he undoubtedly expected to be warned far enough in advance of the bridge to approach with complete safety. But even so, he was traveling at about 20 mph, slow enough to provide ample space and time to stop or otherwise maneuver had the bridge been posted with a reflector. The bridge sat at an angle left of the road and had no elevated structure above four or five inches. This road level bridge was difficult to distinguish from an on-going extension of the road. The headlights were a great aid but even so, there had to be a slight mental delay in perceiving the exact predicament. A slight delay even at the reasonably slow speed of 20 mph was too long to avert the disaster.

It is difficult to fathom what special interest was in the minds of the representatives of justice for the Commonwealth. Could it have been political considerations? They must have realized the impossibility of establishing negligent homicide beyond a reasonable doubt, and after having tarnished the Senator enough to satisfy their purpose, they abandoned their effort to prosecute in anticipation of a Kennedy trial victory which would have lessened the negative impact of the disparagement they had created.

PART II

If Senator Kennedy was not driving the ill-fated Olds, why did he choose to plead "Guilty" to the charge of leaving the scene of the accident?

It is not always possible to ascertain all facts and evidence before a stand, which is almost irrevocable, must be taken. This case appears to have presented just such a situation. If Kennedy first learned of the accident near 9:00 o'clock in the morning on July 19, 1969, several hours after the bridge catastrophy, he was confronted with the dilemma of choice between voluntarily reporting it, or failing to report it. If he failed to report it, being the owner of the car, he was certain to be summoned or apprehended and asked to identify the person having use of the car on the night of July 18th. In either event, Kennedy was faced with making a statement which would effectively determine his only practical choice of plea in the event of a later formal accusation against him.

As a matter of law, Kennedy could have remained silent about incriminating matters at the reporting stage or at an interrogation stage, but in that event it would be only a short time before he would be arraigned on a formal accusation. Kennedy was himself an attorney — as were his cousin, Joe Gargan, and his friend, Paul Markham, and both of them were available to him in the immediate area of Edgartown, and perhaps were with him when he first learned of the fatal accident. Kennedy was confronted with a *legal problem,* and being in the public eye, as he was, he also faced a serious *non-legal decision* which only he could make. Should he risk alienating the voting public by exercising his right to remain silent in order to await developments, or should he, as any official should, take the redeeming course of cooperating with the law enforcement officers? It apparently was no difficult choice for Kennedy the public figure; he decided very soon, within minutes, after he presumably learned of the accident to voluntarily report, and did so by 10:00 a.m. of the 19th, without having inspected and studied the accident site, the recovered body of Mary Jo, or the condition of the recovered vehicle.

Without the knowledge of what inspection and study might reveal, Kennedy must have pondered what his report should contain and he must have come to the uncomfortable, if not agonizing, realization that in the eventuality of trial, the prosecution could make out a case that would seriously militate against him.

The damaging facts provable by a prosecutor were few, but would carry great weight:

1. Crimmins, near midnight on July 18, 1969, had given the keys to the Olds to Kennedy who told him that he was taking Mary Jo in the car to her motel in Edgartown.

2. Officer Look had encountered, at 12:45 a.m. on July 19, 1969, at the cross-road, a car very similar to the Kennedy Olds, being driven by a male and carrying an additional passenger in the front seat. The encountered car bore a Massachusetts license plate having the only letter and first and last numbers identical to the Massachusetts license plate on the Kennedy Olds later found in Poucha Pond; Officer Look reported he had observed that car, with the same occupants, go east on Dyke Road, a dead end road, toward the bridge at Poucha Pond, a minute or so after the encounter.

3. The County Engineer could establish that Dyke Road was legally a public way, that it was the only road to Poucha Pond from the cross-road, and that seven-tenths of a mile to the pond at 20 mph would take about two minutes and six seconds — a greater speed, a shorter time.

4. Sheriff Arena could establish that the Olds was found submerged in Poucha Pond, con-

taining the dead body of Mary Jo. The sheriff could also establish that by 8:00 a.m. on July 19, 1969, no one but the men fishing from the bridge had reported having any knowledge of the vehicle or accident and that no living person was attending the vehicle at the scene when he (Arena) arrived shortly after 8:00 a.m. Thus, if the dead person in the Olds had not been driving, whoever had been driving was not at the scene and had not reported the accident.

5. A representative of the Motor Vehicle Department could establish that the car was registered to Kennedy.

6. The coroner could establish the time of Mary Jo's death within reasonable limits, which would not substantially contradict the time of Officer Look's encounter shortly before 1:00 a.m. of July 19th.

Although not an absolute certainty, based on those provable facts, the great probability was that the car and its occupants were last seen prior to the accident by Officer Look at the cross-road in the near vicinity of the fatal accident, and left the cross-road on the only road heading in the direction of the accident site which could be reached in barely over two minutes driving time at 20 mph.

Kennedy knew he was the driver at the cross-road and that he continued driving and went east on Dyke Road and that in all probability the officer could at least identify the Olds by description or license number or perhaps both.

He also knew that since leaving the cottage with Mary Jo, there had been no passenger nor driver substitution in the Olds up to the time the car left the cross-road headed east on Dyke Road. Surely if any such substitution, except Mary Jo as driver, had occurred there would have been at least one living witness to the fact in addition to Kennedy, which would have changed the entire concept of this case.

What could a prosecutor have put in evidence concerning the trip from the cross-road to the bridge? Very little, if anything. The physical evidence would conclusively prove that the Olds traveled Dyke Road, the only access to the bridge, where it ended the trip in the pond, submerged alongside of the bridge. The prosecutor did discover, after the reporting stage and prior to the hearing on the charges, that a nearby neighbor had heard a vehicle sometime around midnight of the 18th, presumably traveling Dyke Road, but the neighbor had not seen the car and had witnessed nothing pertaining to the vehicle, its direction of travel, its impact with the water, or the identity or number of the occupants in the car. The neighbor's knowledge added absolutely nothing to the conclusive physical evidence that the Olds had traveled the road, had come to rest in Poucha Pond and had contained the dead body of Mary Jo Kopechne.

Whatever may have transpired during travel along Dyke Road would have been in perfect vacuum for a prosecutor. The only living person who could have witnessed the ride toward Dike Bridge was Senator Kennedy; at least, for more than ten years, no other person has come forward with information about the last leg of the trip.

In a criminal prosecution in an American court, the admissible evidence must establish the elements of the charges and guilt flowing therefrom "beyond a reasonable doubt"; otherwise the accused must be acquitted.

The elements of the crime alleged in this case are contained in the language of the charges as follows:

"Edward M. Kennedy ... did operate a certain motor vehicle upon a public way ... and did go away after knowingly causing injury to Mary Jo Kopechne without stopping and making known his name, residence and the number of his motor vehicle."

It is too obvious to further discuss the physical certainty that the Kennedy Olds was the vehicle and that it was operated upon a public way. Also almost beyond a shadow of doubt, medical testimony could establish that Mary Jo was injured (drowned) as a result of the Olds accident. The Sheriff's Office could prove conclusively that no living person at the scene admitted operating the Olds, and that no report to the Sheriff's Office of the accident or that the Olds was missing was made until 10:00 a.m. of July 19 (some 9 to 10 hours after the probable time of the accident) except a report about 8:00 a.m. by a fisherman that he had discovered a vehicle submerged at Dike Bridge.

Thus, if the driver of the Olds was alive, he had not complied with the law.

The only element of the charge which could not be accounted for beyond any doubt was the connection of Kennedy with the operation of the Olds at the time of the accident.

If the matter had come to trial on a plea of "Not Guilty", the prosecutor would have argued to the court that the admissible evidence established beyond a reasonable doubt that Kennedy was operating the Olds as it left the cross-road going east on Dyke Road and that the mere time lapse of two minutes and six seconds to the bridge is no cause for a reasonable doubt that the driver remained the same up to the time of the accident.

In the absence of an offer of proof by the accused that a change of drivers had occurred before the accident, it appears very clear that the judgment by the court or verdict by the jury would have been "Guilty".

It should be emphasized that Kennedy did not have the advantage of having all of the physical and scientific facts which strongly indicate that he could not have been the driver at the time of the accident.

Kennedy knew for certain that he had not intentionally harmed Mary Jo, otherwise, as a normal person, he would have given no aid to potential prosecution. If he had wronged Mary Jo in a criminal sense, his public image would have faded from his thoughts. All of his physical and mental reserve and energy would have been focused on self-survival as distinguished from preservation of his personal status and his public career.

When Senator Kennedy admitted, as he did in the accident report, that he had been the driver of the Olds at the critical time, he supplied the link which tied him to the elements of the charge later filed, beyond any possibility of doubt in so far as the ultimate court proceedings were concerned.

It is inconceivable that he would have done this if he had wronged Mary Jo in any criminal sense. That admission assured his conviction of the later charge of "leaving the scene" which he clearly appears to have been willing to accept. The admission, for practical purposes, was irrevocable. Kennedy, the lawyer, knew the folly of contradicting his admission by pleading "Not Guilty" to the later accusation. He could have entered such a plea; no rule of law would have prevented his doing that. A plea of "Not Guilty" permits an accused to present any relevant defense he has. Had he pleaded not guilty and then attempted to disprove his prior voluntary admission, his credibility within and without the court would certainly have been badly damaged — if not totally destroyed.

Survival in court after such a switch would have required a most plausible explanation and clear proof of the compelling reason for making the voluntary "admission against fact" in the first instance, coupled with convincing evidence that he in fact was not the driver of the car.

Kennedy had no witnesses to support any statement he might have made in his own defense. His testimony would have been viewed as self-serving and undoubtedly would have been greatly discounted unless it was strongly corroborated by other evidence. Certainly some of the physical facts concerning the car, the water and the absence of glass cuts from Mary Jo's body indicate the probability, but not the impossibility, that she was driving. But Kennedy had no knowledge of those physical facts at the reporting stage. Whatever explanation he may have had for leaving the car at some point along the road would not have been at all convincing without corroborating witnesses and supporting physical facts. A witness, he did not have, and he had no knowledge of physical facts which could have been of some support. Thus, at the accident reporting stage the Senator was faced with the appearance of being without a defense that would hold up in a trial.

Had he reported that he was not the driver and had pleaded consistently with the report that he was "Not Guilty", the great probability was conviction. Such a conviction contrary to his testimony and contrary to fact, nevertheless, would have destroyed his credibility for all time in all places.

The court would then have construed his offer of a defense as an attempt to conceal his identity and probably would have imposed a heavier penalty.

Senator Kennedy was in a very unusual predicament; when he reported the accident it appeared that he had no way to prove he was not driving, so he admitted to driving, later pleaded guilty and took the penalty which seemed certain to be imposed upon him in any event. This is a situation in which his admission and plea of guilty does not present a moral issue. He concealed no living person, not even himself, from law enforcement.

The discussion in Part I in this letter regarding negligent homicide and criminal negligence applies equally well here. Whether driving the vehicle was established by admission or by conviction does not change the fact that there was never any evidence presented in any hearing which could have supported negligent or criminal homicide beyond a reasonable doubt.

Very truly yours,

J. L. Long
Consultant

BIBLIOGRAPHY

LEGAL PROCEEDING TRANSCRIPTS
In RE: Kopechne
Petition for Exhumation and Autopsy
No 1114 of 1969
  Clerk of Courts Office
  Luzerne County Court House
  N. River St.
  Wilkes-Barre, Pa 18711
    Attention: Mr. Dan Stadulis
  Send money order or certified check made payable to the
  "Clerk of Courts" for $100.00

Inquest into the Death of Mary Jo Kopechne
Docket No. 15220 1970
  Joseph E. Sollitto, Jr.
  Clerk of Courts
  County of Dukes County
  Edgartown, Mass. 02539
  Send money order or certified check made payable to the
  "Clerk of Courts" for $110.00.
Books
*THE FINAL ASSASSINATIONS REPORT: REPORT OF
  THE SELECT COMMITTEE ON ASSASSINATIONS U.S.
  HOUSE OF REPRESENTATIVES.* A Bantam Book July
  1979
Burns, James MacGregor, *Edward Kennedy and the Camelot
  Legacy,* W.W. Norton and Co. 1976.
Chester, Lewis; McCrystal, Cal; Aris, Stephen; Shawcross, Wil-
  liam, *Watergate.* Ballantine Books, 1973.
Cohn, Roy, *McCarthy: The Answer to "Tail-Gunner Joe,"* Man-
  nor Books, Inc. 1977.
Dallas, Rita, *The Kennedy Case,* G.P. Putnam's Sons, 1973.
David, Lester, *Joan, The Reluctant Kennedy,* Funk & Wag-
  nalls, 1974.
David, Lester, *Ted Kennedy: Triumphs and Tragedies,* Award
  Books, 1971.
David, Lester, *Ethel, The Story of Mrs. Robert F. Kennedy,*
  World Publishing Co. 1971.
Dean, John W., *Blind Ambition,* Pocket Book, 1977.
Epstein, Edward Jay, *Legend, The Secret World of Lee Harvey
  Oswald,* McGraw-Hill Book Co. 1978.
Gager, Nancy, *Kennedy Wives, Kennedy Women,* Dell Publish-
  ing Co. 1976.
Guyton, Arthur C. MD., *Textbook of Medical Physiology,* Phila-
  delphia, Saunders, 1966.
Haldeman, H.R., *The Ends of Power,* A Dell Book, 1978.
Hersh, Burton, *The Education of Edward Kennedy,* Morrow,
  1972.

Honan, William H., *Ted Kennedy: Profile of a Survivor,* Manor Books, Inc., 1972.

Kaiser, Robert Blair *RFK Must Die* Dutton & Co., 1970 NY.

Kelly, Kitty, *Jackie Oh!* Lyle Stuart, Inc. 1978.

Kennedy, Robert F., *The Enemy Within,* Popular Libary 1960.

Kennedy, Rose, *Times to Remember,* Doubleday Co., Inc. 1974.

Koskoff, David E., *Joseph P. Kennedy, A Life and Times,* Prentice-Hall, Inc., 1972.

Lasky, Victor, *It Didn't Start With Watergate,* Dell Publishing Co. 1977.

Leek, Sybil and Sugar, Bert R., *The Assassination Chain,* Pinnacle Books 1976.

Lippman, Theo. Jr., *Senator Ted Kennedy,* Norton, 1976.

Miller, William "Fishbait", *Fishbait,* Warner Books, 1977.

Moldea, Dan E., *The Hoffa Wars.* Paddington Press LTD, 1978.

Nixon, Richard, *The Memoirs of Richard Nixon,* Grosset & Dunlap, 1978.

O'Donnell, Kenneth and Powers, David F., *Johnny, We Hardly Knew Ye* Pocket Book, 1972.

Olsen, Jack, *The Bridge at Chappaquiddick,* Ace Books, 1970.

Opotowsky, Stanley, *The Kennedy Government* E.P. Dutton & Co. 1961, NY.

The Presidential Transcripts, The Staff of the Washington Post, A Dell Book, 1974.

Rather, Dan, *The Camera Never Blinks,* Ballantine Books, 1977.

Reybold, Malcolm, *The Inspector's Opinion – the Chappaquiddick Incident,* Saturday Review Press/E.P. Duton & Co Inc., 1975.

Rust, Zad, *Teddy Bare,* Western Islands, 1971.

Salinger, Pierre (editor) *An Honorable Profession,* Garden City, NY. 1968.

Schorr, Daniel, *Clearing the Air,* Berkley Publishing Corp. 1977.

Schlesinger, Arthur M. Jr., *Robert Kennedy and his Times,* Houghton Mifflin Co. 1978.

Sherrill, Robert, *The Last Kennedy,* The Dial Press, 1976.

Stein, Jean with Plimpton, George. *American Journey – The Times of Robert Kennedy,* Harcourt, Brace Javanovich, Inc. 1970.

Sussman, Barry, *The Great Cover-up: Nixon and the Scandal of Watergate,* The New American Library, 1974.

Tedrow, Richard L. and Tedrow, Thomas L., *Death at Chappaquiddick,* Green Hill Publishers, Inc. 1976.

Turner, William W. and Christian, John G., *The Assassination of Robert Kennedy,* Random House 1978.

Whalen, Richard, *The Founding Father: The Story of Joseph P. Kennedy,* Signet, 1966.

White, Theodore H., *A Breach of Faith: The Fall of Richard Nixon,* A Dell Book, 1976.

Witkin, B.E., *Summary of California Law,* Bancroft-Whitney 1974, Volume V, Chapter XI (178(b))

PERIODICALS

Atlantic Constitution
  August 22, 1969
  September 16, 1974
  October 27, 1974

Esquire
  February 1972, "Chappaquiddick after the bridge."
  February 1972, "Thousand Days of Edward M. Kennedy," B. Hersh.

Good Housekeeping
  September 1969, "An intimate portrait of Joan Kennedy" by Barbara Kevles.

Human Events
  August 2, 1969, "Tragedy at Chappaquiddick."
  January 10, 1970, "Possible charges against Teddy."
  April 18, 1970, "Cover-up at Edgartown?"
  April 25, 1970, "Teddy's friend at court."
  November 2, 1974, "The Chappaquiddick mystery: 40 questions for Teddy Kennedy" by David Franke.
  November 9, 1974, "Liberal Bay State Paper Rips into Kennedy."

Ladies Home Journal
  October 1969, "Girl in Ted Kennedy's car."
  July, 1970, "Joan Kennedy's Story" by Betty Hannah Hoffman.

Life
  August 1, 1969, "Incident at the Dyke Bridge" B. Brower.
  August 8, 1969, "In dread of knowing more" B. Farrell.
  August 8, 1969, "Kennedy: the unanswered questions."

Look
  May 15, 1964
  November 26, 1968, "A visit with the indomitable Rose Kennedy" by Laura Bergquist.
  March 4, 1969, "Ted Kennedy Talks about the Past and His Future" by Warren Rogers.
  August 10, 1971

McCall's
  September 1970, "The Truth about Mary Jo," by Mrs. Joseph Kopechne as told to Suzanne James.
  August 1974, "What happened at Chappaquiddick" V. Cadden.
  November 1975, "Recurring doubts about Chappaquiddick."
  August 1978, "Joan Kennedy tells her own story," by Joan Braden.

National Enquirer
  February 25, 1975, "Interview with Officer Look"
  October 24, 1978,
  July 10, 1979

National Review
  August 12, 1969, "Massachusetts soap opera"
  August 26, 1969, "Occurrence at Dyke bridge"
  August 26, 1969, "On taking the fifth"
  October 7, 1969 "After Chappaquiddick"
  November 18, 1969 "Chappaquiddick mystery"
  May 19, 1970, "Teddy brazens it out."

Newsweek

July 17, 1968

July 28, 1969 "Tragic turn for Teddy Kennedy"

August 4, 1969 "Moon and Pond"

August 4, 1969 "Grief, fear, doubt, panic and guilt."

August 4, 1969 "Guilt by appearance"

August 4, 1969 "Questions about Kennedy"

August 11, 1969 "Scandal that will not die?"

August 11, 1969 "Walk on Chappaquiddick"

August 18, 1969 "Order for an inquest"

August 25, 1969 "Columnist and Kennedy"

August 25, 1969 "D.A. on the spot"

September 1, 1969 "Why the ferry is late."

September 8, 1969 "Blueprint for the inquest"

September 15, 1969 "Listening to the lawyers"

September 29, 1969 "Disinvited"

October 20, 1969 "Plea for secrecy"

November 3, 1969 "On the record"

November 10, 1969 "Quiet inquest"

December 22, 1969 "No autopsy"

January 12, 1970 "Rendezvous in Edgartown"

January 19, 1970 "Inquest"

April 6, 1970 "Back to Chappaquiddick; grand jury inquiry"

April 13, 1970 "Grand jury"

April 20, 1970 "This case is closed; grand jury decision"

May 11, 1970 "Judge's harsh verdict on Teddy Kennedy"

October 7, 1974 "Chappaquiddick story"

November 11, 1974 "Teddy talks"

July 16, 1979 "Court vs. the Press"

New York Times Washington Merry-Go-Round by Drew Pearson and Jack Anderson

August 22, 1969

August 23, 1969

September 1, 1969

September 2, 1969

September 26, 1969

September 29, 1969

New York Times Magazine

July 14, 1974 "Chappaquiddick + 5" by R. Sherrill.

June 17, 1979 and June 24, 1979 "The Kennedy mystique" by Anne Taylor Fleming.

Reader's Digest Feb. 1980 "Chappaquiddick — The Still Unanswered Questions" by John Barron

Time

July 25, 1969 "Wrong turn at the bridge"

August 1, 1969 "Mysteries of Chappaquiddick"

August 8, 1969 "Kennedy case: more questions" & "Public Reaction"

August 15, 1969 "Kennedy's inquest of suspicion"

August 22, 1969 "Living with whispers"

August 29, 1969 "Calling the witnesses"

August 29, 1969 "Anguish of Edward Kennedy"

September 5, 1969 "Kennedy's legal future"
September 5, 1969 "Who's who at the Kennedy inquest"
September 12, 1969 "Kennedy: reckoning deferred"
October 10, 1969 "Back from Chappaquiddick"
October 31, 1969 "Rehearsal for an inquest"
November 7, 1969 "Private inquest"
January 12, 1970 "Back to Chappaquiddick"
January 19, 1970 "Inquest on Chappaquiddick"
April 6, 1970 "Chappaquiddick"
April 20, 1970 "End of the affair"
May 11, 1970 "Chappaquiddick suspicions renewed"
October 7, 1974 "Memory that would not fade"
November 11, 1974 "Back to Chappaquiddick"

The Oakland Tribune
July 15, 1979, "Chappaquiddick: Kennedy faces lingering doubts"

US
June 12, 1979 "Ted Kennedy: Ten years after Chappaquiddick"

U.S. News and World Report
June 24, 1968
August 11, 1969 "To bring the Kennedy case up to date"
August 18, 1969 "Inquest set in Kennedy case"
September 1, 1969 "Kennedy case"
September 8, 1969 "New light on Kennedy case?"
September 15, 1969 "Men who may decide Kennedy's fate"
September 29, 1969 "Autopsy hearing nears in the Teddy Kennedy accident"
October 20, 1969 "Inquest rules Kennedy wants"
November 3, 1969 "New light on the tragedy"
November 10, 1969 "Kennedy's inquiry: it's to be secret"
December 1, 1969 "What voters think of Kennedy now"
December 22, 1969 "As inquest nears in the Kennedy tragedy"
January 19, 1970 "Will Kennedy mystery ever be solved?"
January 19, 1970 "Ground rules for the Kopechne inquest"
April 13, 1970 "New look at Kennedy case and a public airing"
April 20, 1970 "Closed chapter in Kennedy story."
May 11, 1970 "Official report on the Kennedy case; with exerpts from testimony by E.M. Kennedy"
July 23, 1979, "Why Kennedy legend lives on"

Additional copies of *Chappaquiddick Decision* may
be ordered from:
Better Books Publisher

Better Books Publisher
Rt. 2, Box 69
Vale, OR 97918

Please send ___ copies of *Chappaquiddick Decision*
@ $3.50 each ($2.95 plus $.55 mailing) to:

Name _____

Street _____

City _____ State _____

Zip Code _____

312